HOW TO STAGE A COUP

T0035159

Rory Cormac is a Professor of International Relations at the University of Nottingham, specializing in secret intelligence and covert action. He is the author of *Disrupt and Deny* and co-author, with Richard J. Aldrich, of *The Black Door* and *Spying and the Crown*.

'Rich in anecdote and detail... Cormac, you can see, is an engaged teacher, the kind of lecturer who holds his students' attention with illustrative stories of derring-do and dirty tricks. They will like this book, as I do, with its relish of good yarns... A zippy read.' *The Times*

'A compelling history of the dark arts of statecraft – from assassination and sabotage through to disinformation, election interference and cyberattack. Rory Cormac combines the best true-life spy stories with thoughtful analysis of the perils of covert government operations. So full is it of fascinating and astutely examined examples of these murky practices that you wouldn't want his book to fall into the wrong hands.' Jonathan Rugman, author of *The Killing in the Consulate*

'A dazzling journey through the subterranean world of covert action: from assassination, secret wars, cyberattacks and sabotage, to rigging elections, spreading influence, and subverting democracy. This major new book is stacked full of fascinating examples from around the world, perceptive analysis and careful warnings. A must read for anyone interested in international politics and secret statecraft.' Jamie Gaskarth, author of *Secrets and Spies*

'An absolute must read for understanding the wide range of tools states pursue in the realm of covert statecraft. It has immense lessons for cyber operations, the Russian invasion of Ukraine and more.' Michael Poznansky, author of *In the Shadow of International Law*

'An important public service... Cormac's book has an ambitious scope, and its arguments and information are truly timeless.' *International Affairs*

'Rory Cormac offers a delightfully incisive and much needed corrective to the opacity surrounding covert action. He shows that reality is, in fact, far more interesting than fiction... It may sound odd to say, but despite it being about some of the most underhanded behaviors a state can undertake, it is a fun book to read. It is a must read for both practitioners of the dark arts and the curious general public alike.' *Diplomatic Courier*

'A must read for those interested in intelligence, secret warfare and the hidden hand.' *Intelligence and National Security*

*

Also by Rory Cormac

Disrupt and Deny: Spies, Special Forces and the
Secret Pursuit of British Foreign Policy

Confronting the Colonies: British Intelligence
and Counterinsurgency

Also by Rory Cormac & Richard J. Aldrich

Spying and the Crown: The Secret Relationship Between
British Intelligence and the Royals

The Black Door: Spies, Secret Intelligence and
British Prime Ministers

Spying on the World: The Declassified Documents
of the Joint Intelligence Committee, 1936–2013
(*with Michael S. Goodman*)

HOW TO STAGE A COUP

AND TEN OTHER LESSONS FROM THE WORLD OF SECRET STATECRAFT

RORY CORMAC

Atlantic Books
London

First published in hardback in Great Britain in 2022 by Atlantic Books,
an imprint of Atlantic Books Ltd.

This paperback edition first published in Great Britain in 2023
by Atlantic Books.

10 9 8 7 6 5 4 3 2 1

A CIP catalogue record for this book is available from the
British Library.

Paperback ISBN: 978-1-83895-564-9
E-book ISBN: 978-1-83895-563-2

Printed and bound by CPI Group (UK) Ltd, Croydon, CR0 4YY

Atlantic Books
An imprint of Atlantic Books Ltd
Ormond House
26–27 Boswell Street
London
WC1N 3JZ

www.atlantic-books.co.uk

For Finlay and Genevieve,
true masters of the dark arts

CONTENTS

PROLOGUE

'America is back,' President Biden confidently declared in February 2021. Bruised, bloodied and more than a bit broken after four years of disinformation and democratic decay, America, Biden insisted, had returned to the world stage. And had no time to waste.

Democracies across the world are under siege. Hostile forces use propaganda and subversion to sow division, and to promote their own brands of illiberal authoritarianism. The distribution of power across the world is changing. After decades tied down fighting terrorists, the US is no longer the dominant power it once was. China is assertive and on the rise; Russia is intent on maintaining not only dominance over its backyard but also its self-perceived great power status. It wilfully wields disruption and wreaks havoc to do so. The Biden presidency wasted little time promising to compete in this 'gray zone'.[1]

'I made it clear to President Putin,' Biden insisted during an early speech at the State Department, 'in a manner very different from my predecessor, that the days of the United States rolling over in the face of Russia's aggressive actions – interfering with our elections, cyberattacks, poisoning its citizens – are over.'[2]

Just weeks later, the American intelligence community warned of China's push for global power, and of yet more provocative actions by the usual suspects of Russia, Iran and North Korea. Russia, US intelligence predicted, would continue dividing western countries for the foreseeable future. It had already meddled in successive American presidential elections, developed dangerous cyber capabilities able to sabotage targets and conducted assassinations overseas. Meanwhile, US intelligence accused Iran of sabotaging Israeli water facilities during a hot summer in 2020, and, in the same year, of trying to undermine confidence in American democracy.[3] China did not attempt to interfere in the election but did spend much of 2020 pumping out propaganda designed to undercut the west's response to the coronavirus pandemic.

That same spring, across the Atlantic, Prime Minister Boris Johnson made a similar declaration. We are living in a more competitive age, he wrote, and we must change our approach to adapt to the uncertain new world emerging around us. The UK, Johnson promised, would defend against disinformation, cyberattacks, electoral interference and attempted assassinations on the streets of Britain.[4] It would do so, in part, using the hidden hand of secret statecraft: intelligence agencies and discreet forces capable of special operations. The UK would thrive in the grey zone.

Afterwards, the head of MI5 issued a sombre warning: ordinary members of the British public were not immune from the 'tentacles' of foreign states. This is not some game played out by spies in the shadows, he insisted; subversion, sabotage and subterfuge affect all of us.[5]

Much mythologized and heavily romanticized, covert action is one of the most misunderstood aspects of the grey zone within international politics. Few fictional figures have created more confusion than James Bond. 'Britain's real life 007s have licence to kill renewed after 60 year gap,' declared the *Daily Mirror*, confidently but entirely wrongly, in summer 2020.[6] It was certainly not alone in illustrating any story about subversion and sabotage, indeed any aspect of secret intelligence, with reference to the irrepressible James Bond. The following spring, the head of GCHQ, Britain's signals intelligence agency, publicly committed to recruiting more women. It was, he said, 'mission critical' to increase diversity in the service. The *Mail Online* covered this story with a photograph of Bond caressing the naked back of Strawberry Fields, a glamorous fellow intelligence officer featured in *Quantum of Solace*, the 2008 outing of the franchise.[7] Wrong service; fictional officers; and hardly reflecting the diversity requirements highlighted by the GCHQ chief.

The UK is not alone here. In an example of British cultural influence, 007 features prominently in American headlines too. The image is clear: suave men, dashing around the world despatching baddies, driving expensive cars and sleeping with beautiful women. More cocktail party than covert action. Legislative oversight be damned.

In May 2021, the CIA launched a diversity drive of its own. Its campaign featured a cisgender millennial Latina officer with generalized anxiety disorder. Republican senator Ted Cruz was quick to criticize on Twitter: 'If you're a Chinese communist, or an Iranian Mullah, or Kim Jong Un… would this scare you? We've come a long way from Jason Bourne.' Played by the actor Matt Damon in the eponymous films, Bourne is of course another fictional character not entirely dissimilar to Bond.

This book navigates the fact and fiction to cut through the romance of the secret world. It makes three arguments designed to demystify, elucidate and provoke. First, poisonings, disinformation and electoral meddling are all pieces of the same puzzle of covert competition as states try to gain the upper hand on each other without resorting to war. These tactics are not new and can only be understood alongside recent history. The timbre may now be brasher, the tempo faster, the volume louder, but the notes remain the same. Covert action is not new. The internet era has not revolutionized the very nature of subversion and sabotage; neither has it created an entirely new type of covert action.

Second, it is harder than ever before to control global events; covert action is therefore more about disruption. Hidden hands divide, discredit and chip away at authority. Whether secret war or cyberattacks, it often comes back to the same thing: exploiting weaknesses and crippling the adversary. It is the slow drip of steady subversion, of persistent disruption. This can be subtle, to the point of being untraceable; or it can be deliberately ambiguous.

It can also be decidedly bold and far less dependent on secrecy than people realize. Many operations are performative, using sabotage and assassination, as well as propaganda, to send a message to friend and foe alike. Covert action is about so much more than leaders using intelligence agencies to influence events without anyone knowing. It can be a spectacle in which leaders' refusal to acknowledge their operations becomes more important than hiding them. Presidents and prime ministers use covert action for a wide range of reasons, including influencing, disrupting and communicating when they cannot act openly.

Although the promise is seductive, these leaders face significant constraints when wielding the hidden hand. They face trade-offs between secrecy, scale, directness and control. The more deniable, the less impactful; the more control, the less secrecy; the more indirect, the more secrecy, but the less control, and so on. You cannot have it all. Covert action is about carefully calibrating secrecy, scale and signals. Neither can you use covert action in isolation as a magical silver bullet. It forms one part of a policy response, carefully calibrated to the end goal.

Covert action will continue, even increase, in our era of implausible deniability. As secrecy breaks down, exposing covert action will not be sufficient to counter it. Clinging to an enlightenment ideal that laying bare a pure, unmediated truth will cut through and discredit adversaries is outdated. There is too much noise; exposure is not enough. Covert action is becoming messier, the subject of competing cross-cutting claims and counterclaims.

Third, to understand this, it is important to recognize how covert action works and how it is reported. Ambiguity is everything. Covert action is all about illusions and collusion, myths as much as meddling, often viewed through the prism of Bond and Bourne. When states seek to subvert reality, stories and narratives become just as important as the events they represent. These narratives become significant in themselves, breathing life into otherwise moribund operations and shaping policy responses. Fear of Russian meddling can end up more consequential than the meddling in the first place.

Given the subterfuge, secrecy and half-truths involved, covert action is less about objective accounts of events and more about how we interpret them. The grey zone is not some blurred line between war and peace; such a thing has always existed. The real grey zone is epistemic: blurred lines between what we know, what we do not know, and what we think we know. The novelty in all of this comes from the fluctuating space between covert action and public knowledge, the decline of state secrecy and the rise of multiple competing narratives churned out across a kaleido-scopic media landscape.[8]

Perception and paranoia become paramount. Is a hack aggressive sabotage or run-of-the-mill espionage? Is it offensive or defensive? Is a death an assassination or a targeted killing? Did the state even sponsor the assassination at all? Is a coup a legiti-mate expression of internal dissatisfaction with a brutal regime or illegitimate interference by a hidden hand? Can it be both? Is the state sending weapons to terrorists or rebels? Did covert action succeed or fail? None of these are foregone conclusions. Given the classified sources, potential for manipulation and the grey nature of covert action, how we answer these questions is key in wielding and defending against secret statecraft.

INTRODUCTION:
GREY ZONES AND COVERT ACTION

We live in uniquely uncertain and complex times. Wars are changing. They can be won and lost without a single shot being fired, without war even being declared. Threats come from multiple directions: from old foes like Russia and new competitors like China; from regional powers equipped with burgeoning cyber capabilities and from the familiar bala-clava-clad gun-toting convoy of terrorists and insurgents. Demagogues and rabble-rousers are rife. The liberal international order, defined by rule of law, respect for human rights and cooperation, is eroding before our eyes. More worrying still, it is not collapsing with a bang, something clear and obvious against which we can rally. Instead, this decline is gradual and pervasive, marked by a dissolving of acceptable and unacceptable behaviour. It is being silently overwhelmed. The damage is done before we can understand exactly what is happening.

We live in such uncertain and complex times, they require a bewildering bonanza of ill-defined buzzwords to make sense of it all: grey zones, hybrid warfare, ambiguous, sub-threshold, non-linear, liminal warfare… The list goes on.

Except we do not live in uniquely uncertain and complex times. Wars still exist, whilst talk of strategic and persistent competition, of states using proxies to do their bidding discreetly and deniably, and of dissolving lines between war and peace is nothing new. The supposed liberal international order, a romanticized phrase regularly embraced by President Obama, reflects a nostalgia for the recent past which struggles under scrutiny.[1]

In the post-truth world, people interpret facts through the prism of their own ideologies and beliefs. They prize emotion over authority. Myth and reality mix freely as new technology helps disinformation flow with mellifluous ease. The 2020s? Perhaps. But this characterization equally applies to England under the Stuarts in the seventeenth century, a world away from Twitter and Trump. It was a time when the printing press enabled the proliferation of pamphlets to spread rumours about papal plots. Conspiracy was rife and people clung to their own perceptions and prejudices: their personalized truths.

More recently, journalists covering the Troubles in Northern Ireland complained about being 'overwhelmed by a blizzard of facts and atrocities, lies and propaganda, from all sides'. The swirling information made it 'simply impossible to tell truth from fantasy, fact from fiction'.[2] This complaint could have equally applied to the post-truth Trump presidency.

And what of secret statecraft beyond propaganda? In the nineteenth century, US president Thomas Jefferson, a venerated founding father, bribed foreign politicians, toppled a government and provided discreet assistance to insurgent fighters.[3] This all feels remarkably modern. The CIA certainly has been no stranger to such activity; and neither have the Russians.

We live in an era in which states operate ambiguously between war and peace. It is difficult for adversaries to draw a line between the acceptable and unacceptable – and to respond accordingly. The Kremlin in particular sponsors operations which are 'sufficient to keep the wound bleeding but insufficient, thus far, to warrant massive retaliation'.[4] This observation, made by historian Jonathan Haslam, related not to so-called hybrid warfare in Ukraine prior to February 2022, but to Soviet operations against Poland almost a century earlier.

The same goes for election meddling. Amid growing international tension, a Russian intelligence officer looked ahead to forthcoming US presidential elections. Behind closed doors, he briefed his audience of spies about increasing divisions in American society, including what he called the race problem, social issues, unemployment and crime. He urged better understanding of each in order to 'find effective opportunities [to] attack' the election. The year was not 2016, but 1983. The intelligence officer worked for the powerful KGB, Soviet intelligence, and was addressing the East German Stasi.[5] This all feels remarkably familiar, perhaps unsurprisingly given Vladimir Putin's famous quip that there is no such thing as a former KGB officer. Today's relentless use of secret intelligence to achieve foreign policy goals resonates with Cold War spymasters.[6]

So much of the excitable neophilia dominating global politics today was prevalent in the Cold War. 'Positive action' was needed to disrupt Russia, according to British Foreign Office documents way back in 1951; 'covert action', diplomats suggested, could 'bring about changes' inside Russia by identifying sources of tension inside the Soviet Union and then secretly exploiting them to spread division. A senior British diplomat in the 1950s, pointing out that subversion was cheaper than invasion, wondered why countries spent so much money on deterrence when they could just bribe foreign leaders instead. The following decade, British planners concluded that wars were no longer declared or winnable. States therefore turned to the hidden hand instead.[7]

Talk of defending forward is all the rage in the US: a proactive approach to intelligence, engaging enemies on their own turf, bravely working with allies in perilous places and disrupting threats at source. And yet Marc Polymeropoulos, a veteran of CIA operations in Iraq and Afghanistan, insightfully points out that the CIA has been doing exactly this since its inception in 1947. Deployed overseas, moving from country to country, its intelligence officers have recruited agents, led dangerous expeditions and supported allies.[8] We have been here before.

That is not to downplay current events, but rather to keep them in perspective. Neither is it to embrace the seductively nostalgic caress of the past and recast the 2020s as Cold War version 2.0. There are important differences, not least higher levels of global interdependence, even if, in the words of one academic, Hong Kong does have an air of Berlin about it.[9] The Cold War was fluid and played out differently across the globe. It was sometimes incredibly dangerous – the world stood on the brink of nuclear war on more than one occasion – while very real violence broke out from southeast Asia to Latin America.

Our construction of history is equally fluid. We project our own prejudices onto the past and so the Cold War meant something different in 2010 compared to, say, 2016 once Russian subversion and meddling had become mainstream.[10] History may be about the past, but it is also about the present. It reflects our own reality as much as anyone else's.

Although not new, persistent competition, information operations and subversion are clearly prominent features of statecraft today. The loose references to grey zones and hybrid warfare – the Israelis talk of a 'campaign between the wars' – reflect a disorienting range of activities. Most involve the pervasive deployment

of multiple, often covert, instruments of influence – from saboteurs to assassins, from political meddlers to peddlers of lies.[11]
Our confusion and lack of clarity turns on the ill-defined role of
secrecy, exposure, deniability and acknowledgement. We cannot
understand what is going on in the world – the manipulation, the
subversion and subterfuge – without considering covert action.

What does an internet troll factory on the outskirts of St
Petersburg staffed by poorly trained twenty-somethings have
in common with high-end assassins using lethal poison to
despatch problematic leaders? Both are covert actions, unacknowledged interference in the affairs of others.

Covert action evokes many images: dashing James Bond types
whizzing around the world in supercars dramatically exercising
their supposed licence to kill; adventurous CIA officers carrying
suitcases stuffed full of money across the desert to arrange a
Middle Eastern coup; mysterious Russians slipping poison into
a cup of tea in a fancy hotel restaurant; Israeli assassins hunting
down terrorists in the shadows; and thousands of the Chinese
diaspora working discreetly to promote the Communist Party's
interest. Covert action is highly mythologized – and often
misunderstood.

Plots and rumours of plots are all around us. A daily diet of
disinformation feeds conspiracy theories and a broader climate of
paranoia. Trust is in decline, and hesitancy and cynicism are on
the rise. Yet there is a big difference between conspiracy theory
– with all the nonsense about abominable monolithic groups
operating omnipotently from the shadows – and conspiratorial
politics.[12] Real conspiracies do exist. According to one former
CIA official, 'Conspiracy is hard, and it takes a lot of time to do it
right.'[13] And while the CIA has had a lot of practice over the years,

it is in good company. The rap sheet covering the last few years alone is long, varied and global. It spans Chinese propaganda trying to justify Beijing's authoritarian response to COVID-19; Russian and Israeli sabotage of arms warehouses and nuclear sites respectively; Pakistani sponsorship of terrorism; and British disruption of ISIS communication networks.

Subterranean activity – supported, but not controlled, by a hidden hand – ranges from subtle influence work all the way up to assassination and secret wars. It brings together a disparate cast of great powers, regional rivals, rebel fighters, mercenaries and hackers. Competition for power, for influence, for health security, and even competition over the nature of the global (dis) order itself, loom large. Covert action is neither inherently bad nor immoral. It can be a vital tool in the state's policy toolbox, and, like any other, its outcomes depend on how and why it is used. Some states are more reckless than others, some more responsible. It is, however, inherently controversial.

Covert action is generally understood as plausibly deniable interference in the affairs of others designed to bring about political change. For all the cultural ubiquity of James Bond, the US definition of covert action is the most prominent and provides a prism through which we (mis)understand this shadowy form of international statecraft more widely. After all, the US has long been a dominant power, is relatively transparent and, unlike the UK, actually commits definitions of secret work to paper.

The US formally defines covert action as 'an activity or activities of the United States Government to influence political, economic, or military conditions abroad, where it is intended that the role of the United States Government will not be apparent or acknowledged publicly'. This explicitly does not include espionage, traditional military or diplomatic activity, and law enforcement; neither does it include manipulation of domestic audiences. Covert action is generally conducted by the CIA, although it constitutes only a small portion of the agency's activity, with espionage and analysis forming the core mission. It is legally distinct from the Pentagon's special operations, although the line between them blurs in practice and close cooperation between the two is a hallmark of twenty-first-century lethal counterterrorism operations.[14]

Covert action is authorized by the president, usually after copious discussions between layers of policymakers, intelligence officers and lawyers. Lots of lawyers. The idea of the CIA as a rogue elephant running amok around the world is a myth. Operations have formally required presidential approval and congressional oversight since 1974. This might not be particularly romantic or exciting – especially to those well versed in freewheeling spy films – but it is the humdrum, and essential, reality.[15]

The US has turned to covert action since its very founding and the revolutionary war against Britain. George Washington, its first president, was a famously keen practitioner, planning and executing a veritable cornucopia of operations against the crown: kidnappings, including one outlandish plot to kidnap none other than the king's son; at least one operation directed at acquiring a fourteenth colony in Quebec; sabotage of British dockyards; and the creation of newspapers for propaganda purposes.[16]

In the two and a half centuries since, successive presidents have used covert action to protect American power: to see off threats and to maintain the status quo, reaping political, military and economic benefits in the process.[17] Between 1951 and 1975, the US conducted over nine hundred covert actions.[18]

Covert action, technically speaking, is an American legal and bureaucratic term for a specific type of activity with specific authorization procedures. However, these unacknowledged interventions are a global story, playing out on a global stage. Many states attempt to influence political developments while masking their own conspiratorial role. Different countries have different approaches to secret statecraft. Some hands are more hidden than others; some are bounded by bureaucracy, others contorted, even deformed, to meet the norms of liberal democracy; some are aggressive, unrestrained. Some hands are unchained.

The Russians long talked of *aktivnye meropriyatiya* or active measures to cover a range of political influence and subversion operations, from influencing foreign governments to undermining confidence in western institutions.[19] Interestingly, the word 'disinformation', one such active measure and a term widely used today, comes from the Russian *dezinformatsiya* and only entered the English lexicon in the late 1970s.[20] Sharp measures – or *ostrye meropriyatii* – covered a more particular subset of skills: assassination, sabotage and kidnap. This included use of explosives; surprise mines; 'devices for soundless, mechanical shooting of needles containing fast-acting poisons'; and 'strong toxins', as one document recently uncovered in Bulgarian archives matter-of-factly put it.[21]

Russia adopts a broader and more holistic approach in its active measures than US covert action, greying lines between peace and war.[22] Much of this is carried out by Russian intelligence services. The powerful FSB, successor to the KGB and once headed by Putin himself, is domestic-focused but increasingly engages in international operations; the SVR is the foreign intelligence service; and the GRU is military intelligence. All have wide freedom of action, are aggressive, entrepreneurial and, according to Russia expert Mark Galeotti, competitive 'to the point of cannibalism'. The GRU is particularly willing to take risks and evinces an audacious mindset more redolent of special forces than intelligence.[23]

For a supposedly top-secret organization, GRU Unit 29155 is remarkably conspicuous. As we shall see, its brazen – to the point of sloppy – operations allegedly include the poisoning of a Bulgarian arms manufacturer, blowing up a Czech munitions warehouse, orchestrating a failed coup in Montenegro, and the poisoning of a dissident and his daughter in the UK. If that was not enough, its operatives have also been linked to the failed Catalan bid for independence from Spain in 2017 and to accounts of Russians offering bounties to the Taliban to kill Americans in Afghanistan. Their cover stories are sometimes paper thin and they have used the same aliases for multiple operations, leaving a trail of breadcrumbs for online sleuths to uncover more and more of their work. Russia, and especially its GRU, is willing to embrace implausible deniability.[24] According to the chief of MI6, such unabashed activity 'is on an upward trend'.[25]

Although active measures are nothing new and their roots can be traced back to the tsarist secret police of the late nineteenth century, the Russians are becoming more active and less measured, according to Thomas Rid, an expert in Russian disinformation.[26] Confrontation with the west – even warfare in some Russians' eyes – began a long time ago.[27] Facing a mismatch between ambition and assets, President Putin, with his conspiratorial and paranoid worldview, uses these tactics to divide and distract the west, hoping to render it unable or unwilling to prevent his claim to Russia's great power status.[28]

Despite what the headlines and history books suggest, covert competition and secret statecraft are about more than Russia and the US. China, like Russia, blends the overt and covert, the political and military.[29] Unlike Russia, China is on the rise. It is less constrained by a chronic mismatch between ambition and assets, and so is better able to use economic and development programmes to influence others. Unacknowledged, semi-secret, activity complements this where necessary. Its whole of society approach includes propaganda; discreet political donations; subverting academic freedom; and mobilizing broad coalitions of people, from private companies to Chinese diaspora, to promote the interests of the Chinese Communist Party and shape international debate.[30] The latter is known as united front activity and can be traced back to Mao's era; if anything, it has only become more potent since.[31] All of this grey activity combines with what China calls the 'three warfares' – public opinion, psychological and legal – to discreetly shape events.[32]

Influence work is conducted by the party's propaganda department and United Front Work Department among others. Meanwhile, China's formidable intelligence agencies have a broad remit. The Ministry of State Security is responsible for domestic and overseas operations, and the People's Liberation Army (PLA) conducts military intelligence. Little is known about the internal workings of either, but the PLA also engages in united front work, political warfare and offensive cyber. It implements the three warfares.[33] China is a global power with a wide reach. That said, almost half of its covert actions target Taiwan, with many more aimed at Hong Kong.[34]

This is about strengthening political power. China's leaders fear that western forces are actively trying to subvert their sphere of influence by sowing divisions and encouraging revolutions. These perceived threats, especially since the advent of the internet, have become an almost existential struggle for the Chinese Communist Party.[35] The party therefore seeks first and foremost to preserve itself and then to transform the international order in its own image – without a shot being fired.[36]

Smaller powers wield the hidden hand too. We tend to associate western covert action with the CIA, but the British have been doing this since before the CIA existed. In fact, the British have been doing this since before the United States existed, and before even the United Kingdom existed. As early as the mid-sixteenth century, Queen Elizabeth I sanctioned what were then called 'covert meanes' to undermine King Philip of Spain, including discreetly sending money to Protestant rebels waging an insurrection against Catholic rule.[37] By the mid-twentieth century, Britain had developed a formidable reputation among friend and foe alike for meddling, manipulating and blowing things up. It is not for nothing that Iranians refer to the UK as the old fox.

London favours a flexible and informal approach, compensating for its own ever-widening gap between ambition and assets. Successive prime ministers and foreign secretaries have turned to covert action as a cost-effective means to mask decline and project influence on the cheap.

Unlike the US, Whitehall has no official definition. Over the years, it has used a range of phrases to denote different activities including special political action, disavowable action, special operations, propaganda and counterpropaganda, and covert action itself. Whitehall now talks of intelligence effects: the exploitation of intelligence to effect real-world change. Effects can be broad in scope and tactical in scale, including things like neutralizing a cache of terrorist explosives or merely preventing a terrorist suspect from boarding a boat.

Effects operations are undertaken by whichever government agency is most appropriate. MI6 has traditionally taken the lead, but GCHQ has more recently found a role as the internet created opportunities to influence, disrupt and sabotage – what is now called offensive cyber. GCHQ defines effects as 'doing things in cyberspace to make something happen'. And MI6's definition? That remains unknown. Special forces activity also constitutes covert action; unlike the US, the UK does not make a sharp distinction between this and special military operations. Nimbleness is the order of the day.[38]

Across the Channel, French practitioners talk about *action clandestine*. The Directorate-General for External Security, France's overseas intelligence agency, has a dedicated unit known as *Service Action* that specializes in paramilitary operations.[39] It has a well-earned reputation for taking a crude and muscular approach, giving French covert action a more aggressive feel than British special political actions. Much French paramilitary activity, especially that conducted in post-imperial Africa, made the CIA look like a nunnery in comparison. As we shall see, back in the 1950s, the French conducted sabotage and assassination operations targeting arms dealers and Algerian nationalists in West Germany.[40] Paramilitary covert action then spanned Cameroon, Chad, the Comoros, Mozambique, Nigeria, Zaire and elsewhere. The French plotted to assassinate Libya's Colonel Gaddafi. Twice.[41]

One head of intelligence at the end of the Cold War acknowledged the secret services' *droit de mort*, or right of death. It was far from a daily occurrence, and he insisted it was used parsimoniously, but the threat of assassination hung over the heads of targets.[42] More recently in 2016, the French press reported that *Service Action* was working alongside military special forces to disrupt and neutralize ISIS in Libya.[43] The president supposedly had a kill list; it was, according to one journalist, 'ultra-secrète'.[44]

Israel is another country with a muscular – to put it mildly – reputation when it comes to covert actions, perhaps having assassinated more people than any other in the western world. Its particularly aggressive approach derives from the revolutionary roots of the Zionist movement, the trauma of the Holocaust and the perpetual menace of Arab terrorism.[45] Mossad, one of the most famous – indeed legendary – intelligence agencies in the world, takes the lead.

Despite its reputation, there is more to Israeli secret statecraft than targeted assassinations. It includes the rescuing of Jewish people from foreign countries.[46] One wonderful example that surfaced recently is instructive: back in the early 1980s, Mossad helped create a holiday resort on the Sudanese shores of the Red Sea. To all the world it looked like the perfect place to dive among beautiful exotic fish, but the resort served another purpose in secretly facilitating the evacuation of thousands of Ethiopian Jews from Sudanese refugee camps.[47]

The Israeli approach also seems to cover other, more indirect, means of deniably influencing international affairs. On one occasion, Mossad created a fake company to buy French missile boats and contravene an arms embargo. Just twenty-four hours after the Israelis sailed them away, battling unstable weather conditions in the process, the French realized that they had been played.[48]

Israel is currently engaged in a shadow war with Iran, another notable practitioner of secret statecraft. Mysterious sabotage of ships in the Persian Gulf is not uncommon. Pursued by the Revolutionary Guards and Ministry of Intelligence and Security, Iranian activity traditionally prioritizes secretly getting hold of weapons, supporting terrorism and assassinating dissidents abroad.[49] As such, it has generally acted regionally, although, according to US intelligence, Iran attempted to sow division in the US and undercut President Trump's re-election campaign in 2020. This went all the way up to the Iranian supreme leader himself.[50]

Across the border, Turkey has also long turned to the hidden hand. A regional power with great foreign policy ambitions, Ankara uses covert action to influence areas removed from Turkish control by the collapse of the Ottoman Empire after the First World War. Successive leaders, perhaps with heads in the past but wallets in the present, sought to recover their influence without triggering a bigger military conflict.[51] And Turkey is not alone; as we shall see, Saudi Arabia, Qatar, the UAE and others in the region all engage in subversion and subterfuge. Intrigue abounds.

Historically, Egypt has boasted an incredibly ambitious – if unsuccessful – covert action programme subverting and destabilizing Jordan, Iraq, Yemen, Saudi Arabia and Libya. Its post-war operations all followed a similar pattern: lower public confidence in the target regime, boost the opposition and force the creation of a new friendly government. Egyptian intelligence used the entire gamut of covert tactics, from black propaganda – material with a falsified origin – to assassination, from sponsoring bombings to cultivating agents of influence inside the targets' armies, and from sabotage to creating pro-Egypt student and labour movements.[52]

Moving further east, Pakistan and India are regular performers on the covert stage. Pakistan's intelligence agency, Inter-Services Intelligence (ISI), often portrayed as a thuggish behemoth beyond democratic control, has a Covert Action Division.[53] Unsurprisingly, India's foreign intelligence service, the Research and Analysis Wing (RAW), has maintained its own covert action capabilities since its creation back in the late 1960s.[54] Covert actions undertaken by both sides are comparatively local. Pakistan has long assisted Islamist militants in northeast India and channelled aid to extremist fighters in Afghanistan.[55] Most dramatically, plenty of circumstantial evidence points to Pakistani complicity in the devastating terrorist attacks on Mumbai in 2008. At least 160 people died when gunmen assaulted two luxury hotels, a train station and other high-profile targets.[56]

ISI's bitter rival, RAW, played a significant role in the creation of Bangladesh from East Pakistan; trained and armed Sri Lankan terrorists in the 1970s; and, more recently, stands accused of covertly influencing the 2015 Sri Lankan election after the government became worryingly close to China.[57] India also has the capabilities to target Pakistan – and probably China – with cyber sabotage.[58] Secret warfare and subterfuge constitute an essential dimension of the fraught geopolitics of south Asia.

Nefarious Russian meddling dominates headlines, and CIA-sponsored coups dominate the history books, but they are not alone. This is a global game. Although not all countries practise such secret statecraft, enough meddle and manipulate, subvert and sabotage, to make it a serious activity worthy of our attention. Although states have different approaches to secret statecraft, much of what we are talking about boils down to a single – if broad – activity: unacknowledged interference to create political change; to subvert, pressure, cripple and undermine adversaries. This is international politics at its most discreet and devious, but also its most creative and ingenious. When states choose to use covert action is shaped by three overlapping factors: insufficient clout to get away with intervening openly; mismatch between ambition and assets; and reputation and risk management.

Covert action is a policy tool, complementing others from the state's toolbox. It nestles, often glistening seductively, alongside the more expensive, risky or protracted options of economic sanctions, diplomatic negotiations and military force. Covert action is not espionage; rather, as the name suggests, it is active: going out and shaping events; it is influence not information. By contrast, espionage is more passive: silently watching, reading and listening. They do often go hand in hand, though, in so far as intelligence agencies conduct many covert actions, covert action exploits intelligence, covert action can generate intelligence, and, as we shall see, it can be difficult to tell espionage from action in the cyber age. This is problematic because, as a former MI6 director of intelligence and operations put it, the blurring of espionage and action dissolves 'already weak distinctions between war and peace and favours the approach of states which believe, like Thucydides, that peace is merely an armistice in a war that is always ongoing'.[59]

Covert action is hard to pin down; it evades understanding. How do we know what we know about it? Where does our knowledge of these operations come from? And this uncertainty – this mental grey zone – is partly what makes it so intriguing and, at times, so frustrating to study. It is secretive, operating in the shadows, and many cases remain classified. Understanding a significant feature of global politics in which most examples are off limits is particularly challenging, albeit a challenge to which intrepid (or foolhardy) scholars are increasingly rising.

The CIA's chief historian says that the fifty or so US operations that have been officially declassified offer a representative sample of the broader universe of US covert action – but, to paraphrase the famous quip of Mandy Rice-Davies, 'he would say that, wouldn't he?' At least the US does declassify historical activities. The UK is notoriously parsimonious and is only getting worse, as the government clamps down on freedom of information requests. Australia is worse still. France, meanwhile, seems intent on gagging its ghosts by going further and *re*classifying various historical documents.

Historians rely on snippets and fragments like jumbled pieces of a puzzle with no picture and no box. Covert action is that which we cannot see: brief shadows burned into the pages of the thousands of mundane diplomatic papers released annually into historical archives.

Those covert actions we do know about, those shadows we have gathered, might create a sample bias and skew our understanding of the broader activity. Paramilitary operations and secret wars are inevitably harder to keep secret, while their dramatic bombs and bangs generate more news stories and Hollywood films than, say, low-key influence work. Accordingly, paramilitary operations take on a disproportionately prominent place in the public imagination even though they constitute only a tiny percentage of covert actions.

Similarly, we are more likely to know about covert actions which went wrong, especially if they attracted criticism in parliaments and the press. Foreign Secretary William Hague fumbling at the despatch box in 2011 is a case in point. A secret mission to make contact with Libyan rebels had gone disastrously wrong, with the team ending up handcuffed in a Benghazi farmyard. Hague squirmed nervously as the press invoked the usual Bond tropes and questioned whether the foreign secretary had 'lost his mojo'.

Covert actions are even more likely to attract widespread attention if their failure or extravagance results in government inquiries. The most famous example is the investigations of the US Senate select committee chaired by Frank Church, the Democratic senator for Idaho, back in the 1970s. Church and his colleagues rummaged through recent CIA history, publicly airing its dirty laundry, including alleged assassination attempts. Successes remain hidden for longer than failure, propaganda longer than paramilitary, thereby skewing our understanding of covert action and whether it works and what types are best.

Surprisingly, secrecy and eye-wateringly high levels of classification are not the main factors making covert action difficult to pin down. More than secretive, it is inherently elusive. Like the wind, visible in the movement of branches on trees, you can only feel its effects. Covert actions rarely have obvious beginnings or ends. They might start literally years before a coup overthrows a government and continue long afterwards through funding certain political parties. They exist alongside larger open instruments of policy, such as economic pressure or a military threat, making it difficult to isolate covert from overt, especially when assessing impact.[60]

Covert action exists in relation to other actors. It nudges along internal forces in the target state – dissidents, revolutionaries and opposition parties – sometimes with a deft fleeting touch, sometimes with a shove. It is incredibly difficult for observers, even those with full access to classified material, to isolate the impact of the hidden hand. How do we separate covert action from events that would have happened anyway? How do we know it was Russia that made all the difference in the 2016 election and not disaffected Americans? Covert action lives through others, shaping what it encounters. Most of the wind, to borrow from the Irish poet Paul Muldoon, happens where there are trees.[61]

It is difficult to pin down because it operates in the grey zone between war and peace, between militaries and civilians, and between the acceptable and unacceptable. It is unbounded by geography, with much taking place in cyberspace. Information defines and shapes what is known, yet covert action is all about the interplay between appearance and reality. It is a cognitive grey zone. It involves performance. As we shall see, states use covert action to send messages; they collude in the fiction of secrecy, and even in the fiction of potency. Covert actions are told through stories or myths, which can then become as important as the actual events they represent. In the 'covert sphere', as one professor of English literature calls it, stories and the public imagination, fantasies about secret statecraft, can end up shaping policy.[62]

Covert action is difficult to pin down because our knowledge of it is constructed through so many different filters. It is less a wilderness of mirrors, a phrase often used to describe secret intelligence, and more a funfair world of mirrors, warped and distorted. It is confected; reflected through Bond and Bourne, through memoirs and selected declassifications of once top-secret documents.

This evasiveness leaves a rather daunting question: where to start on our journey around the dark corners of secret statecraft. Methods of manipulation are limited only by meddlers' imaginations: from cyberattacks to social media bots, bribing politicians to subverting academia, sponsoring rap and graffiti artists to arming rebel fighters. Assassination, slipping poison into a cup of tea, lies at the extreme end of the scale, while slipping a factually accurate article into a friendly news-paper lies at the more mundane other. Assassination is far less common than low-key influence work and yet dominates the headlines owing to its macabre gadgetry, 007 connotations, or sheer lethal brazenness. Given its prominence in the public imagination, and a worrying rise in recent cases, it is from here where we will embark. Crucially, however, low-key influence work forms the cornerstone of secret statecraft, and is by far the most pervasive of these 'most unusual measures' (as one British diplomat once euphemistically put it). We will, therefore, travel from killing to propaganda before climbing back up the ladder of escalation, through subversion, electoral rigging, coups, secret warfare and sabotage.

Covert action is a global game. Mythologized and misunder-stood, this secret statecraft is not new, but paradoxically it has featured prominently in global politics over the last decade. This is a guidebook to the grey zone for the armchair éminence grise. It draws on intriguing international tales, past and present, to offer key insights into this murky subterranean world. What goes on beneath the surface; how states lie, subvert and sabotage; and what works. Let us begin with the most dramatic and controver-sial measure of all: assassination.

1

HOW TO ASSASSINATE YOUR ENEMIES

I n the early hours of 3 January 2020, the powerful Iranian general Qassem Soleimani landed at an airport outside Baghdad. As his convoy of two cars set off through the dark to meet the Iraqi prime minister, a US drone hovered above, closely watching his every move before launching Hellfire missiles. Both cars exploded. Soleimani was killed.

The following August, the Russian opposition leader Alexei Navalny became violently ill on a flight. After doctors placed him in an induced coma, it soon became apparent that someone had poisoned him with a deadly nerve agent, Novichok, the very same substance used in earlier attempts to assassinate other Russian dissidents and defectors. Navalny survived, and, in a remarkable twist, later posed as a senior Russian official and telephoned one of the assassins to demand why the poisoning had failed. Through subterfuge of his own, he learnt that they had applied the poison to his underpants in a hotel room, but that it had failed to penetrate his skin as planned.

In November, just three months later, Mohsen Fakhrizadeh was ambushed, shot and killed outside Tehran. This was no ordinary murder. Fakhrizadeh was Iran's top military nuclear scientist, and, rather mysteriously, the gunmen were nowhere to be seen. His heavily armed bodyguards could only haplessly shoot back into thin air. The murder weapon – a robotic machine gun – was equipped with artificial intelligence and controlled by satellite to target Fakhrizadeh, and only Fakhrizadeh. His wife, sitting centimetres away from him in the car, escaped unharmed. A stray dog wandered into the line of fire; the bullets missed. The attack was remarkably precise, leaving no collateral damage. Iran quickly accused Israel of assassination. These three high-profile attacks – two of which succeeded – spanned the year 2020. Each was conducted by a different state using different methods. Whether they constituted assassinations or targeted killings is debatable, but one thing is clear: state killing of high-profile targets remains a feature of international politics today.

Remote-control machine guns may offer a glimpse of the future, but the history of assassinations is littered with equally ingenious – and often more gruesomely outrageous – stories. The Soviets euphemistically called it 'wet work' – a crass reference to the spilling of blood – and, in one particularly shocking example, dissident communist Leon Trotsky met his end in Mexico when a Soviet agent smashed in his skull with an ice pickaxe. Many remember the umbrella modified to carry poison which the Soviets used to kill a Bulgarian dissident on Waterloo Bridge in 1978. The KGB developed a range of lethal gadgetry, much of which would have been at home in a Bond film. Alongside the umbrella sat an equally devious lipstick gun, giving new meaning to the kiss of death, and a gun disguised as a packet of cigarettes.

Over the years, the Americans have turned to poisoned toothpaste, poison-lined scuba diving suits and, most famously of all, exploding cigars. Meanwhile, the Israelis have launched over two thousand assassination operations. Methods include snipers, car bombs, parcel bombs, explosives hidden in a phone, and poison.[1] They were not always successful. On one infamous occasion, back in 1997, Mossad operatives travelled to Jordan on a mission to assassinate the leader of Hamas, the Palestinian militant group. The top-secret plan was to insert poison into his ear, but it went spectacularly wrong. The perpetrators were caught and, as the target fell dangerously ill, Israel had to provide the antidote as a diplomatic row broke out.

There may be a thousand ways to die, but there are only really two ways for states to kill: directly or indirectly. States can use their own forces – usually paramilitary, intelligence or special forces – to take out the target. In the examples cited above, the US, Russia and Israel did just that. Soleimani was killed by a US drone; Russian intelligence poisoned Navalny; and Israeli intelligence organized the assassination outside Tehran, smuggling ground-breaking technology into the country. In fact, Russia passed a law in 2006 permitting its military and special services to conduct just such extrajudicial killings abroad, targeting those accused of 'extremism' and 'hooliganism'.[2]

A direct strike has the benefit of greater control over the operation and a higher chance of success. State assets are well trained, equipped and funded. But there is a catch. Greater control comes at the cost of decreased plausible deniability. Direct involvement, getting hands dirty, will more often than not leave the state's fingerprints all over the operation, making it much more difficult to deny. Who else other than Israel could have set up a remote-control semi-autonomous gun amid the villas of an upmarket district outside Tehran? It hardly looked like an accident or the work of a random run-of-the-mill terrorist. Given the risks of exposure, states are more likely to kill directly if they deem it legal, if they are not too concerned about secrecy, or, as we shall see, if they think the benefits outweigh the negatives.

Presidents and prime ministers contemplating a lethal strike grapple with this macabre trade-off between directness and deniability.[3] Drones and special forces sit at one end. Next, a spymaster might recruit an agent to carry out the assassination, thereby giving some deniability. In 2013, a young Turk living in France shot dead three Kurdish activists in Paris. One was Sakine Cansız, a political refugee and co-founder of the PKK terrorist group, established to fight for Kurdish independence from Turkey. Press reports strongly suggested that Turkish intelligence had recruited the assassin, but it was difficult to prove.[4]

The agents could even be unwitting. In 2017, North Korea assassinated the dictator's half-brother, Kim Jong-nam, in a bizarre operation. Jong-nam had arrived at Kuala Lumpur airport, travelling under a fake name, on his way back from a picturesque tourist island off Malaysia's west coast. He was a wanted man, having become a critic of the regime – and a reported CIA source. Indeed, he may have been travelling back from meeting an American intelligence officer. Kim waited in the busy terminal for a flight on to Macau when, all of a sudden, a woman swooped in behind him thrusting a wet cloth into his face. His eyes burned; he felt dizzy. The liquid was a deadly nerve agent and Kim died shortly afterwards.

A twist followed. When arrested, the woman and her accomplice claimed that they had no idea what they were doing, instead believing it was a prank for a hidden-camera television show. They had earlier been seen performing similar pranks in a nearby mall. The supposed TV producers who had recruited them quietly fled the country.

Moving further down the macabre scale of directness and deniability, an intelligence agency sometimes supplies a rebel group with weapons – but issue no orders and ask no questions. The CIA has a track record here. Back in the 1950s, it covertly supplied pistols, ammunition and grenades to dissidents seeking to overthrow Rafael Trujillo in the Dominican Republic. Trujillo was a thug of a dictator, amassing a personal fortune while unleashing terrorism and massacre at home and abroad. Rumour has it he fed the bodies of his dead opponents to sharks. His cult of personality – visible through a superabundance of statues and even the renaming of the highest mountain in the country after himself – made him a perfect target for assassination. If he fell, so too would the entire regime.

Armed with weapons and ammunition from the CIA, but without explicit American instruction, conspirators ambushed Trujillo's car along a dark highway in May 1961. A vicious gun battle left the dictator sprawled dead on the road. The US did not technically order the assassination, but some in Washington knew it was coming and fully approved.[5]

Twenty years later, with assassination now illegal under US law, the CIA covertly supported rebels in Nicaragua seeking to overthrow the leftist government. As part of the operation, the CIA famously prepared a training manual which highlighted what it obliquely called the benefits of selective violence for prop-aganda purposes. In other words, assassination. Critics decried it as a murder manual. At around the same time, CIA officers covertly supporting the Afghan mujahideen against the Soviet invasion sent sniper rifles and other lethal weapons to the rebels – but asked no questions about how they would be used.[6]

If special forces and drones lie at one end, then collusion lies at the other end of our directness/deniability scale. This might even

be as passive as simply turning a blind eye to terrorist activity or
not investigating crimes properly. Collusion is particularly associated with UK activity in Northern Ireland; however, it extends well
beyond this arena. Loyalists and collaborators played an important role in the rise and fall of the British Empire, from surrogates
in nineteenth-century India killing on behalf of the crown, to
collusion with friendly local forces during dirty end-of-empire
counter-insurgencies in places like Palestine, Cyprus and Kenya.

As part of the covert operation to overthrow the Iranian
prime minister in 1953, MI6 used propaganda to smear Iran's
chief of police and whip opposition forces into a fervour. He was
kidnapped (as part of the plan to provide a morale boost for the
opposition) but ended up tortured and murdered. Two years later,
MI6 tried to start a row within the Hanoi politburo intended to
spark a chain of events leading to the assassination of the North
Vietnamese president Ho Chi Minh. No order had to be given;
the death would not be traced back to Britain. In 1960, Britain
ran a covert campaign to destabilize the Congolese leader Patrice
Lumumba. It included propaganda, bribery, smears and even use
of stink bombs. Alongside the CIA, MI6 conspired to create a situation whereby the death of Lumumba was practically inevitable.[7]

Collusion in Northern Ireland led to the deaths of numerous
republicans. Most notoriously, in 1989, loyalist terrorists burst
into the home of a thirty-nine-year-old nationalist solicitor, Pat
Finucane, and shot him dead in front of his wife and children.
The most recent government inquiry into the attack is damning:
'a series of positive actions by employees of the State actively
furthered and facilitated his murder'. And Finucane was not a
one-off. While there was no central policy of collusion stemming
from Downing Street, various security policies and use of propaganda to discredit certain targets enabled it.[8]

Colluding with rebel and terrorist groups is the most indirect way a state can kill. Collusion has a clear benefit: it becomes difficult, if not impossible, to prove the hand of the state. No orders are given and neither is collusion a policy which can be uncovered, rather a witting – or even unwitting – consequence of a wider culture or approach to a particular conflict. As ever, though, it comes with significant legal and practical problems: the state's intelligence services will have little influence or control over the deaths. Violence could spiral; innocent people could end up dead. Whether going direct or indirect, or indeed any point on the scale between them, assassinations, like all covert actions, create tough choices. Leaders cannot have it all. An increase in secrecy creates a decrease in control and impact.

Even when working directly, it is crucial to remember one thing: the real James Bonds do not have a licence to kill. Any use of lethal force would need to be signed off by the foreign secretary or prime minister. The 1994 Intelligence Services Act does allow MI6 to engage in 'other tasks' beyond gathering intelligence, while a particularly sensitive section, often referred to as the James Bond clause in the press, gives the foreign secretary power to authorize criminality overseas. At the time, Number 10 worried that excitable journalists might interpret it as a licence to kill and so Prime Minister John Major annotated the draft text with a single word, 'Hitler', offering the classic Whitehall analogy of when lethal force would be considered.[9]

Even if MI6 officers could kill people (and they cannot) – it hardly amounts to a licence given the amount of ministerial oversight required. And besides, MI6 does not have paramilitary capabilities. If ministers did authorize lethal force, intelligence officers would rely on their close relationship with special forces to carry it out.

In summer 2021, *The Sun* breathlessly hyped the existence of 'the real 007s... a unit of real-life James Bonds so secret [the] government won't admit they exist': the elite E Squadron, which works at the disposal of MI6 and the director of special forces. It is a very real unit, staffed by brave personnel and doing important, dangerous work. The journalist quoted one operative: 'Is it a licence to kill? It is certainly not carte blanche. But the nature of soldiering means it's sometimes necessary to take life. Everyone is trained in deadly force.'[10] The article – and plenty of others like it – is a classic example of constructing specialness, peddling myth and misperceptions about the licence to kill. Suggestive photographs of Princess Diana (whom MI6 did not assassinate) and interviews with special forces 'legends' describing their 'mad ops' provided plenty of innuendo. It is little wonder that myths emerge.

Neither do MI6 *agents* have a licence to kill. Although officers and agents are often wrongly conflated, intelligence agents are those individuals – usually foreign nationals – recruited by officers to spy for the UK. Under certain circumstances, agents can commit crimes in order to protect their cover while gathering intelligence. For example, an agent inside a terrorist group would look suspicious if he or she consistently refused to engage in any criminality. Indeed, almost every successful counterterrorist operation in recent years has involved some sort of undercover human agent hidden inside the group. Agents have engaged in serious criminality in the past; however, the government claims that it is carefully monitored with proportionate red lines imposed. Despite sensational newspaper headlines to the contrary, it does not amount to a licence to kill.

Thanks to the fictional exploits of James Bond, and rampant

mythologization in the tabloid press, the infamous licence to kill is most associated with British intelligence. It is a myth elsewhere too. The CIA does have paramilitary capabilities and a more gung-ho reputation than MI6, but CIA officers do not have a licence to kill either. Any covert use of lethal force – even a risk of accidental death as a by-product of a paramilitary operation – requires the explicit advance approval of the president. In something known as a finding or, in this case, a lethal finding, the president must inform certain members of Congress in writing, preferably in advance of the operation. In Israel, only the prime minister can give the go-ahead to a targeted assassination.[11]

Even in non-democracies like Russia and North Korea, it would be remarkable if authority did not come from the top especially regarding high-profile targets. State-sponsored killings may be on the rise, but it is a closely controlled activity. Intelligence agencies do not have a carte blanche licence to kill.

Putting ethics to one side, any leader contemplating assassination would be wise to temper their ambition. History suggests that thinking big – targeting presidents, premiers and popes – to overthrow a regime tends to end in failure. We can say with confidence that the US had a particularly appalling track record during the Cold War. Not a single plot in which the US directly sponsored the assassination of a leader succeeded. Of all the underhand tactics Washington used to overthrow regimes covertly, assassinating leaders had the lowest success rate by far.[12] This is because covert action cannot be both very secret and very impactful.

Numerous examples have come to light over the years: a catalogue of errors and excess. In 1957, the US – alongside British intelligence – drew up a list of Syrian officials to be removed as part of a ludicrously convoluted operation to overthrow the leftist government. 'A special effort should be made to eliminate key individuals,' as the planning documents euphemistically put it. The plot fell apart; it had been utterly penetrated by Syrian intelligence.

In autumn 1960, the CIA plotted to kill Patrice Lumumba, the leader of the Congo. Amid army mutinies and breakaway rebels, Lumumba faced a breakdown of order at home and committed the crime of turning to the Soviets for help. A scientist from the CIA's banally named 'technical services division' turned up in the capital, Léopoldville, armed with a special poison which would cause a fatal disease. It was to be slipped into Lumumba's toothpaste. The senior intelligence officer on the ground dithered and refused to go through with the plan. Lumumba survived for another year before being shot by separatist fighters (with the complicity of Belgium). All that remained of him was a single tooth.

The most infamous name on the American hit list was of course Fidel Castro, the cigar-smoking, charismatic, communist leader of Cuba. Some of the botched assassination attempts were laughably farcical and have since become legendary – and heavily mythologized. The earliest known plot targeting the leaders of the Cuban revolution has only recently come to light. In the summer of 1960, just a year after his brother assumed power, Raul Castro was due to fly back to Havana from Prague alongside other high-profile revolutionaries. Sensing an opportunity, the CIA developed 'The Accident Plot'.

Intelligence officers recruited the pilot of the plane, Jose Raul Martinez, and paid him $10,000 to arrange an accident. This would be an incredibly risky venture, given the dangers to the pilot's own life, and the lives of his crew, if the plane crashed. Martinez was willing to take the calculated risk but made the CIA promise that, if he died, his two sons would receive a college education.

Martinez set off to Prague to collect the Cuban delegation and fly them home. When he was mid-air, the CIA dramatically backed out. 'Do not pursue,' instructed a cable sent to the Havana station. By this time, it was too late and there was no way of reaching the pilot. Intelligence officers waited nervously for news of a plane with engine burnout or crashing into the water. In the end, the plane arrived home safe and sound with all passengers alive. Martinez told his CIA handler that he had 'no opportunity to arrange an accident such as we had discussed'.[13]

Other, better known, plots revolved around cigars, of both the exploding and poisoned variety. Another plan proposed that an agent would slip poison into Castro's milkshake or ice cream. Yet another involved a poison pen, which came equipped with a hidden hypodermic needle so fine that the Cuban leader would not have felt it when a nearby official, recruited by the CIA, injected him. The agent, who coincidentally received the pen on the same day as the Kennedy assassination, did not think much of the gadget. It apparently lacked sophistication.

The bizarre list goes on. The CIA exploited Castro's love of scuba diving by plotting to sabotage his wetsuit with some sort of fungus which caused a skin disease. If that was not enough, it also planned to lace his breathing apparatus with tuberculosis. The devious idea never left the laboratory. Another, equally devious, scheme involved booby trapping a particularly exquisite seashell. It would be painted with such beautiful colours that Castro would simply be unable to resist swimming towards it for a closer look. As he approached, the shell would explode. Officials later discarded the idea as impractical.

And on still. The CIA worked with mobsters from the underworld to bump him off, exploiting mafia anger at Castro's closure of Havana's casinos. It also supposedly recruited one of Castro's former lovers to slip poison pills in his drink. She got cold feet and backed out (but would have failed anyway given that she stored them in a cold-cream jar, causing them to lose their potency). All these attempts failed. Assassinating foreign leaders was harder than it looked. US Attorney General Robert Kennedy, President Kennedy's brother, was losing patience: 'why can't you gentlemen get things cooking the way 007 does?' he asked.[14]

The US clearly had a poor track record. We might debate the CIA hand in the deaths of Trujillo in the Dominican Republic or Diem in South Vietnam, both of which led to a change of government. But the Americans explicitly sanctioned neither. The US supported the removal by South Vietnamese generals of the autocratic leader and one time US-favourite, Ngo Dinh Diem. Kennedy hoped for a bloodless coup, but the plotters ended up murdering Diem and his brother in the back of an armoured personnel carrier. These lie very much at the indirect end of the assassination scale.

Despite the US experience dominating history books, it is important to look beyond the CIA before concluding that state-sponsored assassination does not work. Examples of unequivocal success are hard to find. Some might point to the assassination of Archduke Franz Ferdinand on the streets of Sarajevo in 1914. A young nationalist stepped out from the crowd and pulled a pistol at close range. This was a consequential killing given its role in the countdown to the First World War, but, while the assassins enjoyed support from Serbian military intelligence, the Serbian government did not direct or sanction the assassination. Its prime minister got wind of armed men crossing the border into Bosnia but did not know the details of what was planned. Thinking it dangerous anyway, he disapproved and even apparently sent an unofficial, if vague, warning to Vienna.

The prelude to the Second World War offers its own candidate. In July 1934, Austrian Nazis shot and killed the chancellor Engelbert Dollfuss. Across the border in Germany, Hitler denied knowledge, but evidence found decades later suggested that he did, in fact, order the coup when a historian found scribblings in Joseph Goebbels' notebook: 'Austrian question. Whether it will work. I'm very sceptical.'[15] The assassination succeeded when a gunman entered the chancellery and shot Dollfuss twice. However, the wider Nazi coup failed. It cannot therefore be seen as a success, at least in the short term.[16] 'Lost!' Goebbels wrote afterwards.

We might look instead to the aftermath of the conflict and the emerging Cold War, as the Soviets consolidated power over eastern Europe. In February 1948, the Soviets backed a communist takeover of the Czechoslovakian government. The following month, Jan Masaryk was found dead on the cobbled streets of Prague. The only non-communist left in the Czechoslovakian government, he had – officially at least – committed suicide by jumping from a window of the Czech foreign ministry building. Is this finally an example of a successful and consequential state-sponsored assassination? There are two problems. First, despite very strong suspicion, it is not clear whether he was murdered and by whom. Second, even if he was assassinated by the Soviets, and he might well have been, Masaryk was not the leader and died two weeks after the coup.

There are plenty of other inconclusive cases. In August 1988, the leader of Pakistan, Muhammad Zia-ul-Haq, died in a plane crash. The plane had taken off smoothly but soon nosedived and crashed. Local investigators concluded that it had likely been sabotaged, and pointed to evidence of an explosion inside the aircraft. Perhaps a bomb detonated inside the cockpit; perhaps someone had hidden nerve gas in a crate of mangoes. Pakistani intelligence accused a foreign power of conspiring to assassinate him. Over the years, fingers have pointed to the usual suspects of the Soviets, Israel, Afghanistan and India, but in the absence of hard evidence much of this labours in the realm of speculation.[17]

And there have been near misses: in 1995, senior members of the Sudanese government conspired to assassinate President Mubarak of Egypt. Sudanese intelligence officers provided passports to terrorists, transferred the weapons via state airliner, and then stored them in the Sudanese embassy in Ethiopia, where Mubarak was due for a meeting of the Organisation of African Unity. It was here the assassins would strike. As Mubarak approached, gunmen stepped out into the street and fired their AK-47 assault rifles. Fortunately for him, they fired at the wrong car; his armoured limousine, third in the convoy, quickly spun around, and his bodyguards bundled him back into the plane.[18] It backfired for Sudan. The United Nations Security Council denounced it for sponsoring terrorism; its Islamist government became increasingly isolated; and a regional alliance emerged aiming to topple it entirely.[19]

Given this litany of half-baked failures, near misses and inconclusive cases, can we say that covert assassination does not change regimes? Not quite. The two clearest cut examples, of which we know, happened within three years of each other. The first comes from Afghanistan in December 1979. After a communist coup in Afghanistan the year before, followed by another coup in September, the Soviets wanted to ensure their unstable neighbours had a friendly, more predictable, regime in place. The KGB infiltrated the kitchen staff of the Afghan leader, Hafizullah Amin, and managed to poison his food. Doctors frantically saved his life but, as he lay in bed recuperating, a handful of Soviet special forces stormed the Tajbeg Palace in Kabul and assassinated him.[20]

The Soviets invaded the very same day. Moscow quickly tried to separate the two events and denied involvement in the assassination. They insisted it was an internal coup, and Kabul Radio officially claimed – wrongly – that the president had been tried and executed for crimes against the regime.[21] If the devious and plausibly deniable Plan A fails, sometimes a more brazen Plan B is necessary.

The second example comes from Syria in 1982. A bomb, planted by a Syrian agent, killed Bashir Gemayel, the president-elect of Lebanon. Technically, it was not a regime change because it prevented the new president from taking office rather than removing the serving leader, but it still had huge consequence in scuppering the promise of better relations between Lebanon and Israel. Syria is widely blamed for directing, or at the very least knowing in advance and approving, the assassination. Senior US and Israeli intelligence sources have pointed the finger at the very highest levels of the Syrian government.[22]

The lack of clear examples is revealing. On the one hand, some deniable or untraceable operations are surely yet to come to light (rumours persist, for example, about secret French complicity in the assassination of the revolutionary leader of Burkina Faso in 1987) and, as outlined earlier, sometimes this can be done indirectly without the state instructing an assassination. Back in the mental grey zone, how can we call an assassination covert action given a lack of evidence of state sponsorship? There is a big difference between directing, sponsoring and turning a blind eye.

On the other hand, covert state-sponsored assassination designed to overthrow governments is not only illegal but very difficult. Even if – and it is a very big if – a president, prime minister or chancellor is killed, it is unlikely the wider regime will change in a manner favourable to the sponsoring state. Just as killing Dollfuss did not bring the Nazis to power in Austria, many in the CIA knew that, had they killed Castro, someone else would have taken his place. Even killing Castro, his brother and Che Guevara, the legendary revolutionary, would not have been enough. There is a clear difference between change of leader and change of regime. If a leader chose to go down this route, not only would they need a Plan B but they would also need conventional armed forces to ensure a new, more favourable, government. Assassination does not succeed on its own.

Assassinations and targeted killings obviously do succeed some-times – but at a less ambitious level. The Russians had enjoyed plenty of success killing dissidents over the years, including on the streets of the UK, as the fatal poisoning of Alexander Litvinenko in 2006 demonstrated; the Israelis have killed many terrorists and scientists over the decades; the US drone programme, from Somalia to Pakistan, has killed thousands since 9/11. Apartheid-era South Africa was also notoriously aggressive. Its security forces successfully assassinated up to one hundred people between the late 1970s and early 1990s, with many thousands more dying in the wider violence.[23]

Assassinations can remove an imminent threat. They can disrupt and reduce the technical expertise of adversaries. Israeli operations targeting Iranian scientists illustrate this well. In 2007, a forty-four-year-old Iranian nuclear scientist mysteri-ously died. Three years later, another Iranian nuclear scientist died when a booby-trapped motorcycle exploded as he tried to open his car door. In 2012, a motorcyclist pulled up alongside a car and quickly stuck a magnetic bomb on its door before speeding off. The driver, yet another Iranian nuclear scientist, died of his wounds shortly after the explosion. The fatal ambush of Fakhrizadeh in 2020 is simply the most recent in a long line of assassinations in which Israel targeted the technical expertise of an adversary – expertise which is difficult to replace.

Despite hesitancy among intelligence professionals, Presidents Bush and Obama saw targeted killings as a pragmatic option to disrupt and remove the terrorist threat. They thought so partly because the US swiftly overthrew Afghanistan's Taliban regime in late 2001 forcing the surviving terrorists to reorganize into secret cells and hide in rough mountainous terrain. Others fled across borders. This made it difficult for the US to fight them using conventional military power.

Moreover, by the middle of the decade, the domestic population had grown tired of the never-ending wars in Afghanistan and Iraq. Targeted killing offered a more surgical and detached alternative to ever more boots on the ground. As a leading thinker on ethics and war, Michael Walzer, put it: targeted killing 'is clearly better than untargeted killings'.[24] All the while, advances in technology enabled pilotless drones to stay airborne for longer periods of time and to carry missiles. Choosing armed drones to remove a stubborn and evasive terrorist threat seemed like the obvious option. There is a danger here, though: the US turned to targeted killing because it seemed a simpler alternative, not because it obviously worked. Too often leaders turn quickly and uncritically to the tools at hand.[25]

Assassinations can disrupt, but they can also send a message. They are theatre. Leaders are not so woefully naïve as to think that certain covert actions are completely secret and that nobody is aware of who is behind them.

In 2018, an elderly man and his daughter were found slumped on a park bench in Salisbury. They slipped in and out of consciousness. He was Sergei Skripal, a former Russian intelligence officer who had betrayed the Kremlin and become an agent for MI6. Two days earlier, a pair of Russians, flying under false names, had arrived at Gatwick airport. In an era of advanced technology and biometric data, such international undercover activity is becoming more difficult, but not impossible. It appears that Russian intelligence pressured a source to manipulate British visa systems to allow their officers to slip past customs.[26] They then travelled west to Salisbury, likely on a quick last-minute reconnaissance mission, before returning to a two-star hotel in east London.

The next day, the pair took the train back to Salisbury where CCTV showed them in the vicinity of Skripal's home. They contaminated his door handle with a lethal nerve agent which they had hidden inside a Nina Ricci perfume bottle specially converted into a dispenser. That night, the two men quietly flew back to Moscow. The Skripals survived, but a local woman, Dawn Sturgess, who had also come into contact with the perfume bottle, died shortly afterwards.

A Russian dissident-turned-spy poisoned on the streets of the UK sparked intense media interest and inevitably triggered an investigation. The deadly substance, Novichok, could easily be traced back to Russia – it was almost a calling card – while the subsequent denials of the alleged perpetrators were laughably implausible. Two nervous-looking men appeared on camera to recount their visit to the wonderful city of Salisbury specifically to see the cathedral's famous clock, the first of its kind, and the 120-metre spire.

But this is to miss the point. The attempted assassination required an audience.[27] Exposure was necessary to send a message to other defectors and would-be defectors. There are at least a dozen or so former Russian intelligence officers who have spied for the British currently living in the UK. The message to them was clear: you cannot escape the past; we can come for you; you can never relax. The message to other intelligence officers, in fact to any government official tempted to defect, was equally clear: do not be disloyal. Or else. MI5 also interpreted it as a message to the UK more generally, warning it against recruiting more Russian spies. The head of MI5's Russia counterespionage desk, known only as Tom, was shocked at the brazenness and ruthlessness of the attack but ultimately knew it was more about the message and less about the assassination.[28]

Putin's pantomime secrecy was performative power. The very public assassination attempt sought to enhance his image as a bare-chested horseback-riding strong man.[29] It threw down a challenge to the west. Attempted assassination on the streets of Salisbury was not an act of war but it did shamelessly flout international sovereignty and important principles against the use of chemical weapons. This grey zone made a response difficult.

Putin was not alone. The failed assassination of Skripal was sandwiched between two successful assassinations conducted by other authoritarian regimes. The bizarre North Korean assassination of Kim Jong-nam in 2017 sent an equally powerful message to critics, and using the cover of a game show really did have an element of performance in more ways than one. Then, in October 2018, just months after the attack on Skripal, Jamal Khashoggi, a dissident Saudi journalist, entered the Saudi consulate in Istanbul and never came back out. He was assassinated and dismembered before a body-double stepped outside wearing his clothes in a crass attempt to trick the security cameras. Saudi denials became increasingly implausible as evidence piled up.

But it did not matter: the case attracted international media coverage – the message had been sent. As Khashoggi's fiancée put it, 'I cannot really imagine what the Saudi state thought it could achieve by killing Jamal but, maybe, after the Arab Spring, they were saying: Either you are with us or, if not, look at what will happen to you.'[30] Assassination is political theatre, often with pantomime secrecy.

This idea is not lost on Israel either. Meir Dagan, a former head of Mossad, strongly believed that assassinations 'have an effect on morale, as well as practical effect'. Killings removed direct threats to Israel but also sent a wider message: 'If you are an enemy of Israel, we will find and kill you, wherever you are.' Mossad's aggressive and merciless reputation only helped deter enemies further.[31] It was attritional: chipping away at authority, crippling terrorist groups and other adversaries.

Assassinations and targeted killings can clearly succeed: in removing threats, in disrupting authorities and in sending a message. But what difference does it make and how do we judge success? It is relatively straightforward to determine whether a drone strike, for example, has killed its target, but it is incredibly difficult to determine the effect. In the US context, lethal findings covering targeted killing are self-evidently binary. Unlike in earlier decades, when language suggesting assassination was euphemistic (such as removing or neutralizing targets), the goal is unambiguous: a stated target either dies or survives. Success or failure. Or so it seems.

Once again, there is a catch: success – even regarding killings – is subjective. Take French assassination operations back in the 1950s as an example. As revolutionary war raged in Algeria, France turned to dirty and brutal tricks in an attempt to turn the tide. The lethal tactics, still familiar today, included undetectable poison, a booby-trapped radio set, underwater explosives, and firearms in the street. French intelligence analysts boasted of success after success. Their boasts seem outlandish given that some operations designated 'partial success' did not actually kill their targets. Two merely injured the targets; another killed the mother of the target, rather than the target himself, an arms dealer; and another hit the family of the target, a man who had provided support to Algerian insurgent sympathizers. Other, less biased, observers might well have labelled each as an outright and embarrassing failure.

Meanwhile, whoever was doing the evaluation deliberately played down failures. The analyst cannily separated failed assassinations from those that were cancelled due to security concerns or because the target was not where intelligence said they would be. Two cancelled assassinations targeted the same man, Ahmed Kamal, an arms trafficker. Unfortunately for the assassins, Kamal had left his hotel in Madrid before they arrived on the first occasion, and was too closely surrounded by other people on the second. This sounds distinctly like a failure.[32] Success and failure are in the eye of the beholder. How to assassinate? Aim low and claim success.

Complicating matters further, lethal covert actions often take place in a broader foreign policy vacuum. A one-off tactical hit might successfully kill the target, providing a flickering victory, but it is difficult to ascertain its place in the broader strategy, and, by extension, its cumulative impact. Covert action risks becoming a never-ending game of whack-a-mole.[33]

US drone strikes have killed between eight thousand and sixteen thousand people since the 9/11 terrorist attacks. Each one that hit the intended target will have been claimed as a success.[34] What does this actually tell us about the success of the drone programme? What difference has it made? It is hard to know for sure.

Different observers use different definitions of targeted killing; determining the numbers of civilians killed is tricky; and isolating the impact of the strike from a host of other factors when assessing the terrorist threat is almost impossible.[35] At best, and moral considerations aside, targeted killing can disrupt the capabilities and communications of terrorist groups. It can weaken morale and lower professionalism.[36] According to Ronen Bergman, who wrote the definitive account of the Israeli assassination programme, 'on numerous occasions, it was targeted killing that saved Israel from very grave crises'.[37]

However, assassination can also be counterproductive in the long term and, like all forms of covert action, does not succeed on its own. Targeted killings are a siren call for angry young recruits seeking vengeance, and so can increase radicalization. They can create a less restrained, more radical leadership. Groups like al-Qaeda and the Taliban became less discriminate and more violent, increasingly targeting civilians, following targeted killing campaigns. The number of terrorist attacks increased following the deaths of al-Qaeda leaders such as Osama bin Laden and Anwar al-Awlaki, an American-Yemeni preacher. Terrorist groups, especially those that are older, larger and more established, adapt and become resilient. Killing the leader does not make the collapse of the organization any more likely.[38]

Apartheid-era South Africa offers an interesting historical example from which, thanks to hindsight and declassifications, we can draw conclusions about impact. Facing an existential threat from revolutionary guerrillas and hostile neighbours, the state turned to a notoriously aggressive strategy featuring covert assassination across borders and at home. Methods were particularly brutal, including stabbings, letter bombs, and even a bomb planted above the Cabinet Room in Harare, Zimbabwe (the Cabinet did not meet there in the end). Security forces eliminated multiple targets in an attempt to remove threats, send a symbolic message to opponents, and sometimes for reasons of mere retribution. Importantly, though, the campaign self-evidently failed to preserve apartheid. At best, it convinced the African National Congress not to move into the final phase of revolutionary warfare: open conflict. Even so, assassination – and the wider brutality – did great reputational damage to South Africa during the transition years of the early 1990s. It was a failure. And its legacy was noxious.[39]

Assassination is illegal, difficult and dangerous. Killing others, especially outside of an obvious battlefield or legal process, is among the most serious action a state can take. Leaders contemplating lethal action face thorny dilemmas: whether to go covert or brazen; whether to be direct by using drone strikes or sending in hitmen; whether to be indirect by passing weapons to rebels and turning a blind eye, or somewhere in between. Whatever they choose, significant trade-offs around control and deniability abound. They cannot have it both ways. Besides, assassinating presidents and premiers in an attempt to change their regime is unlikely to work anyway. And even if it does, it likely requires some sort of military action to shore things up afterwards. Covert action can only do so much.

Perhaps, then, and moral issues firmly to one side, lethal operations work better against terrorists and dissidents. Such killings can disrupt targets and send a powerful message, although, to achieve this, leaders need to think carefully about secrecy, audiences and levels of exposure. You cannot send a message if nobody suspects your involvement. However, targeted killings can also be reprehensibly counterproductive. Leaders tempted by this route, whether through drones or letter bombs, must think carefully about the wider aims and how it fits into a broader strategy. Once leaders – and it is often political rather than intelligence leaders – agree that a target should die, the question then becomes: how on earth do they expect to get away with it?

2

HOW TO GET AWAY WITH MURDER

In early May 2011, President Obama and his national security team huddled around a screen in the White House situation room. They sat waiting for updates as elite Navy SEALs dramatically stormed a Pakistani compound where they believed Osama bin Laden to be hiding. Authorizing a raid deep inside Pakistan was a huge decision for Obama; he feared that, had he got it wrong, he would have ended up a one-term president. What if bin Laden was not there? What if the Pakistani military intercepted American forces? What if the SEALs ended up being taken as hostages?[1]

About two dozen SEALs and a dog boarded two specially equipped Black Hawk helicopters at a US airbase in Afghanistan and secretly flew over the Pakistani border towards the town of Abbottabad. One helicopter crash-landed in the compound. The SEALs were met with gunfire as they entered and searched the windowless building.

Back in Washington, Obama found the wait excruciating. Then, all of a sudden from their respective locations, the director of the CIA and the commander of special forces uttered – almost in unison – the words he had been desperate to hear: 'Geronimo

ID'd... Geronimo EKIA.' Geronimo was bin Laden's codename; EKIA stood for enemy killed in action. The SEALs had found bin Laden on the third floor, shot him dead, removed his body, and left. Within just forty minutes, it was all over. Gasps went up in the small conference room, inside which Obama's team squeezed to watch events unfold. 'We got him,' Obama said.[2] Thousands of Americans later gathered outside the White House and at Ground Zero in New York to celebrate as he announced the news publicly.

The president, eloquently as ever, insisted that the death of bin Laden was lawful. It was not an assassination, but formed part of the war against al-Qaeda, the leader of which was a legitimate military target: an enemy commander in the field. Critics argue that there was never any realistic chance of capturing him alive and so the mission was effectively a summary execution. He was surrounded by his family, and – holed up in a fortified compound – hardly posing an imminent threat. Neither was he actively participating in hostilities at the time, although even in hiding he still served as a potent recruitment tool for terrorists worldwide. To make matters worse, the US militarily breached Pakistani sovereignty without permission.

Because of this, the operation was a legal fudge. It was a covert action partly for diplomatic reasons because, if it had been a military operation, it could have constituted an act of war. Who knows how Pakistan would have responded? CIA authority provided the legal justification for it being deemed a covert action – the military was merely seconded to execute it.[3] The director of the CIA, Leon Panetta, was not really in command, though; that was the job of William McRaven, in charge of special forces and commanding the mission from Afghanistan. Perhaps if it was exclusively a CIA operation, the killing might have been misconstrued as an assassination. It is fitting that both McRaven and Panetta claimed mission accomplished virtually simultaneously.

Still, Osama bin Laden was the most infamous terrorist leader of all time. He was reviled in the US for his role in the 9/11 attacks and there was little incentive to push back against the White House's self-defence enemy combatant line. It was a success and criticism was inevitably muted. On other occasions, though, the target is neither so infamous nor reviled, and so the state must work that little bit harder to justify extrajudicial killing.

Assassination is illegal; targeted killings are not. The US has banned assassination since the mid-1970s when tales of hapless attempts to kill Fidel Castro hit the headlines. Many perceive assassinations as inherently immoral. They conjure images of President Kennedy shot in an open-top car in Dallas; Abraham Lincoln shot in the theatre; Mahatma Gandhi shot at point blank range in New Delhi; and Martin Luther King shot on the balcony of his motel room. They are politically motivated killings, often associated with treachery and tragedy. In Shake-speare's *Julius Caesar*, the eponymous Roman ruler famously utters the words 'et tu, Brute?' upon realizing, at the moment of his assassination, that his friend Brutus is a conspirator. Assassination has become intertwined with betrayal ever since.

Targeted killings are deemed legal. Like assassinations they involve the extrajudicial death of a pre-selected individual. Crucially, unlike assassinations, they are supposedly value-neutral: an act of self-defence against an imminent threat, usually an enemy combatant in a hostile foreign environment. These threats predominantly derive from international terrorists, and consequently the number of targeted killings conducted by the US rose dramatically during the War on Terror. Abu Musab al-Zarqawi, a Jordanian terrorist leader, was one of the most high-profile examples. In 2006, he was killed by laser-guided bombs while attending a meeting at a safe house northeast of Baghdad. He was one of many. President Obama ordered a whopping ten times more drone strikes than President Bush. President Trump increased drone strikes in Somalia and Afghanistan further still. All three administrations insisted they were lawful.

Israel has long conducted targeted killings. In 2006, its approach received unanimous legal backing from its Supreme Court. Clearly not every targeted killing complied but, in principle, so long as every effort was made to prevent injury to innocent people, so long as the strike was based on excellent intelligence, and so long as less harmful means could not be used, targeted killings could be judged legal on a case-by-case basis. The military saw it as a vindication of an established practice.[4]

Evidently, there is a large and undeniable difference between the political assassination of someone like President Kennedy and the targeted killing of a terrorist. In practice, the difference is not always so clear cut. Blurred lines exist. How can states get away with assassination? Call it a targeted killing. Human rights organizations have strongly condemned targeted killings as violations of international law: they have killed many civilians over the years; the targets do not get a fair trial; and Obama's stretching of the definition of imminent threat can only be described as Olympic-standard linguistic gymnastics.

Imminence is like makeshift goalposts demarcated by jumpers on a field: their improvised parameters only hold until a controversial goal challenges them. Obama leapt on the concept of imminence, clung on to it, and wrestled it into submission when justifying targeted killings. Many critics, with some justification, accuse the president of stretching its definition to the point of meaninglessness in a desperately transparent (or transparently desperate) attempt to legitimize the killing of terrorists abroad.

Obama's rationale was logical enough. Successive presidents have long sought to expand the justification used for killing people overseas, and constantly emphasizing imminence allowed them to do so while demonstrating respect for conventions surrounding the legitimate use of force. At the same time, the White House updated and expanded the concept of imminence itself. According to the scholar of assassination Luca Trenta, the focus on imminence, however makeshift or stretched, cleverly resolves this contradiction between a legal footing and aggressive activity.[5]

The death of Qassem Soleimani in January 2020 encapsulates this debate. It was certainly more problematic and controversial than the death of Osama bin Laden almost a decade earlier. As we have seen, a US drone killed the Iranian general as his convoy left Baghdad airport late at night. Critics cried assassination; the White House insisted it was a legal and proportionate targeted killing designed to remove an imminent threat.

Soleimani was the commander of the Quds Force, roughly equivalent to the CIA and US special forces combined, an elite unit within the Iranian Revolutionary Guard Corps. An incredibly powerful figure both in Iran and the wider region, he commanded a unit specializing in unconventional warfare, including sponsoring terrorist groups across the Middle East and supporting President Bashar al-Assad's brutal regime in Syria. Soleimani operated in the shadows, directing the subversive campaign against American influence across the region. He oversaw a network of militant groups responsible for the deaths of hundreds of Americans in Iraq; his forces assassinated many more local foes.[6]

Although options to kill Soleimani had been on the table since early in his presidency, Donald Trump seemingly authorized the operation impulsively, against the advice of some of his senior advisers with whom he discussed the strike on the golf course. One golfing partner, Senator Lindsey Graham, urged Trump not to take such a huge and recklessly dangerous step. Iran might respond aggressively by assassinating members of friendly royal families in the region, by sabotaging oil installations, or by fomenting coups in neighbouring countries.[7]

The CIA worked with spies in five states to monitor the movements of Soleimani carefully. The shadowy commander travelled cautiously, always fearful of attack. His name never appeared on passenger lists; aircraft crew did not know if he would be travelling until the last minute. He switched phones three times in the hours before his death. Israeli intelligence helped monitor his mobile phone patterns. This was a team effort. An elite Kurdish unit helped guide US snipers, operating from nearby buildings and vehicles. They would serve as backup in case the drone strike failed.[8]

Soleimani arrived at Baghdad airport shortly after midnight. His flight from Damascus was delayed by two hours – a delay deliberately created by US intelligence because the drone they planned to use was suffering a technical glitch. Kurdish operatives posed as ground crew, directing the plane to a halt. Other undercover Kurds, posing as baggage handlers, positively identified him as he descended from the plane onto the tarmac. The CIA watched overhead, tracking his vehicle as it set off towards the designated kill zone.[9]

Drone operators fired two missiles, taking out both cars in the convoy. Ten people died, including Soleimani, whose remains were identified informally by a ring on his finger. Another victim was Abu Mahdi al-Muhandis, leader of a local Hezbollah militia group – an unexpected bonus for Trump.

Trump quickly and gleefully acknowledged the successful strike. Although planned in intense secrecy, the president and his advisers ultimately opted for an overt killing, eschewing more devious methods on which the CIA had been secretly working. Impact and scale came at the expense of secrecy, but for Trump it was worth it. He knew the US would be blamed anyway, and he wanted to take credit to bolster his re-election campaign. He wanted his bin Laden moment.[10]

Trump publicly accused Soleimani of plotting 'imminent and sinister' attacks on American targets, including four US embassies.[11] His secretary of state, Mike Pompeo, floundered when reporters pressed him on the question of imminence. The chairman of the House Intelligence Committee, who had supposedly received extensive intelligence, publicly expressed doubts. As Trump and Pompeo changed their stories, Democrats demanded the release of intelligence demonstrating the imminent threat and justifying the death.[12]

Under pressure, the US government continually repeated the mantra: it was a legal targeted killing executed in self-defence against an imminent threat. Soleimani undoubtedly had blood on his hands, having headed the much-feared Quds Force and having developed plenty of links to terrorist and militia groups over the years. Trump repeatedly called him a terrorist. The US ambassador to the United Nations cited Article 51 of the UN charter to justify the strike: self-defence. Iran had subjected the US to continuous threats and attacks.

Critics grew more vocal. After all, Soleimani was a high-ranking military official representing a government with which the US was not at war. For the first time, the US expanded its targeted killing to a state official.[13] Justifications of self-defence and imminent threat seemed stretched to breaking point. Indeed, Pompeo now implied that imminence constituted anything that put US lives at risk. Even Obama would have blushed.[14] The UN's special rapporteur on extrajudicial killings was unimpressed, concluding that the strike was 'a violation' of the UN charter 'with insufficient evidence provided of an ongoing or imminent attack'.[15]

Trump unsurprisingly dug in his heels. He told Republican donors that US intelligence had intercepted audio footage of Soleimani discussing plans to target Americans. If true, this would have been a huge intelligence coup and a decent return on the millions of dollars spent targeting the communications of senior Iranians. However, just because the Iranians had plans did not actually mean they would execute them.[16] Equally unsurprisingly, Trump also turned to Twitter, attacking his critics and anyone else demanding proof of imminence as peddling fake news. In characteristic style, he then suggested it did not matter anyway, because Soleimani was a terrorist with a bad past. Within merely a couple of weeks, his attorney general even dismissed imminence as a 'red herring'.[17]

Details are still sparse, and the intelligence underpinning the decision to kill Soleimani will not be declassified for decades. One thing is for sure: while targeted killing and assassination are legally distinct, they exist in a slippery grey zone conceptually. In practice, the differences between them can be wafer thin and down to the perceptions of observers. There is one other certainty: even if the killing of Soleimani did constitute an illegal assassination or extrajudicial execution, it is highly unlikely that the US will face significant consequences. Power talks.

On the questions of imminence, threat and legality, states get away with lethal strikes by controlling the narrative. The US exploits quasi-secrecy to normalize its targeted killing policy

– and differentiate it from assassination in the public mind. Frustrated officials realized that the intense secrecy surrounding lethal drone strikes in places like Yemen was proving counterproductive. On the one hand, it was – and remains – very difficult to plausibly deny such visible and explosive deaths brought about by hi-tech weaponry. With reporters sniffing around and locals equipped with smartphones able to film the bloody aftermath, consistent denials by the White House made it difficult to rebut damaging claims of high civilian casualties. On the other hand, Obama's team wanted to take credit for what they saw as a successful policy.

To resolve this, they carefully crafted a twilight zone of quasi-secrecy. Senior officials gradually began to praise the programme's effectiveness – and legality – without acknowledging that it even existed. On one occasion, the CIA director refused to discuss particulars about 'covert and secret operations', before adding that 'these operations have been very effective because they have been very precise in terms of the targeting and it involved a minimum of collateral damage'.[18] It is reminiscent of Tony Blair's quip that 'We never talk about intelligence matters… except when we want to, obviously.'

More controversially, the Obama White House used leaks and unattributable briefings to ensure friendly press coverage and gradually legitimize the covert killings. Multiple newspaper stories emerged which revealed the classified drone programme in a controlled way. The idea was to keep the American people minimally informed and to artfully frame the killings in a manner designed to boost support without compromising security. Leaking details in this manner also aimed to prevent domestic watchdog groups from securing additional details about sensitive internal procedures, collateral damage estimates and legal debates. This was the case regarding the classified drone programme in Yemen. Obama had promised his local allies that he would keep it secret, but that did not stop his team from planting information in the press.[19]

The secret state relies on half-knowledge. Covert action requires public approval and massive public investment, which clashes with the need for operational secrecy and so covert actions cannot be fully disclosed. As the academic Timothy Melley puts it, 'the covert state has an interest in generating a public that *thinks* it has a general knowledge of such work but *does not* and *cannot* know in detail'. This tension explains why states leak information, why the CIA has a large public relations department, and why military agencies loan their equipment to Hollywood studios. The CIA even gave classified material to the director and screenwriter of *Zero Dark Thirty*, the film about the killing of bin Laden.[20]

Even if states cannot control the narrative, they can muddy it through ubiquitous messages meandering between obliquity and obfuscation. This is how Russia and Saudi Arabia have tried to get away with recent attempted assassinations. Given the fragmented media landscape and competing commercial pressures, even a non-democratic state like Russia struggles to micro-manage journalists' coverage of high-profile deaths.[21] Instead, and amid much finger-pointing following the poisoning of Sergei Skripal in 2018, Russia put out dozens of competing stories. MI6 was to blame; a secret laboratory in Wiltshire was to blame; the poison came from Sweden, the Czech Republic or even the US; the Kremlin itself was a victim of 'hostile action'; the two suspects were innocent tourists; someone had doctored CCTV images of the suspects arriving in Britain; UK allegations were 'insane'. The list went on and on.

Russian diplomats simultaneously turned to sarcasm and humour. The embassy in London tweeted a picture of the fictional detective Hercule Poirot beneath the caption, 'In the absence of evidence, we need Poirot in Salisbury!' Pro-Kremlin Twitter users adopted the hashtag #IamfromGRUtoo, mocking both the #metoo movement and allegations that the suspects were undercover Russian intelligence officers.

On the surface the bewildering range of contradictions seems farcical. But the aim was not to make people believe all these things. Rather, Russia sought to chip away at the British version of events, to sow doubt, and to encourage people to question what was true and what was false. The humour and mockery lowered the level of discussion and made a serious message accessible, memorable and well suited to social media. Flooding the internet with competing stories ensured nothing made sense; people shrugged and wondered if anything was real anymore.[22] Propaganda and assassination go hand in hand; we cannot understand one means of covert action without understanding them all.

Saudi Arabia attempted something similar – albeit with far less humour – following the murder of Jamal Khashoggi in October 2018. The prominent journalist had once been close to the Saudi government but fell out with the royal family and became a vocal critic of the regime, writing a regular column in the *Washington Post*. At around lunchtime on 2 October, he entered the Saudi consulate in Istanbul but never emerged.

The Saudi story kept changing. At first, the government insisted that Khashoggi had left the building perfectly alive. Two weeks later, it accepted that Khashoggi had in fact died, but after a fight. Later still, it added that he had died from a chokehold.

The following month, Saudi prosecutors acknowledged that (what they decorously called) a 'negotiations team' had ordered the assassination after failing to bring Khashoggi back to Saudi Arabia peacefully – and that his body had been dismembered.

Crucially, though, the murder was supposedly not planned. Behind closed doors, a Saudi court sentenced five people to death. All the while, prosecutors insisted that the crown prince, the de facto ruler, had no knowledge.

The Turkish president accused a Saudi death squad of committing a premeditated murder in cold blood. It was, he continued, ordered at the highest levels of the government. Istanbul's chief prosecutor claimed Khashoggi was suffocated and his body dismembered. It turned out that Turkish intelligence had a recording of the killing in which Saudi officials discussed how to cut up the body before what they called the 'sacrificial animal' had even entered the building. He was likely injected with a sedative and suffocated using a plastic bag. Turkish intelligence claims to have heard the sound of a saw about twenty-five minutes after Khashoggi entered the building. The plausibility of Saudi denials quickly wore thin. In the UK, a former head of MI6, John Sawers, said it was inconceivable that the hit was not ordered by the highest levels of the Saudi government.[23] In early 2021, US intelligence assessed that the Saudi crown prince had approved the operation to kill or capture Khashoggi.[24]

The competing versions of events spread wildly on social media across the Gulf and beyond, sowing confusion and doubt. A network of over fifty websites, posing as authentic Arabic-language news outlets, spread disinformation. Khashoggi had long been the target of vicious smears himself, but mentions of his name skyrocketed on social media in the month following his death, with the content monopolized by a narrow clique of influencers rather than being an organic broader discussion. Twitter removed a network of thousands of bots sharing pro-Saudi positions on the killing.[25]

Clearly there is a stark and significant difference between American use of quasi-secrecy to normalize the targeted killing policy and Russian contradictory spamming or Saudi lies deployed to cover up attempted assassinations. All three cases do, however, emphasize the importance of the narrative to avoiding criticism.

States get away with killing because other states get away with killing. As more leaders turn to lethal drone strikes as a seemingly cost-efficient way to disrupt threats, and as other, more perfidious, leaders go unpunished for using poison or suffocation to despatch enemies, the taboo against killing erodes.

Before the terrorist attacks targeting the World Trade Center and the Pentagon in September 2001, the US had strongly criticized Israeli targeted killings as illegal and illegitimate. A year earlier, at the start of the Second Palestinian Intifada, or rebellion, Israel had begun to respond to suicide bombings with the daily use of armed drones, launching over one thousand strikes.[26] In the summer of 2001, the US ambassador to Israel bluntly denounced this lethal practice as constituting 'extrajudicial killings'. Just days before 9/11, the director of the CIA condemned any idea of covertly using armed drones to eliminate targets as being 'a terrible mistake'.[27]

Things changed overnight. After September 2001, the US stopped criticizing and instead turned to Israel for inspiration as Washington ramped up a targeted killing programme of its own.

The United Kingdom followed suit, albeit to a far lesser extent. British special forces engaged in targeted killing operations in both Iraq and Afghanistan, operations which, following the US lead, became increasingly up-tempo in their attempts to disrupt terrorist organizations. As they grew more proactive and aggressive, buying strategic credits with the Americans in the process, policymakers in Whitehall struggled to keep up. More recently, Prime Minister David Cameron supposedly had a kill list of his own, naming some twenty-four terrorist leaders who could be eliminated as a last resort.[28]

Things escalated in 2015 when, in an unprecedented and exceptional operation, a British drone strike in Syria killed a British ISIS fighter outside of military operations. Reyaad Khan was a twenty-one-year-old straight A student from Cardiff who had travelled to Syria in 2013 after becoming radicalized. An RAF drone strike killed him and two others, in a move which human rights groups noted emulated US policy. According to multiple intelligence reports, Khan was a prolific terrorist recruiter and attack planner. Over a period of nine months, he, and another man, provided practical instructions to terrorists around the world, encouraging them to make bombs and conduct attacks on British and allied targets. He undoubtedly posed a serious threat.

Questions remained over the key issue of imminence. Intelligence revealed that the timescale between Khan contacting operatives and providing targets could be very short and the intelligence agencies faced significant pressure to disrupt these attacks. Ministers decided he posed an imminent threat, but this is subjective, and the government refused to provide evidence to the parliamentary oversight body, the Intelligence and Security Committee. Neither did the government share evidence of how it concluded that Khan's actions constituted an armed attack on the UK or Iraq, which, it noted, was 'clearly a subjective assessment'. The committee publicly expressed its profound disappointment at being unable to do its job properly.[29] How do states get away with targeted killing? Follow the American lead, then impede proper oversight.

France – never one to shy away from aggressive covert operations – also followed the American lead. Like the US, France drew up a terrorist kill list and has been particularly active in hunting down jihadists in Syria and in the Sahel region of Africa.[30] In the eighteen months from January 2013, the Élysée ordered the elimination of more than fifteen high-value targets in Mali alone. According to one journalist, France put itself into the slipstream of the Americans post-9/11.[31]

The expanding US drone programme has influenced military activity, both covert and otherwise, well beyond American allies. In 2015, Pakistan used an armed drone it had built itself to kill what it called three high-profile terrorists in the tribal regions bordering Afghanistan. Turkey has used plenty of drones to kill separatist Kurdish fighters in Iraq and Syria, as well as inside Turkey itself. Meanwhile, China is building ever more lethal drones, and is happy to export them far and wide. Iraqi forces have used such Chinese drones to attack ISIS militants, sharing footage of a Chinese Cai Hong-4 blasting a terrorist position in Ramadi in 2015. The following year, Nigeria used a Chinese Cai Hong-3 to attack Islamist terror group Boko Haram. It was Nigeria's first ever use of an armed drone. The UAE and Egypt are also customers. What started as a practice dominated by the US and Israel is going global.[32]

The terrorist attacks of 2001 might have dramatically altered the White House's attitude towards Israeli targeted killings and led to wider use of drone strikes worldwide, but it is simplistic to see 9/11 as revolutionary in its impact. We need to go further back. Attempts to erode the norm against assassination did not begin as the Twin Towers fell, although clearly the War on Terror turbocharged debates on targeted killing. In the 1980s, President Reagan's administration manoeuvred to undermine the ban on assassination. Typically gung-ho when it came to covert action, even when using lethal force, Reagan's team established historical precedents for the likes of Obama to draw on decades later. Reagan, his gruff and buccaneering director of the CIA, William Casey, and others believed that various reforms imposed during the 1970s had neutered the CIA. They longed for a throwback to the glory days of the early Cold War and a more aggressive posture. Shortly after taking charge in 1981, Casey pushed back against the suffocating rules and regulations, scrapping one particularly long and bureaucratic manual on covert action in favour of simply using common sense.[33]

Under Casey, the CIA recommended that rebels in Nicaragua 'neutralize' targets. When the CIA wanted to arm rebels in Afghanistan with sniper rifles in order to kill Soviet leaders and generals, it claimed that the ban on assassination did not cover paramilitary covert actions. It followed this with a second argument: the ban only covered *intent* to assassinate. Casey bullishly told CIA lawyers: 'if anyone asks don't tell them these are sniper rifles for assassination; tell them they are hunting rifles: that's our intent. What they choose to hunt is their decision, not ours.'[34]

Casey used counterterrorism operations to redefine – and limit – the ban further. The CIA trained Lebanese teams, one of which went on to launch a car bomb that killed eighty civilians in an ill-fated attempt to take out a terrorist suspect. This did not count, they argued, as US complicity in assassination. In short, the Reagan administration worked tirelessly to reshape – and weaken – the ban on assassination, by excluding a range of activities. It helped lay the foundations for twenty-first-century strikes on terrorists and the likes of Soleimani.[35]

The taboo erodes further with each high-profile killing. The more democracies kill people, the more non-democracies deploy whataboutism – however unfairly – whenever criticized for killing people. And even those states engaging in prominent illegal assassinations tend to get away with it in the big scheme of things. Russia faced few serious consequences following the attack on Sergei Skripal. Plenty of countries rightly condemned the attempted assassination and many, following the UK's lead, expelled Russian diplomats believed to be intelligence officers. The British royal family boycotted the 2018 football World Cup hosted in Russia. None of this hit Moscow where it hurt, and the UK's Intelligence and Security Committee later questioned whether the intelligence community was taking the threat to other Russians living in the UK seriously enough.[36] According to one former CIA officer, the Kremlin knew that the west was complicit enough in the flow of Russian money for them to get away with it.[37]

A few months later, President Trump pointedly reaffirmed the US alliance with Saudi Arabia despite compelling intelligence directly linking the crown prince to the assassination of Jamal Khashoggi. After eulogizing the benefits of Saudi–US trade, Trump stated that 'King Salman and Crown Prince Mohammad bin Salman vigorously deny any knowledge of the planning or execution of the murder of Mr. Khashoggi. Our intelligence agencies,' he went on, 'continue to assess all information, but it could very well be that the Crown Prince had knowledge of this tragic event – maybe he did and maybe he didn't!' It was classic post-truth Trumpism. Both sides are equal. Who knows what is true anymore? The Saudi regime would hardly have felt rebuked. Quite the opposite. It was a classic case of realpolitik trumping moral leadership. As if to underscore this point, the incoming Biden administration did not impose any punishment on the Saudi crown prince either and, on the contrary, also emphasized ongoing interests in the country. Across the Atlantic, one Foreign Office minister knew that the murder should have been a 'game changer' and wanted the UK to take the lead in criticizing the crown prince. 'We should,' he wrote in his diary, 'but we can't afford to… so we won't.'[38]

*

Assassinations and targeted killings are not necessarily the same thing, and there is a clear difference between Russian and US activity not least in terms of means, motive and proportionality. There is an equally clear difference between active and direct attempts to kill a target using special forces or drones and passive, indirect, collusion with violent non-state actors. Unfortunately, the messy world of international politics is often not so clear cut.

A fine line exists between some targeted killings and assassinations, especially those taking place off the battlefield. Critics can engage in whataboutism, falsely claim equivalence, or muddy the narrative using the classic 'everyone is as bad as each other' trope. If some states continue to normalize targeted killings and other states get away with assassinations, we can expect them to remain a growing, murky, part of international politics as states compete in the grey zone.

How do states get away with killing? By controlling, or muddying, the narrative, by hampering oversight, by finding safety in numbers, and by being too economically powerful to be held to account. This is all the more important if leaders choose to sacrifice secrecy for more control and a bigger impact.

Assassinations and targeted killings are the tip of the covert action iceberg. Although they grab the headlines and dominate the public imagination, they are by far the least frequent form of secret statecraft. Most covert action does not involve bombs and bangs, rather it encompasses subtle influence work. And even on those occasions when someone is bombed or poisoned, the attack is wrapped up in layers of propaganda to shape the narrative. They work together to persistently discredit and disrupt. As we continue our journey through the grey zone, the most important stop is the particularly shadowy world of influence and information operations.

3

HOW TO INFLUENCE OTHERS

I n early 2020, western populations blithely went about their business barely noticing news reports about some mysterious new virus spreading quickly in a Chinese city of which few Europeans had heard. The idea of putting an entire country under effective house arrest was utterly alien. Unfathomable. Something out of a dystopian film.

China, the epicentre of COVID-19, quickly began a propaganda campaign through Twitter. Thousands of similar messages criticized pro-democracy campaigners in Hong Kong for exaggerating the severity of the outbreak. China, the propaganda insisted, had it all under control. The campaign was crude: many of the thousands of accounts lacked profile pictures or biographies; they recycled the same names repeatedly; and many were created on the same day. It was also swiftly overtaken by events.

When China could no longer hide the magnitude of what was going on, the message changed tack. Accounts began to praise China's authoritarian response to the outbreak instead. The government had put Wuhan, a busy city of eleven million people, under house arrest. Streets emptied. Masks became mandatory. Police guarded motorways. Authorities rigidly enforced these radical and stringent measures despite the World Health Organization initially stating that quarantining such a large city was unprecedented and certainly not a recommendation it had made.[1]

In March, as cases spread across Europe, Chinese propaganda challenged the idea that Beijing had delayed telling the world about the virus. Instead, it insisted that the government had acted quickly, transparently and successfully. China was a serious and responsible country, it claimed, sitting at the bedside of the world, providing medical equipment. Its leadership had supposedly helped all countries prepare for the pandemic.

As Italy became the new epicentre, propaganda bombarded Italian audiences. It encouraged them to copy China's unprecedented authoritarian response and be grateful for Chinese assistance, using hashtags such as #GoChinaGoItaly and #thankyouChina. Propaganda praised the efficient and effective response of the Chinese, sharing videos of empty streets being disinfected. On one occasion, China manipulated genuine footage of a video showing Italians coming together to thank healthcare workers. It added the Chinese national anthem in the background and claimed the Italians had come together to thank China; that Romans were spontaneously appearing on their balconies shouting 'Grazie, Cina!' This simply was not true; still, the campaign spread across Europe to France, Serbia and Spain.[2]

As cases rose, propaganda became more sophisticated and began to criticize other countries' weak responses. Legions of suspicious accounts attacked the US for putting the economy over the value of human lives and for failing to provide adequate healthcare. All of this, of course, was presented as a stark contrast to China.[3] The pandemic became so politicized that China could easily exploit existing divisions: those pushing back against lockdowns were deemed Trumpists. At the same time, Chinese propaganda (alongside that of Russia and Iran) provocatively questioned whether the US was responsible for the outbreak of COVID.

Earlier, in late February, the *People's Daily*, the largest newspaper in China, had published an article about the potential US origins of the virus. This was picked up in the *Helsinki Times* and *New Zealand Herald*. A few days later, a noted Chinese epidemiologist told a press conference that the virus indeed may not have originated in China. The Chinese foreign ministry quickly amplified these sentiments: it was not 'made in China'.[4]

By mid-March, the foreign ministry's information spokesman began peddling conspiracies about the US origins of the virus. Perhaps, he claimed, the Americans had brought COVID to China when competing in the world military championships which, by coincidence, took place in Wuhan in November 2019. He tweeted: 'When did patient zero begin in US? How many people are infected? What are the names of the hospitals? It might be the US army who brought the epidemic to Wuhan. Be transparent!'[5] This was retweeted some ten thousand times. He then shared articles and blogs about the supposed US origins of the virus, which were then cited almost one hundred thousand times in at least fifty-four different languages, helping to bring them to a worldwide audience from Venezuela to Saudi Arabia.

At the same time, the *Global Times*, an English-language Chinese tabloid, accused the US of waging information warfare against China. Stories and suggestions, many of them untrue, continued to be amplified via social media; they circulated among the Chinese diaspora in countries such as Italy and France as well as on WeChat, a Chinese instant messaging platform.[6]

The propaganda campaign criticized the US pandemic response and called on countries to put aside political bias and work together – unsurprisingly under Chinese leadership. All nations should learn from China's ruthlessness. In April, as western countries began an extraordinary shutdown of their economies and collapse of civil liberties, Chinese accounts emphasized that back in China the situation was now under control. They claimed that Chinese 'unity' and 'national spirit' had led to the 'rebirth' of Wuhan. Propaganda praised the Chinese government, criticized the US, and attacked anyone who supposedly discredited the Chinese Communist Party.[7]

Fake news circulated across Europe. The EU accused China of spreading disinformation, including stories about selfish care workers abandoning jobs in France and leaving residents to die.[8] Across the Atlantic, US intelligence reportedly uncovered secret Chinese attempts to create panic about rising cases using text messages and messaging apps.[9]

The aim of all this was to promote China as a global leader while obfuscating the origins of the virus. Alongside sowing confusion and conspiracy, China, as well as Russia and Iran, argued that democracies were failing in their response to the virus and, implicitly, that only authoritarian responses could control it. In June 2020, Twitter removed almost 24,000 accounts deemed part of a coordinated influence campaign, as well as a further 150,000 accounts designed to amplify the content. None of this is to say that propaganda caused lockdowns. The virus was serious and states' responses were influenced by scientific advice interpreted against the backdrop of internal divisions and politics.

The COVID influence campaigns evolved into 2021 to reflect the next stage of the pandemic: vaccine rollout. Both China and Russia sought to promote their own vaccines, again portraying themselves as innovative and responsible world leaders – and discredit western vaccines in the process.

Pro-Kremlin media sensationalized reports and laundered narratives linking the AstraZeneca vaccine to rare blood clots. They gleefully emphasized the side effects, however rare, and spread doubts about vaccine safety more generally. Both Russia and China accused the European Medicines Agency of politicizing and mishandling the issue in yet another attempt to demonstrate the failure of democracies. They sought to divide and discredit the European rollout, disrupting its unified attempts to secure vaccine supplies.[10] We must not exaggerate the impact, but they did seek to influence whole populations, to manipulate hearts and minds.

Influence operations are all around us, constantly seeking to sway, sever and smear. They exist on a global and industrial scale. More than eighty countries, from Azerbaijan to Zimbabwe, have sponsored covert influence campaigns over the last couple of years. Most of these countries use propaganda to manipulate their own citizens. In Kenya, for example, the main opposition candidate boycotted the second presidential election of 2017 amid claims of disinformation and deceit. He angrily ranted against manipulation conducted online: 'These leaders are chicks, chicks of computers, computers laid them as eggs, computers lay on the eggs, computers hatched them… chicks of computers… computer-generated leaders.'[11]

Fewer – but still plenty of – countries try to covertly influence audiences beyond their borders: propaganda as foreign policy. They include China, Ecuador, Egypt, France, various Gulf states, India, Iran, North Korea, Pakistan, Russia, Saudi Arabia, the UK, the US and Venezuela. In Ecuador, for example, a network of inauthentic social media accounts sought to influence presidential campaigns in neighbouring countries by promoting certain candidates and criticizing others until Facebook removed it in July 2020.[12] Each state using cross-border influence operations does so in very different ways, at very different volumes, and for very different purposes. Russia's 'firehose of falsehoods' remains unusual, and we should be wary of extrapolating too much from it. Iran comes in a distant second. Democracies are much more restrained.[13]

States leverage covert influence operations to bolster their diplomacy. Propaganda and diplomacy are not separate things operating in isolation from each other. China exploited the COVID crisis to enhance its reputation and undermine adversaries. Something similar is happening in the Gulf, where disinformation has exacerbated tensions between Qatar and four neighbouring states, Saudi Arabia, the UAE, Bahrain and Egypt. In June 2017, a diplomatic crisis broke out as the quartet severed relations with Qatar, accusing it of supporting terrorism. Saudi Arabia closed Qatar's only land border, while other countries barred Qatari planes from entering their airspace and ships operating under the Qatari flag from docking at many ports. This was a serious issue for a tiny oil-rich state, jutting out into the Persian Gulf, dependent on imports from land and sea.

A month earlier, the Qatari emir had supposedly praised Islamist groups Hamas, Hezbollah and the Muslim Brotherhood. Qatar quickly said the quotes, which appeared on the state news agency website, were fake. Someone had hacked government media platforms to spread inflammatory disinformation. Saudi Arabia continued reporting them anyway, even as Qatar threatened to sue. Although Russia and Saudi Arabia were early suspects in the hacking, US intelligence soon pointed the finger at the UAE. Ever since, the UAE has sponsored anti-Qatar, anti-

Turkey and anti-Iran narratives online, associating them with terrorism, often by outsourcing propaganda to marketing firms.[14] Others in the Gulf quartet have also weaponized social media. Trolls and bots spread doctored news stories, manipulate Twitter trends and exaggerate the levels of opposition.[15]

In March 2020, disinformation, allegedly originating in Saudi Arabia, spread rumours of an impending coup in Qatar. Doctored video footage showed gunfire on the streets, as people rose up in protest against the regime. If this was not dramatic enough, a digital rent-a-crowd of automated bots amplified the footage and, in doing so, exaggerated the size of opposition. Interestingly, the propaganda provided a fig leaf for those genuinely seeking regime change; it allowed them to threaten the authorities by pointing to the supposed mass opposition. Such coup-baiting blurs the line between indisputable facts and downright lies, between what was to happen and what has happened. We might call it truth creation: creating facts rather than stating them.[16]

Saudi propaganda has become increasingly sophisticated. The kingdom has built an electronic army – known as an Army of Flies – to advance the crown prince's agenda and suppress dissent. Alongside targeting Qatar, it has discreetly influenced debates in the UAE, Bahrain, Egypt, Morocco, Palestine, Lebanon and Jordan. Automated bots tried to cast doubt on the idea that Saudi Arabia had assassinated the journalist Jamal Khashoggi, himself a campaigner against the regime's disinformation, who, as we have seen, was brutally killed when visiting the Saudi consulate in Istanbul in 2018. At least fifty-three websites posed as a network of genuine Arabic-language news outlets spreading Saudi denials.[17]

Across the Red Sea, Egypt also used covert influence activity. Fakes, bots and impersonated accounts – as well as real accounts

– spread a range of messages including disinformation, doctored photos and deliberate amplification of hashtags. Messages have recently included pro-Palestinian and anti-Muslim Brotherhood hashtags, as well as material attacking Qatar, Iran, Turkey and Libya. They also support controversial Saudi intervention in the ongoing Yemeni civil war.[18]

These regional actors use propaganda, intertwined with diplomacy, to bolster their own regimes while attacking rivals.[19] To achieve this, many of these countries choose to outsource their propaganda. Disinformation for hire is a booming growth industry. Private firms operating in almost fifty countries have deployed propaganda on behalf of political actors; more than sixty-five firms offer computational propaganda as a service and have spent almost $60 million on hiring staff to do so over the past decade or so.[20]

In 2019, Twitter removed a network of around eighty thousand pro-Saudi accounts spreading propaganda against the regime's critics. The campaign was run by a genuine digital marketing company, which also had Dunkin' Donuts as a client, with links to the Saudi royal family. In the same year, Facebook removed over three hundred accounts linked to an Egyptian marketing firm, New Waves. The company had created a network of fake accounts, posing mostly as women, which combined humour with political content to target Libya, Sudan, Somalia and Turkey.[21] Another Egyptian company, Bee Interactive, created an inauthentic network to support the Egyptian government, as well as criticize Turkish foreign policy and Ethiopia's construction of a dam on the Blue Nile.[22]

Outsourcing increases deniability by making it difficult to trace propaganda directly back to a state, and even then, there are scales of state endorsement and involvement, from turning a blind eye to actively commissioning work. An increasingly fine line exists between genuine firms' routine marketing work and their covert activity. Some contractors, once caught, claim that they acted without their client's knowledge or that they were simply trying to win future business. Outsourcing also helps outmanoeuvre social media companies, which are becoming better and more proactive at removing propaganda content.[23] This is a trade-off, though: the quest for deniability, through outsourcing, comes at the cost of control.

Propaganda is a global business. Importantly, this activity cannot exist in isolation, but is intertwined with diplomacy. States use propaganda – directly or indirectly – to bolster their foreign policy, build up their regime and discredit rivals.

States can – and do – influence others in many ways. They spread lies, lies of omission, half-truths and carefully packaged facts. Sometimes they use lies to spread truths; and sometimes they launder lies through unwitting stooges or useful idiots. Rarely, however, do they admit to creating propaganda.

Propaganda has become a dirty word. It simply means the spread of ideas intended to convince audiences to think and act in a particular way for a particular purpose. However, we associate it with the totalitarian regimes of the twentieth century (and North Korea today). Even before Nazism and Stalinism, liberal-minded people baulked at the very thought of it. Writing in 1926, the Labour politician Lord Ponsonby famously viewed it as 'the defilement of the human soul' which is 'worse than the destruction of the human body'.[24] It is about mind control, brainwashing and dirty tricks. Propaganda certainly has a 'sinister ring' to it but, as Prince Philip once quipped, we should not condemn all propaganda just because 'we did not like the way' the Nazis used it. 'After all,' Goebbels 'presumably drove in a Mercedes car, but that does not really condemn the motor car.'[25]

Philip was right. Propaganda simply involves attempting to influence audiences for better or worse. Nonetheless, its sinister ring and unhelpful breadth mean that practitioners do not tend to talk of propaganda. Instead, they use a range of terms often inconsistently, confusingly and euphemistically: influence operations, information operations, psychological operations and effects work.[26]

The vast majority of this activity constitutes attributable material in the form of a government PR or public health campaign. Stay at Home; Protect the NHS; Save Lives. Propaganda only becomes covert action when government sponsorship is concealed – or at least is unacknowledged.

This includes the deliberate spreading of unattributable information; information which might well have been gleaned from secret intelligence gathered and laundered for public consumption via friendly relationships with journalists. It might be generally accurate but packaged or selectively edited to make a particular point and evoke a particular response. It might include what is now named malinformation: exploiting accurate lines or real pictures repackaged out of context to damage or discredit the target, essentially what the Russians call *kompromat* material.

The US and the UK spread plenty of unattributable material during the Cold War. The Foreign Office's secretive, yet banally named, Information Research Department spent the best part of three decades writing press releases and newspaper articles exposing Soviet hypocrisy, aggression and imperialism, and then sending them out to be published by friendly journalists as far afield as India and Mexico. They expanded to target nationalists, domestic subversives and anyone else who threatened British interests. It was a sizable operation but has since been dismissed as the shandy drinker's covert action, especially when compared to other more potent and controversial options available.

Alternatively, states can lie. Disinformation is the deliberate spread of false information to manipulate targets' perceptions.[27] Russia has been promulgating fakes and forgeries since the time of the tsars, often targeting revolutionary Russian nationals operating overseas.[28] The more recent Soviet AIDS campaign, Operation Denver, is the most infamous example. In 1983, the Soviets planted a story in the Indian newspaper *Patriot* blaming the US for creating the virus which, by then, was spreading fast. Around a thousand people had reportedly died in America alone. According to the propaganda, US scientists had created it during genetic engineering experiments in Maryland involving biological weapons. Moscow then asked allied intelligence services in Bulgaria, Czechoslovakia and East Germany to spread the story by fabricating lies and publicizing the sensationalist claims of others.

This was, of course, a lie. But, to some, it was a believable lie. The US had only shut down its very real chemical and biological weapons programme fifteen years earlier. And the US did have a track record of experimenting with drugs, like LSD, and medicines. One case involved assessing the impact of syphilis on African American farm workers in Alabama without offering effective treatment. The AIDS lie exploited these truths.[29]

Moscow and East Germany then slowly and patiently spread the story to Africa, South America and Europe by using front organizations and journalists to amplify the investigations of an East German biologist who supposedly verified the link. They exploited ambiguity, amplified misinformation and emphasized the work of any journalist or scientists who cast doubt on the truth. Other foreign journalists then reported the claims independently as the 'news' spread. The KGB was rather pleased with itself and rated the propaganda as having achieved particular resonance in Africa.

Eventually, the Soviets backtracked, but even after the KGB stopped spreading the lie in 1989, the East German Stasi carried on. The Stasi had taken on a bigger role in the latter half of the decade and, as fingers pointed towards the Russians, enjoyed the plausible deniability created by hiding behind its larger ally. The Stasi even claimed to have covertly co-financed a film on the subject which aired on West German television in 1989 and in the UK the following year. The English-language version was called *Monkey Business* and broadcast on Channel 4. It covered the unproven origins of AIDS and developed the line that western scientists pointing the finger at Africa were perpetuating racist stereotypes of the continent. The film then shifted gear to examine the potential US origins, at Fort Detrick or another research laboratory, before raising questions about the dangers of genetic research and biological weapons more generally. Those involved in making the film deny collaborating with the Stasi, and it is possible that the East Germans may have hidden the funding in such a way that the filmmakers were genuinely ignorant of it.[30]

There are some clear similarities with Chinese exploitation of the COVID pandemic thirty years later. It is too soon to ascertain the damage caused by Chinese disinformation, but we do know that, despite eventual Soviet acknowledgement, the AIDS lie still reverberates around the internet, like some lumbering zombie refusing to die. Kanye West took it up as a theme in his 2005 song 'Heard 'Em Say', bringing it to a whole new generation.

Choosing to spread falsehoods is obviously more morally problematic than inadvertently spreading misinformation without intent to cause harm. However, the line between the two blurs when unwitting third parties inadvertently share and launder disinformation. It also blurs when states deliberately amplify misinformation in an attempt to influence their audience. Whether Soviet propaganda about AIDS or Chinese propaganda about COVID, states deliberately exploit the lies and mistakes of others, or simply take their words out of context in order to make a particular point.

Dividing operations up into truth and lies, with or without intent to manipulate, is incredibly difficult. Measuring people's intentions is extremely problematic – motives may never be proved – and so this becomes a poor line in the sand when differentiating between acceptable and unacceptable behaviour. Similarly, deciding what is true or a lie is often subjective and resource intensive (and one of the biggest issues in western philosophy).[31] Talking about false or distorted information implies the existence of an original pristine state of truth which has been deliberately altered.[32] Some might argue that propaganda is in fact the deliberate spreading of truths, not all of which may be *factually* accurate.

Sometimes states, notably the Soviet Union during the Cold War, compelled audiences to believe in something that felt right regardless of the evidence by appealing to emotional truths or beliefs as a form of ideological supremacy.[33] As the scholar Thomas Rid writes on Soviet active measures: 'There has always been another truth, one that corresponds to beliefs not facts.' States might spread lies but see them simply as a more clearly articulated or neatly distilled truth. Soviet disinformation, for example, used forgeries to portray NATO as a well-armed, imperialist aggressor. For the communists, this did not distort the truth.[34]

Indeed, the Russian language has a choice of words for what in English would be defined as truth. *Pravda* relates to facts or events; *istina* denotes truths beyond worldly facts. The truthfulness of Russian propaganda, in the words of Russia expert Keir Giles, 'can be measured by two entirely separate criteria'.[35]

Although we need not get too relative about the existence of facts and truth, people do process the same information differently, depending on their own experiences, biases and exposure to misinformation.[36]

Liberal democracies engage in covert influence work but, and this is a big but, they insist they do not spread lies. Dating back to the First World War, when Britain set the standard in modern propaganda, the UK eschewed deliberately lying. Propagandists prudently believed that lies would ultimately be exposed and end up undermining the credibility of facts that had been carefully released. In the words of one leading expert, 'The Government preferred to lie by omission, not by commission.'[37]

A century later, the UK now apparently has a secret team, housed within GCHQ, specializing in discrediting targets as well as doing a whole host of other 'Ds': promoting distrust, dissuading, deceiving, disrupting, delaying, denying, degrading and – in theory – deterring. Leaked documents suggest that this team engaged in propaganda (or, in British jargon, offensive cyber effects operations) targeting Argentina. Operation Quito seemingly sought to shape regional opinion about the Falkland Islands from around 2010 and prevent Argentina from taking control.

It seems the programme was global. GCHQ apparently used propaganda to discredit the Zimbabwean regime of Robert Mugabe – potentially even with the aim of bringing about its downfall. Meanwhile, its Iran team apparently both targeted the general population and discredited the leadership in order to undermine the nuclear programme and disrupt Iranian access to technology. Other countries targeted allegedly include Pakistan, North Korea and Russia.

Influence operations targeted non-state actors too. With ISIS, the team tried to discredit extremist sites, recruiters and terrorist leaders. With the Afghan Taliban, they supported special forces in the theatre by manipulating the Taliban's online environment, such as sending fake directions to fighters. Other influence operations targeting non-state actors include discrediting cyber criminals, disrupting their front companies and disrupting those sharing child pornography online.

GCHQ supposedly uses a range of methods to achieve these goals. They include anonymously uploading YouTube videos, constructing fake personalities on social media platforms to engage in online debates, and creating spoof online material – such as books or magazines – providing inaccurate information. GCHQ also apparently sends spoof messages, via email or social media, 'from a fake person or mimicking a real person' in order to discredit or disrupt a target.[38]

On the military side, the British army recently created a 77th Brigade specializing in 'non-lethal engagement and legitimate non-military levers as a means to adapt behaviours of opposing forces and adversaries': in short, influence operations. Specializing in 'behavioural change', it combines regular army personnel and reservists, and was active during the coronavirus pandemic in 2020.[39] Details are unsurprisingly vague, with the military unwilling or unable to communicate its purpose clearly. This is counterproductive and creates ammunition for conspiracy theorists as much as it protects secrecy.

In each case, officials would no doubt claim to be acting defensively and using fake sources to spread truths. Theresa May, as home secretary, correctly recognized that it is far more effective to work through groups that are perceived to have an authentic voice than it is delivering messages stamped with government branding. The use of disguised – perhaps even fake – sources was simply to ensure credibility and non-attribution rather than to spread deceitful content. In this case, secrecy can actually increase impact.

The UK has outsourced to private companies information operations designed to influence British Muslims. One such company curated a tailor-made social network called 'This is Woke' which targeted discussions about aspects of Muslim faith. Its flashy Instagram content included slogans such as 'You can be both a Muslim and a feminist' alongside inspirational quotes from the likes of terrorism victim turned youth activist Malala Yousafzai. It amassed 75,000 followers online before being exposed as discreetly sponsored by the British government.[40]

Despite denials from civil servants,[41] historical examples do exist of liberal democracies, including the UK, spreading lies. For example, when two young nationalists were killed in Northern Ireland while making a bomb on a particularly cold night, British propagandists spread rumours that the gelignite was particularly volatile at that temperature. The Irish Republican Army (IRA) quickly disposed of what it thought were suspect stocks by using them against soft targets.[42] At around the same time, British propagandists spread false rumours in Uganda that President Idi Amin faced a coup and even an assassination threat if he left the country to travel to a Commonwealth meeting in London. They spread a lie to deter him from coming and having to shake the queen's hand.

Even if we take them at their word, that the UK did not spread lies, there is still a question of whether using fake sources to spread truth constitutes deceit. Is it possible to influence others by deceit, without actually lying? Obviously, using lies to spread truths is more acceptable than the old Soviet approach of using lies to spread more lies, but it still intends to deceive the audience. In addition, and perhaps more importantly, the context shapes how audiences interpret and respond to the factual content. Fake sources, and the emotion they create, can affect audiences' interpretation of facts. This is neither to say that the facts are irrelevant nor that the propaganda abandoned them, but facts can be presented in a way that favours a particular interpretation. As the philosopher Lee McIntyre puts it, context can subvert the truth, while still being factually accurate.[43]

Two recently declassified examples from Cold War history demonstrate this philosophical conundrum. In the 1960s, British propagandists created an entirely fake organization, the Freedom for Africa Movement. Supposedly a neutral francophone group, it became the vehicle of choice to attack nationalist leaders and Soviet imperialism in Africa. Every pamphlet began with the rallying cry 'Loyal African Brothers!', before attacking individuals the British deemed too close to the Soviets. The Brothers purportedly posted hundreds of copies of four leaflets attacking Diallo Telli, the secretary-general of the Organisation for African Unity. The first accused him of becoming 'delirious for power' and being biased towards the Chinese. It closed with another rallying call: 'DIALLO TELLI MUST BE REPLACED BY A PERSON WORTHY OF OUR TRUST'. Four months later, the second leaflet stepped up these accusations (alongside a swipe at the UK for credibility purposes), accusing Telli of being a self-serving tyrant 'PLACING ALL OF AFRICA IN THE MOST GRAVE PERIL'.[44]

When that did not work, the 'Brothers' played the Soviet card: Telli 'visited Moscow for SECRET NEGOTIATIONS with the leaders of the Soviet Union'. He 'received SECRET DIRECTIVES relative to MANIPULATING the OAU to serve the expansionist political exigencies' of the Soviet Union. British propagandists then complemented these attacks with propaganda from another notional group, this time supposedly based in Accra, Ghana.[45]

In the same decade, the same propagandists forged Muslim Brotherhood pamphlets, using aggressive religious language to attack nationalist leaders in the Middle East. Much of the content – about Egyptian gas attacks in Yemen – was factually accurate, but they stirred anti-Israeli sentiment to appear credible. Angrily criticizing Egyptian aggression in Yemen, one asked, 'If the Egyptians have to go to war and fight, why don't they direct their armies against the Jews?' Egyptian bombs used against Yemen, the forgery pointed out, would have been enough to 'destroy Israel completely'. All of this was written 'in the name of God, the compassionate, the merciful'. Except it was not. It was the Foreign Office.[46]

In both cases, the content was broadly accurate, but the facts were hardly open, transparent, unfiltered and unvarnished, the high standard an absolutist would set for truth.[47] More importantly, the facts would be reinterpreted through the context of the fake source. In seeking to encourage a reaction, truths mixed with emotion, encouragement and instruction. They coupled facts with statements of intent: what *was* to happen with *what had* already happened.[48] The fake source deliberately resonated with the emotional or religious beliefs of the target audience and created a prism through which facts would be reinterpreted. It blurred truths or beliefs with animation.[49] Accurate claims made by fake resistance groups implied a false sense of opposition which the propagandists hoped would inspire others to take confidence from the misleading impression that they were not alone.

This is not merely a philosophical question about the nature of truth, interesting though it is. It has practical consequences if inciting a change in behaviour, a rebellion even. Practitioners grapple with questions of credibility, consistency and attribution when designing influence operations. They know that lies decrease credibility and can doom an operation to failure. According to NATO, 'indisputable facts' are necessary to withstand scrutiny, and false information can undermine the credibility of future operations, leading to short-term wins at the expense of longer-term problems.[50] But what constitutes an indisputable fact? If increasing secrecy can, unlike with other covert actions, increase impact – by being more credible – it still comes at the cost of control because the propagandist is compelled to write in a certain tone and use certain language.

In the first decades of the twenty-first century, the era of Brexit and Trump, pundits have been falling over themselves to point out that we now live in a post-truth world, in which emotion and ideology eclipse fact.[51] Audiences rely on perception, personal beliefs and gut reaction more than on evidence and data. We have lost touch with reality. Influence operations, exacerbated by social media, have chipped away at authoritative voices we can trust, such as the media, experts and politicians, leaving audiences without shared modes of validation.[52] It is disorienting: without a true north, we are compass needles swinging wildly in all directions.

This is not new; and neither is there a dichotomy between reason and emotion, fact and belief.[53] There never was a world of truth from which society has departed. Even if we accept this, others argue that the worrying novelty of the present rests on the idea that truth has become less relevant and that facts are now subordinate to political beliefs.[54] Again, however, propaganda has long made facts subordinate to political beliefs, emotional truths and the need for credible messaging. The genuine novelty of the present is more the idea that leaders increasingly do this openly without consequence, rather than having to resort to fakes and forgeries. Covert influence operations require careful thought about truth, lies and deceit. It is much more complex than asking: to lie or not to lie?

Propaganda does not have to be written down or transmitted through the media, and here we start to see overlap between various forms of covert action. Shortly after the Second World War, in the jungles of the Philippines, local communists were mounting an insurrection against the US-backed government. When a group of fighters went on a routine late-night patrol, the last man did not return.

Nervously retracing their steps to find their missing comrade, the men were horrified to discover a corpse dumped on the trail. It had been drained of blood, with two bite marks in the neck. It must have been the Aswang, they concluded, a mythical monster similar to a vampire in local folklore. The fighters fled.

The Aswang attack was staged by American operatives to influence the fighters. It might sound ridiculous but there are actually numerous examples of propaganda exploiting deeply held superstitions – things audiences believe are true – and appealing to what philosophers might call emotional or eternal truths, something felt almost viscerally by believers.[55]

Some influence plans were so bizarre that they did not get off the ground. In the early 1960s, the CIA proposed Operation Elimination by Illumination. Intelligence officers would spread propaganda via Cuban media and leaflet drops predicting that the second coming of Jesus Christ – an arch anti-communist – was imminent and that this spelled the end for Fidel Castro. An American submarine off the coast of Cuba would then discreetly surface and fire star-shells into the night sky to signal Christ's arrival and spark an insurrection.[56]

Others, like the Aswang attack, did get approval. In the same decade, the British created ghost ships to rise out of the mist and terrify Indonesian soldiers to deter them from attacking Malaysia. In the early 1970s, British intelligence faked a satanic altar in Northern Ireland. It came complete with upside-down crucifixes and enough animal blood to suggest some sort of ritualistic sacrifice. The aim was to sever the link between the IRA and the Catholic community. All of this is designed to appeal to the emotional truths of the target audience. For some, truth derives from scripture or ideology; it is, according to Thomas Rid, 'relative to a specific community with shared values'.[57]

These examples are not necessarily relics of some bygone era. More recently, a senior US air force officer wondered about projecting a giant hologram of Allah over the Baghdad skies.[58] Like the earlier Cuban operation involving Christ, it would have supposedly inspired an uprising against the regime. For obvious reasons, the suggestion proved infeasible. In 2005, the CIA developed a prototype Osama bin Laden doll. It had a removable head depicting him as a demon, complete with green eyes and red skin. A decade later, American intelligence blasted ISIS terrorists with eerie sounds designed to unsettle them.

These stories may be filed away under the category of bizarre but true, yet there is an important point. Propaganda is not limited to newspapers, the media and social media. The ways to influence people's thinking are limited only by the scale of our imagination. And, equally importantly, the propaganda might well appeal to emotional truths over factual accuracy: to put ideology and belief before objectivity.[59]

Propaganda is vague, amorphous and all around us. States influence others by exploiting ambiguity, amplifying the misinformation of useful idiots, or by selectively repackaging facts and publicizing them out of context. They appeal to broader emotional truths or superstitions. They also lie.

In theory, lying is counterproductive; lies get exposed and thus risk undermining the credibility of facts. However, there is a fine line between facts, lies, laundered mistakes, exaggerations, spin and plausible deniability, especially when states outsource disinformation. States need to mask the authorship in order for their message to be credible to the target audience, but creating a fake source alters the nature and interpretation of the message (even if it is broadly factually accurate). Secrecy – and the need to write in someone else's voice – decreases control over the message. Sophisticated covert influencers think carefully about all these permutations. They determine how to make something credible, what hook to hang it on, and calibrate levels of truth/ lie, plausible/implausible deniability accordingly.

They also recognize that influence work rarely exists as an end in itself. Instead, it complements diplomacy and, as we shall see, forms the cornerstone of covert actions. Manipulating opinion enables other, more aggressive, operations. A coup would not work without propaganda laying the foundations. Sabotage or assassinations would lack impact if not exploited by propaganda. And there is a fine line between sabotage and propaganda: blowing something up can send a rather loud message.

Influence operations closely intertwine with other forms of covert political work – from funding political parties to meddling with currencies – to subvert target governments. Meanwhile, the internet has made influence operations bigger, brasher and more disruptive than ever before. This not only subverts governments, but, even more than that, risks fundamentally undermining liberal democracy.

HOW TO SUBVERT GOVERNMENTS AND UNDERMINE DEMOCRACY

'FAKE NEWS,' screamed Martin Kossipé in the comments beneath an online article about the shady relationship between a political party in the Central African Republic and French mercenaries. Kossipé, hiding behind a Muhammad Ali profile picture, was a vocal and aggressive critic of disinformation spread on Facebook about the African country.

It was the summer of 2019 and locals were deeply divided about the future direction of francophone Africa. Some looked towards Russia, approvingly sharing smiling photographs of the Russian foreign minister meeting local politicians. Others looked towards France, the old colonial power which maintains a strong interest in the region. When a post appeared praising Russia's 'precious gifts' of tanks and $1 billion in cash, Kossipé again pounced: 'fake news'. Increasingly frustrated by the manipulation of his newsfeed, Kossipé turned amateur detective. He used open-source research techniques to expose various Facebook pages as Russian propaganda. He revealed one, called Future African Leaders, as having a Russian phone number, and accused it of exploiting and manipulating young people.

Meanwhile, a children's cartoon on YouTube depicted a wholesome story of a group of animals whose farm had been raided by villainous hyenas. The lion, representing the Central African Republic, bravely tried to fight them off. The hyenas (the US and France) outnumbered and overpowered him. The lion called for help from his old friend the bear (Russia). Waking up from hibernation, the bear heroically rushed to save the lion and the farm.

Many viewers, including Martin Kossipé, were livid. Once more, he derided it as Russian propaganda. Another commenter posted that the cartoon was astonishing; it sought to brainwash the young.

Shortly afterwards, another video appeared on YouTube. Equally lacking in any subtlety, this one mocked the animal cartoon. It depicted an ignorant but beautiful Russian blonde and her alcoholic manager busily making the Russian propaganda. In the video, the woman did not even know the name of the country they were targeting. It was all the same to her. Someone, somewhere, was fighting back against the Russians with propaganda of their own.

Kossipé's persistent investigations and exposés were irritating the propagandists. Another Facebook account accused him of being a French agent – paid to destabilize the Central African Republic. This account was a Russian fake: the profile picture had been lifted from a Nigerian user of a Russian social media platform.

In a bizarre twist, the allegation was true. Kossipé did not exist. He was indeed a persona used by the French.

France and Russia had spent the best part of a year covertly trying to influence Facebook users in the Central African Republic. Remarkably, this evolved into an outlandish scenario in which bogus accounts were interacting, arguing and trying to expose the other side as fake. Often, their allegations of deceit were accurate – if highly hypocritical. On other occasions, they smeared legitimate accounts, spreading confusion and undermining debate.[1]

Fake news – and allegations of fake news – was flung from both sides. In this Kafkaesque world of fakery fighting fakers, truth becomes the first casualty. When reality is subverted, how do we know what is true anymore? How do we know who to believe? What to trust? The second casualty is democracy.

For all the impulsive hyping of a new digital post-truth world, propagandists' aims are reassuringly familiar: exploit divisions, widen gaps in the population and undermine trust in authority. Subvert the government. None of these are new. To understand how so-called fake news can subvert governments, we should avoid fetishizing the global and revolutionary impact of social media.[2]

There are, though, important differences when using propaganda today compared to the centuries of propaganda that came before, all of which further undermine trust and challenge authority. First off, the internet era dramatically increases the tempo and volume of operations. Propaganda is quicker and noisier than ever before. Much of it is also dramatically less skilful, with armies of unprofessional trolls churning out volumes of trashy content. This is hardly a well-crafted and finely honed art form.

Famously, or rather infamously, Russia has waged the largest and most sustained internet-enabled propaganda campaign. Based in St Petersburg and allegedly financed by a close ally of Putin, the Internet Research Agency was the most notorious example of industrialized low-grade propaganda. By late 2015, its American department was headed by a twenty-seven-year-old nicknamed Jay Z. He oversaw an annual budget of around $1 million.[3]

Specialist departments sat alongside the geographical ones. One focused specifically on producing internet memes, another on commenting on posts made by other users. Its scope and scale were vast, targeting all major social media platforms. Individual operators ran multiple fake accounts, making around fifty comments on news articles every day. Some ran six Facebook pages at any one time, posting on each at least three times a day; others ran around ten Twitter accounts each, tweeting at least fifty times daily.[4]

Rather than being doyens of deception or masters of manip-ulation, many of these covert operatives were apathetic young students who did not necessarily believe in the cause. Under pressure to churn out as much as possible, they cut corners and made mistakes. Professionalism was low; turnover was high.[5]

The reach was impressive, though. Facebook and Twitter accounts run by Internet Research Agency trolls acquired tens of thousands of American followers, including political figures who eagerly retweeted their content. Facebook estimated that, as of 2017, the Internet Research Agency had reached as many as 126 million people through its website. Twitter claimed that nearly one and a half million of its users had interacted with around four thousand Internet Research Agency accounts. The Russians recruited US citizens to amplify their messages; for example, operatives targeted genuine black activists by posing as a group called Black Matters US. They also recruited conserva-tives to perform political acts, such as, somewhat curiously, walking around New York City dressed up as Santa Claus with a Trump mask.[6]

Russian messages were often blunt and clichéd. One fake account, supposedly run by a Texan called John Davis, offered little more than generic statements intended to appeal to conservatives: pro-veteran, anti-Islam, anti-Clinton etc. The same young operatives in St Petersburg would then switch stereotyped personae. A Kentucky redneck one minute, a hard-working tax-paying Minnesotan white guy the next. And then a New Yorker speaking in black slang. It is little wonder the messaging was simplistic.[7]

In November 2015, one Twitter account, with the display name Jermaine, warned residents near the University of Missouri that the police were 'marching with the KKK!' through the campus. 'They beat up my brother,' he added alongside a photo of a severely bruised black child. Dozens of bots automatically retweeted his messages, and so too did real users outraged by what they were reading. Shortly afterwards, Jermaine's account changed its name to FanFan. The profile picture changed from a young black man to a German Iron Cross. The account now spread, in German, rumours about Syrian refugees and the violent and sexual risk they posed to young women. After that, FanFan turned to the 2016 US presidential election.[8]

It was not an entirely slapdash outfit, however. The Russian trolls tried out their ideas on the unwieldy fora of Reddit first, before using the more effective ones on Twitter a week or so later. They knew that many journalists and politicians use Twitter, thereby increasing the likelihood of rapid retweets to an ever-greater audience. The propagandists then monitored polling data in the run-up to the 2016 election and calibrated messages accordingly. However sophisticated the outfit may or may not have been, it was fast, bold and exploited the newfound ability to go viral.[9]

Contrast this to the hard, slow and painstaking disinformation work of the Cold War – a time when success required outstanding intelligence on everything from the type of paper and even the brand of staples used in a particular forgery. A file recently declassified in the British archives gives us a fascinatingly detailed example. In 1972, at the height of the Northern Ireland Troubles, MI5 uncovered a forged pamphlet with an innocuous title: *Ulster Guide for Tourists*. Inside were photos of the bucolic landscape, singing children and a radiant Queen Elizabeth. Ulster was safe and open for visitors. To prove it, the pamphlet included photos of what its authors called 'dangerous Catholics' being taken away by riot police and of soldiers controlling a crowd of 'subversive Irish Catholics'. It looked like it had been created by local authorities and was convincing enough to take in many a reader.

Rather than innocently promoting Ulster as a holiday destination, the pamphlet sought to discredit Britain's role in Northern Ireland: to subtly portray the British as aggressive and oppressive in equal measure, targeting unarmed Catholics as much as violent nationalists. It was a work of art, leaving the intelligence services stumped about the forger's identity. They deemed it too sophisticated for Irish terrorists and began investigating the origins of the staples and paper. The former proved inconclusive; the latter probably came from Yugoslavia. Perhaps, they concluded, it was the East Germans. They could not be sure.[10]

Running a radio station, pretending to be, say, Egyptian exiles, during the Cold War was equally complicated. It was almost impossible to conceal the location of the transmitter. To make matters worse, intelligence services needed to recruit foreign nationals to work as broadcasters so that the propaganda was credible, but doing so raised thorny issues of loyalty and security.

And if that was not enough, it was hard to reach receptive audiences given the susceptibility to jamming. Black propaganda and disinformation were slow going.

To be sure, forgeries still exist today. Between December 2014 and July 2016, the Russians inserted twenty-six forgeries into the Swedish media ecosystem. Reminiscent of the Cold War, some used fake letterheads and purported to be written by Swedish decision-makers. They targeted a range of contentious issues not limited to Sweden: NATO disagreements with the UN; a Polish politician being mentally ill; and western countries lobbying for a Ukrainian politician to become the next UN secretary-general. Despite this, the bigger, bolder and brasher propaganda work typified by the Internet Research Agency dwarfs this more skilful activity. And even forgeries have become less of an art form: the internet has made it less time consuming and some of those targeting Sweden were littered with mistakes.[11]

Somebody targeted neighbouring Denmark with a forgery in late 2019. Greenland's foreign minister supposedly sent a letter to US Republican senator Tom Cotton, shortly before she and her Danish counterpart met the US secretary of state. The letter, written in English and on official headed paper, asked Cotton to help fund a referendum to gain Greenland independence from Denmark. Any such cooperation – even just the request for cooperation – would stir trouble at the impending meeting in Washington.

Cotton was a well-chosen recipient. He had earlier suggested that President Trump buy Greenland to access its natural resources untapped beneath melting ice. Meanwhile, tensions between Denmark and Greenland – an autonomous dependent territory – provided exploitable context. The Danish press and Greenland authorities quickly outed the report as a forgery, and

Danish intelligence later pointed the finger at Russian agents
of influence seeking to create confusion and possible conflict
between Denmark, Greenland and the US.[12] As one of many
forgeries, the language was stilted and had the distinct whiff of
an online translator about it.

The industrialized scale decreases professionalism and also
makes it harder for states to control their disinformation operations. In our interconnected world, propaganda takes on a life of
its own, replicating into media viruses. They can be tweeted and
retweeted ad infinitum and end up inadvertently influencing
domestic populations who were never the target. The CIA has
a special term for just this unintended consequence: blowback.
The agency is not authorized to manipulate domestic media,
but fake news sent abroad risks being picked up and reported
back home. Propaganda in the internet age is higher tempo and
less controllable; moreover, the boundaries between foreign and
domestic are almost non-existent.

Our age of big data and computational propaganda creates the
second core difference between current and historical activity,
undermining governments further still. Both terms exploded
into the public consciousness after the 2016 US presidential election. On the one hand, the Trump campaign deftly exploited
big data on US voters; on the other hand, Russia used targeted
political propaganda and automated bots to create and spread
messages which undermined Democratic candidate Hillary
Clinton.[13] Both produce problems for democracy.

Our constant use of social media creates dizzyingly vast
digital profiles generated through clicks, likes and retweets, even
through something as innocuous as an online quiz promising to
tell you which *Friends* character you are. It allows advertisers –

and those with more malign intentions – to build up a detailed understanding of individual users' preferences and behaviour. Messages can now be targeted at particular individuals more receptive to their content and more susceptible to persuasion. Mass data allows micro-targeting.

Despite wielding plenty of blunt clichés, the Russians did have access to easy-to-use targeting capabilities available on each of the social media platforms. The trolls deliberately targeted voters outside of key electoral battlegrounds in places like Baltimore, New York City and Washington, D.C. This was likely because they knew that anything happening in these places generated national media attention. In July 2016, for example, Russian operatives organized a 'Down With Hillary' protest outside her New York City offices.

They became more adept at targeting as the election unfolded. One campaign was aimed at specific individuals in Pennsylvania with the words 'coal miner' in their job title, reminding them that Trump would end Obama's supposed war on coal.[14] They also tried to use knowledge of their audience to tailor messages: infographics worked better on liberals; conservatives were more active early in the morning.[15]

Big data also allows tailored intimidation. Russia used personal data, probably harvested from social media accounts, to intimidate Ukrainian soldiers at the height of the war between the two countries in 2014. It sent personalized text messages warning: you are about to die; go home to your family. In some cases, the Russians managed to make it look like the message was coming from a relative. Soldiers' families back home also received intimidating texts. Such targeting would likely not be possible without the world of social media and big data.[16]

And Russia is not alone here. Just two weeks before the 2020 US presidential election, Iranian operatives sent fake emails to voters in key states pretending to be from a far-right extremist group, the Proud Boys. They threatened to come after recipients if they did not vote for Trump.[17]

Other actors use big data in a more sophisticated manner. The influence industry is growing at a worrying pace, yet generates surprisingly little serious attention.[18] Data analytics companies can build psychographic profiles of voters' behaviour and intentions. One firm that made the headlines, Cambridge Analytica, used data harvested from Facebook to help the Trump campaign micro-target its political messaging. Its chief executive, Alexander Nix, boasted shortly before the 2016 election that 'Today in the United States we have somewhere close to four or five thousand data points on every individual.' Each on its own revealed little, but together they gave a detailed picture of a person's likes, dislikes, hopes and fears. 'We model,' Nix continued ominously, 'the personality of every adult across the United States, some 230 million people.' This was the future. The traditional campaign in which fifty million people receive the same blanket advert is being replaced by individualized targeting.[19]

Before being shut down amid scandal in the aftermath of the 2016 US election, Cambridge Analytica was a global firm which, alongside its parent company SCL, had worked on more than one hundred election campaigns across five continents, from Italy to Mexico and from Brazil to India.[20] This includes divisive and hotly contested elections in Kenya in 2017 during which Cambridge Analytica worked for the ruling party. Its involvement raised questions about ethics, legality and a form of digital neocolonialism extracting local data for profit but investing nothing.[21] Such activity is unimaginably more sophisticated than Cold War propaganda, which involved dropping thousands of identical leaflets over a particular community or using the same story in multiple newspapers and hoping for the best. Exploiting big data offers all sorts of possibilities to influence – or subvert – democratic processes.

The third core difference between today's propaganda and that from the Cold War is the radically changed media landscape. Over the last twenty years, we have seen a dramatic demassification – or fragmentation – of the media, characterized not only by hundreds of new channels but also informal reporting by legions of bloggers. The ability to broadcast is no longer the preserve of elites.[22] The unstoppable rise of social media has added millions more sources of information to the ecosystem. Consumers have become producers, blurring the line between audience and creator. This is another unfathomable change from the height of the Cold War when passive audiences would have had access to just a few newspapers or radio stations. Back then, controlling just one could make a huge difference.

This relentless fragmentation, this kaleidoscope of content, makes it much harder than ever before to construct a narrative. International relations are being disrupted; new modes of communication, a new media ecology, have upset the very nature of how power works and dislocated the earlier flows that intelligence agencies had learnt to manage.[23] With so many sources of information available to audiences, old techniques have become almost obsolete. Placing a story in an obscure newspaper somewhere in the hope that newspapers in the target country will then pick it up and generate sufficient coverage to shape voters' perceptions seems unrealistically linear, almost naïve. Millions of people – and millions of stories – all compete for attention. Propaganda can no longer be so neat, so reliant on a deterministic golden thread (if indeed it ever was). Cacophonous competition is overwhelming.

It is easier to be destructive: to attack targets and democratic authority instead of promoting a positive narrative. Rather than building up your own version of events, it is easier to spread so much confusion that your adversary's versions cannot gain traction. Subverting someone else's reality is more straight-forward than creating – and convincing others of – your own. Much propaganda today is therefore less about Voltaire's famous maxim that 'those who can make you believe absurdities can make you commit atrocities', although there is still a bit of that as Russia and China push conspiracy theories. Instead, we are witnessing the rise of propaganda as paralysis. Whether achieved through spreading cynicism or giving people the licence to believe anything regardless of evidence, the overall outcome is the same: apathy and a lack of resilience.

With so many stories and perspectives swirling around the internet, it becomes ever more difficult to distinguish truth from lie. Exploiting the chaos, propaganda dismisses the opposing narrative, distracts attention with something else, and expresses dismay at the allegations. This all has the effect of distorting and subverting reality. Disruption is as important as influence. Operations are numbing; they undermine trust in truth, authority and reality.[24] Propaganda seeks, as two scholars recently put it, to induce audiences 'into a state of self-defeating and endemic scepticism by undermining the very criteria on the basis of which they develop their cognitive abilities to make sense, interpret and shape social reality'. States are not battling over interpretations of a policy which can easily be dismissed or rebutted. They are battling over something much more funda-mental: truth and trust.[25] As Thomas Rid points out, a peaceful transfer of power after a contested vote requires trust in electoral officials, vote counters and the media. Disinformation slowly but surely undermines this like some opiate dulling and smothering the senses.[26]

To be sure, countries do use propaganda positively to promote their own narratives, but it often goes hand in hand with a more negative campaign of confusion. Iran, for example, uses news accounts which appear to be independent and based in other countries to spread content playing up Iranian culture and the Iranian government. It intersperses these with stories stolen from credible news sites to create an impression of authenticity.[27]

At the same time, Iran also denigrates Saudi Arabia, Israel and the US. In the first half of 2021, Iranian disinformation operations targeting the US apparently increased. They spread discord, especially exploiting racial and religious tensions. When conflict broke out between Israel and Gaza, Twitter accounts linked to Iran amplified English-language messages including 'Hitler was right' and 'kill all Jews' at a rate of 175 times per minute. These high-speed low-skill campaigns were rudimentary and somewhat sloppy in their tradecraft, making them relatively easy to spot. But they were loud, provocative and divisive.[28]

China offers another interesting example. Although the overwhelming majority of Chinese influence activity is aimed at domestic audiences and designed to protect and promote the ruling party and the Chinese system of government, it still poses a serious and growing threat to democracy.[29]

Taiwan has become an unfortunate testing ground for China's so-called three warfares. The first, public opinion warfare, seizes the initiative and sets the terms of debate by, say, influencing political positions or building international sympathy. The second, psychological warfare, shapes the behaviour of a given audience. The third, legal warfare, sets the legal conditions to validate Chinese activity, including, for example, around disputed territory.[30] Against Taiwan, China sought to undermine support for President Tsai Ing-wen by accusing her of mismanaging the military and damaging Taiwan's traditional culture.[31] Credible allegations surfaced of Chinese attempts to undermine Taiwanese democracy once again in 2018,[32] and its propaganda has become more aggressive in recent years.[33]

When targeting western audiences, China has traditionally tried to be more positive than Russia. Working from a position of strength and wanting to shape the international order around its own interests, it supposedly cares more about its reputation and uses propaganda to shape western debates favourably. Its huge troll farms promote positive stories about the Chinese government in order to distract attention away from criticism rather than engaging in divisive arguments online. In comparison, Russian disinformation is more negative, divisive and destructive; it revels in the beauty of a burning skyline.[34]

That said, Chinese propaganda is becoming more divisive and damaging in its attitudes to democracy. It increasingly uses online networks to amplify misleading information coming from Chinese government accounts, including attempts to discredit the BBC after high-profile reports of systematic rape in Chinese internment camps. Coordinated disinformation campaigns portray the BBC as spreading lies, not being trusted by British audiences, and as having secret links to British intelligence.[35] And, as we have seen, it launched a widespread propaganda campaign to bolster its image and undermine democracy during the COVID-19 pandemic.

This activity is becoming more sophisticated. Networks of fake social media accounts are increasingly organized into cells with fewer obvious links between them, making them more difficult for Twitter's algorithms to detect. Stealing accounts that once belonged to real users, another recent adaptation, further increases the resilience of Chinese disinformation and facilitates genuine engagement with targets. One such Spanish-speaking account successfully generated retweets by Venezuelan government accounts, including one run by the foreign minister. Elsewhere a video of someone supposedly burning voter ballots in Virginia was shared by none other than President Trump's son Eric. It came to his attention indirectly via a web of accounts.[36] The ecosystem includes a dangerous mêlée of positive propaganda, divisive disinformation and swirling confusion designed to undermine trust in democracy.

North Korea also uses disinformation negatively to deny, distract and divide. In 2010, North Korea sank a small South Korean warship and then launched a sophisticated disinformation campaign using fake accounts to deny doing so and broadly generate sympathetic opinion that the South was scapegoating the North. In the same year, and lasting until 2013, North Korea also allegedly targeted a popular South Korean internet platform called dcinside, using proxies and aliases to post up to nine hundred messages a day. They sought to divide South Korea from the US by criticizing the president, criticizing the American military presence in the country and condemning UN sanctions on North Korea. Although the North Korean hand was never proved, it seems likely that this was an attempt to divide and inflame.[37]

We must, of course, be wary of forgetting history here. KGB disinformation aimed not simply to influence, but to spread confusion which, in turn, would entice the target to act in Soviet interests.[38] The current wave of postmodern propaganda is propelled by trends emerging since the 1970s. Public trust in the media to report the news accurately and impartially has been steadily declining for half a century. It is exacerbated by increasing polarization; the proliferation of partisan media platforms since the advent of cable television; the need to fill airtime in never-ending twenty-four-hour rolling news broadcasts; and a decline in journalistic standards brought about in part by digital adver-tising and the rise of clickbait headlines.[39] Even the new aspects of current disinformation are rooted in trends going back decades.

Current 'fake news' follows in this tradition; it did not magi-cally arrive out of nowhere. More recent developments allow sponsors to sow even more confusion given the fragmentation and proliferation of new media channels. This creates a potent environment in which democracy, for so long treated compla-cently, is under threat.

Social media and other emerging technologies have not empowered democracies. Quite the opposite: they have coarsened public discourse and aided authoritarian regimes by facilitating influence campaigns on an industrial scale. Constant exposure to more and more information disorients as much as it educates. This, in turn, spreads doubt and cynicism. No matter what the issue, whether public health or race relations, there is always an alternative viewpoint somewhere online; a counter-narrative, a personalized truth, a conspiracy. This confusion undermines trust in official information, inducing weariness, fever and fret in equal measure. It challenges democratic institutions and democratic legitimacy. Why listen to the president when a self-proclaimed expert, or a useful idiot, is telling you what you want to hear on Twitter?[40]

Russia's aggressive targeting of western democracies is often the go-to example, but the Kremlin does not have a monopoly on such activity. A senior US National Security Agency adviser on cyber security put it rather worryingly: Russia is just bad weather; China is climate change.[41] The Chinese Communist Party poses a long-term threat. Together China and Russia, along with Iran, use propaganda to erode trust in democratic authority and institutions. The internet era has not fundamentally and existentially transformed propaganda, but it has helped states undermine democracy. Defending it from foreign interference now forms a growing part of intelligence work.[42]

More worryingly, and despite the huge amounts of attention devoted to disinformation and the mountains of books written on the subject since 2016, it is only one form of covert action. It is an enabler – a megaphone amplifying other operations. Propaganda is dry tinder facilitating other forms of subversion.

Covert influence operations work hand in glove with covert political action: sowing confusion, breeding insecurity and uncertainty, undermining faith in institutions of authority. It is continuous and intangible, taking place well below the level of regime change. It exploits divisions and loopholes. A gift here; a bribe there. Contacts in the clergy. Gradual influence through everyday subversion.

Although we focus on headline-grabbing coups and cases of electoral interference, the vast majority of attempts to weaken governments and undermine democracy do not end in a big bang. They are nebulous, gradually chipping away at authority. In the words of one former MI6 officer, there is more to covert action than crudeness: 'one must not think in terms of spectacular coups, or dramatic feats of irregular warfare, but rather of a continuous sapping process'.[43] This kind of secret statecraft is as old as time.

The process to exert covert political influence is threefold. First, states need to penetrate key political and social groups within the target; they need to insert agents of influence. This is so much more than simply spying. Rather than gathering secret material, these agents covertly distort political events, decisions or public opinion. They might simply be individuals already operating of their own accord, thereby requiring, at most, some light coordination, or they might be directly controlled by the state. Or they might be unwitting idiots, ignorant of the hidden hand supporting their career from a distance.

They might be bigger than individuals and exist as front organizations. The Soviets used a range of nominally independent organizations during the Cold War to discreetly pursue the Kremlin's interests around the world. These included the banally named World Peace Council (WPC) and the World Federation of Democratic Youth (WFDY).

Then, once they have penetrated the target, states will seek to exploit divisions. Setting groups against each other by attacking weak spots helps to soften up – or even disintegrate – social structures and institutions. Targets are plentiful. Those sponsoring subversion could increase intercommunal tensions, religious tensions or class tensions. They could go after government hypocrisy, economic tensions or expansionism. Or target immigration, or 'wokeism' or Brexit, or the union of the United Kingdom.

Third, after divide comes conquer. States use subversion to undermine – and potentially even detach – loyalty and to weaken the target's will.[44]

Everyday subversion, operating alongside routine foreign policy, takes many forms. Indeed, the possibilities are almost limitless and can be tailored to the target country's specific weak spots or internal tensions. The goal is not always – or indeed often

– regime change; that might be too ambitious, improbable or risky. Instead, it might be to exert influence over particular policies or to shape political debate; to disrupt, distract and divide a target government; or to destabilize and keep it off balance. Covert political action complements open diplomacy and economic activity.

Plenty of Soviet examples exist from the Cold War. Alger Hiss was a US government official who sat at President Roosevelt's side during the Yalta negotiations, dividing up Berlin at the end of the Second World War. He was later convicted for perjury after lying that he was not a Soviet agent. Hirohide Ishida was a Japanese labour minister, outed by a former KGB officer as a Soviet agent of influence. In 1976, when a Soviet spy plane landed in Japan, he lobbied the prime minister to return it to the Soviets without inspecting it first. In 1981, Malaysian authorities arrested a senior political adviser to the deputy prime minister for being a Soviet agent. Two years later, West Germany expelled a Soviet intelligence officer for attempting to recruit agents of influence inside the anti-nuclear movement.[45]

And this is to say nothing of the Soviets' wider front organization activity. Founded in 1949, the World Peace Council was the largest of these groups. In the words of one Soviet diplomat: 'it swarmed with KGB officers'. It arranged summits to shape opinion, UN debates – and ultimately policy. On one occasion, in 1978, the WPC helped organize a supposedly organic grassroots campaign against the American neutron bomb. It used a sub-front to organize a symposium in Vienna in collaboration with an official United Nations body, the International Atomic Energy Agency. More than forty thousand activists took to the streets in Europe. The Soviets helped make the mysterious neutron bomb a household scare word. President Carter ultimately decided to delay its production.[46]

Afterwards, the Soviets tried to distort disarmament policies too. They continued recruiting agents of influence inside US peace movements, shaping demonstrations to ensure that protestors criticized US arms control policies but, crucially, not Soviet missile programmes. Meanwhile, the Stasi supported a group called Generals for Peace, which included former NATO officers and even registered as a non-governmental organization with the United Nations.[47]

Of course, the west also used covert political operations to influence – and subvert – democracies, especially when it perceived those democracies to be under threat. CIA activities in Latin America are the most well known, but British operations in the region from the 1960s are starting to come to light. For example, operatives worked through contacts in the Catholic Church to put pressure on leaders from Bolivia to Brazil. In Ecuador, British intelligence boasted that they could bring a five thousand-strong mob of Catholic youth, led by priests, out onto the streets of Quito. They hoped protests would not be needed, because the mere 'fact that such a mob could be organised provides the right-wing groups with a useful counter weapon to impose a check on [President] Arosemena who appears to be regarded as a thoroughly unprincipled and undesirable character'.[48]

Meanwhile, in Chile, British operatives developed contacts inside the governing and opposition parties to influence the political process.[49] This complemented overt political and economic activity: the British wanted to capture a slice of the growing Latin American export market.

Fast forward to the present day and critics accuse China of using covert political action to discreetly further Beijing's interests around the world. Alongside economic investment designed to create political leverage,[50] China aggressively uses the United

Front Work Department to charm, co-opt or attack individuals in order to advance Chinese interests. Run from a vast, unmarked building in Beijing, the United Front works through the Chinese diaspora living in almost 180 countries overseas, many of whom have non-Chinese citizenship, unobtrusively providing funding to various groups deemed valuable.[51]

United Front Work Department personnel sometimes operate under diplomatic cover as members of the Ministry of Foreign Affairs to guide all sorts of activities, from student associations to cultural events. President Xi Jinping has turbo-charged these efforts to achieve a global economic order centred around China.[52]

The aim is to unite friends of the Communist Party, and recruit (or coerce) the diaspora, to fight its enemies. In doing so, Beijing makes little distinction between foreign and domestic spaces: only those with the party and those against.[53] Grassroots activities might include, for example, rallying pro-China students to take to the streets to drown out an anti-China demonstration.

They also include more direct political influence by, for example, working with members of the Chinese diaspora who have reached influential positions in foreign countries. The United Front manual states: 'We should aim to work with those individuals and groups that are at a relatively high level, operate within the mainstream of society and have prospects for advancement.'[54]

In 2010, Canadian intelligence warned that several provincial cabinet ministers and government employees were Chinese agents of influence. In 2014, an Australian senator accepted money and gifts totalling around AU$1.5 million from Chinese entities, some of which seemingly exploited loopholes in restrictions against foreign donations.[55] In 2017, New Zealand intelligence began investigating one Chinese-born politician who had served on New Zealand's select committee for foreign affairs, defence and trade. It turned out he was a United Front operative who had earlier spent time teaching at a Chinese military intelligence academy.[56]

The threat is growing. In November 2021, the head of MI6 in the UK made a rare public speech in which he warned that the Chinese 'monitor and attempt to exercise undue influence over the Chinese diaspora'. China, he added ominously, is attempting to 'distort public discourse and political decision-making across the globe'.[57]

Just two months later, MI5 warned MPs that an alleged Chinese agent had infiltrated parliament and sought to interfere in British democracy. The woman, Christine Lee, had developed links with serving and aspiring parliamentarians from across the political spectrum, and made financial donations to certain politicians. MI5 accused her of covertly coordinating with the United Front Work Department and using money provided by foreign nationals in China and Hong Kong – but making it look as if it came from inside the UK.[58] Interestingly, this warning came only days after Canadian intelligence began briefing Canadian politicians to beware of interference operations.[59]

President Xi has lauded this work as 'magic weapons'.[60] Critics call it covert, corrupting and corrosive. Such political influence is difficult to counter because it spills across the borders between public diplomacy, information work and covert action. It can be difficult to even identify a United Front group, not least because the Chinese Communist Party's hand in all of this can be deceptive or covert. A blurred line exists between bribery and donations; legal funding and corruption; and between covert action and open influence.

A former Australian intelligence chief, Duncan Lewis, spoke out. He warned that China was trying to take over Australian politics by fair means or foul. This was neither a dramatic coup nor regime change through electoral interference. Instead, Chinese activity included quietly winning economic influence in business circles, covertly funding political parties and influencing media and university debates. It was slow burning and long term. Lewis added that the effects might not be present for decades to come. By this time, it would be far too late to stop anything. 'You wake up one day,' he warned, 'and find decisions made in our country that are not in the interests of our country.' China was 'basically pulling the strings from offshore'.[61]

Subversion takes many forms. China also stands accused of trying to subvert academic freedom. In late 2019, staff at the University of Nottingham's politics department received an odd email from an outspoken colleague and critic of China with a subject line that began: 'Informing you of my departure and resignation…' It went on: 'this email is to notify you that I am resigning my position' to take up a 'higher lecturing position at another university in Hong Kong'. As gossip rumbled down the corridor, the email was realistic enough to convince some colleagues it was genuine. But there was a red flag. This lecturer always wrote the date underneath his signature. The resignation email did not. It was a forgery attempting to discredit and disrupt an individual – and not especially senior – academic, demonstrating the lengths to which pro-China actors would go to protect the regime.

It may seem strange that a university lecturer was targeted like this, especially when high-profile politicians receive the same treatment. Indeed, the chair of the British parliament's

Foreign Affairs Select Committee, Tom Tugendhat, supposedly sent a similar error-ridden email to colleagues: 'I have tendered my resignation to the Prime Minister and Boris Johnson has accepted my letter of resignation. An announcement will be made at the next sitting of the Prime Minister in Parliament.' Tugendhat blamed Chinese 'psyops'.[62]

Picking on an academic seems small fry in comparison; however, universities are battlegrounds for covert political influence in an age of persistent competition. As the head of MI5 warned recently, 'regular people' are targets for foreign espionage and subversion. Nobody is too unimportant.[63] China and other autocracies seek to shape the research agenda and curricula of western universities, and to limit the activities of researchers on campuses.

As tensions between Washington and Beijing flared in 2020, America labelled the Confucius Institute headquarters in the US capital a foreign propaganda mission. Confucius Institutes operate on university campuses and are partially funded by China to conduct language and cultural programmes. Secretary of State Mike Pompeo accused them of manipulation and of discreetly exerting malign influence over US academia. One American university cancelled its plan to invite the Dalai Lama for a talk; another deleted a reference to Taiwan from a speaker's biography.[64] Confucius Institutes help foster self-censorship in western universities.[65]

In Belgium, the Chinese embassy tried to hire students to express their disapproval of a Uyghur demonstration on a Brussels campus in 2018.[66] Meanwhile, senior British politicians have accused China of providing financial support for academic research but stealing findings and placing limits on the scope of the subjects studied. Parliamentarians accuse the Chinese Students and Scholars Association, supported and partly funded by the Chinese government, of interfering in the UK by trying to stop discussion of Taiwan, Tibet and the Tiananmen Square protests.[67] This particular network is not controlled and directed by China; as ever, we must be wary of overplaying the hidden hand. But the ruling party is both present and discernible, manifesting itself on issues of particular interest.[68]

Spies, subversion and higher education have an interesting history; the cloisters and common rooms of universities were unlikely fields of combat when the battle for young minds became a front line in the Cold War. The CIA used to covertly fund the US-based National Student Association in an attempt to influence worldwide student opinion by sending American students to international conferences. Once upon a time, the CIA used professors to write propaganda or even participate in covert action overseas. This was highly controversial because it undermined academic freedom and integrity. More worryingly still, if the relationships had come to light, all scholars would suddenly have been tarred as potential subversive secret agents. Nobody would have believed a word they wrote. Such use is now banned.[69]

Chinese activity today bears more resemblance to Soviet activity during the Cold War. The International Union of Students, supposedly independent, had gradually fallen under communist influence and become reliant on Soviet funding. It was an important front through which to manipulate students.[70] The World Federation of Democratic Youth was another Soviet front which promoted a left-wing agenda among students critical of western imperialism and warmongering. On the Chinese side, the All-China Youth Federation aimed to promote the Chinese worldview among students. It still exists.

Recent archival releases offer interesting detail on how the UK countered such Soviet and Chinese covert political influence campaigns. Foreign Office diplomats went after the International Union of Students, exposing its links with international communism and disrupting its meetings. Distributed to students worldwide, forged booklets highlighted communist infiltration of international higher education networks and played up Soviet interference in its own universities.

British propagandists incited unrest. On one occasion, in 1963, African students in Bulgaria clashed violently with police after local authorities banned their attempts to establish an all-African students' union. Watching from London, diplomats exploited the opportunity by forging a WFDY response. Among flowery platitudes about anti-racism and Soviet–African friendship, it defended the Bulgarians while denouncing the Africans as uncivilized, 'primitive' and morally weak. They then posted copies from anonymous addresses to various universities and student groups, hoping to 'intensify indignation' among African students – and it proved successful. The forgery received press coverage across the continent, with many newspapers reacting violently. It led to at least one college directly protesting against the WFDY.[71]

Forgeries of International Union of Students material attacked China too, aiming to drive a wedge with the Soviets. They criticized the closure of Chinese universities under the Cultural Revolution and then protested against the expulsion of foreign students from China by offering them alternative places inside Soviet bloc countries. This had the added benefit of embarrassing the IUS.

Forgeries could only do so much. Sometimes a more direct approach was required. The UK covertly influenced universities across South America as part of its efforts to counter Soviet encroachment into the continent. The aim was simple, if wildly optimistic about professorial influence on young minds. Diplomats hoped that 'getting politically conscious British professors appointed to Latin American universities' would prevent local students from veering towards communism. They scoured British universities for a tough anti-communist who spoke excellent Spanish, preferably a graduate from the London School of Economics who was socialist and lectured in law or economics. It was a very specific shopping list. They knew that fiddling university appointments, alongside organizing lecture tours, student exchanges and subsidizing student pamphlets, needed to be done in an unattributable manner. Academic freedom was at stake. Or at least the perception of academic freedom.[72]

Subversion can also be economic. States use propaganda and political action to aggravate economic cleavages and exploit competition between economic interests so as to put pressure on target governments.[73] This was more prevalent in the Cold War given the less complex and interdependent global trade and financial systems of the twentieth century, but it still exists today.

Past operations have fixed currencies, manipulated supply chains, fomented strikes and sabotaged factories. President Kennedy encouraged the longest strike in history to undermine the troublesome leader of British Guiana back in 1963. He deemed Cheddi Jagan, the elected prime minister, a communist and feared another Cuba. Some in the US even – and entirely wrongly – thought he was a possible Soviet sleeper agent. Jagan faced economic problems, and, amid a tough austerity programme, a general strike began in April, yet he was confident it would not last long. The strikers had few funds and, once the money ran out, they would soon be back at work.

He was wrong. Shortly after the start of the strike, a CIA operation got into full swing to sustain the strikers. Working alongside American labour organizers and unions, the CIA helped funnel around $800,000 to the strike fund (almost $7 million in today's money). The strike continued into the summer, amid escalating violence.[74]

In the same decade, the US plotted to undermine the Cuban economy by sabotaging sugar cane, disseminating counterfeit currency and fake ration cards, and by inserting defective repair parts of machinery and cars into the supply chain.[75] In the 1980s, President Reagan, a big fan of covert action, prevented sensitive emerging technologies from reaching the Soviet Union and mined harbours to discourage commercial shipping from entering Nicaragua. Economic problems can cripple governments.

And we should be clear: economic covert action was not solely the preserve of the Americans, even though we know most about their secret history. When the small west African country of Guinea voted for independence from France in 1958, the colonial power did not take it well. The retreating French quickly severed ties and took as much as they could home with them, rather pettily unscrewing lightbulbs and stuffing them into suitcases. Guinea then dared to look towards the Soviet Union for assistance instead. In response, French intelligence introduced fake currency into Guinea to topple its financial system and put pressure on the new government.[76]

Today, in our globalized world, it is trickier to execute some of these plots and ploys. Manipulating currencies is now much more complex than even a few decades ago given the interdependent global financial system. There are simply too many possible – and unpredictable – effects. Similarly, inserting defective parts into a supply chain is problematic. Mapping out such chains in the first place is hard enough, but then a state would have to manipulate them, and, more importantly, to understand the effects. Economic subversion is risky; the chances of inadvertently harming yourself or your allies are too high.

Despite the constraints, economic actions conducted for political effect do still exist in the post-Cold War world – although evidence is murky and allegations are plenty. In November 1991, the governor of Iraq's central bank cried conspiracy: 'Foreign quarters were behind the pumping of forged money for circulation in Iraq with the aim to sabotage the country's national economy.' He was right: the allegation was beyond doubt. Millions of dollars' worth of fake banknotes came from Sweden and Poland, smuggled across the Jordanian, Saudi, Turkish and Iranian borders and contributed to Iraq's monetary disorder, exacerbating inflation. The only question was who was behind it. The CIA was the most likely culprit; the US was seeking to undermine Iraq at the time and had previously counterfeited North Vietnamese currency in the early 1970s. Alternatively, it might have been Saudi Arabia, Israel or Iran.[77]

In the run-up to the 2003 invasion of Iraq, the CIA again allegedly considered destabilizing the local currency. According to newspaper reports, this time the plan involved spreading rumours to foster a run on the dinar.[78] Some experts suggest that even in our globalized world, covert currency manipulation will continue – but it will largely target less commonly held or traded currencies.[79]

Elsewhere, India has accused Pakistan of pumping fake currency into the country. In 2014, according to Indian intelligence, forensic analysis revealed that the paper used in a flood of counterfeit notes matched that used in Pakistani currency. Since then, India has continued to accuse the Pakistani government of forging currency and smuggling it over the border via staging posts in the Middle East and southeast Asia. The aim is supposedly to destabilize the economy and finance both terror organizations and sabotage operations.[80]

Although in some ways it complicates economic subversion, in other ways the complexity of the modern world offers new malevolent opportunities. States, directly or through criminal proxies, can target banking websites or personal accounts. Iran, Russia, North Korea and China are the biggest culprits here, but this is more than about theft or espionage. It is politically motivated disruption. Consider three quick examples. First, in 2007, a wave of attacks targeted the Estonian banking sector, including a particularly sustained attack on the Estonian bank Hansabank. It forced the bank to suspend online banking operations, hit ATMs and prevented use of Estonian bank cards outside the country. Estonia blamed Russia. Second, in 2012, an Islamist hactivist group targeted American financial websites, including big names like Bank of America and Wells Fargo. It was an unprecedented attack in terms of scale and the number of banks hit, and so the disruption and remedial measures cost millions of dollars to fix. The US has privately blamed Iran. Third, the following year, malware disrupted three South Korean banks by deleting data, knocking out ATMs and paralysing mobile payment services. South Korea attributed the attack to North Korea.[81]

This matters because disrupting a bank can inconvenience millions of people and worse. More than that, the fear that credit cards will not work, that savings will vanish, or that stocks might fall can undermine confidence; and confidence underpins the entire banking system. By exploiting this vulnerability, disruption and subversion can create political pressure.

*

Like propaganda, covert political action is intangible. Murmuring beneath the surface, a susurrant undercurrent, it works alongside more conventional forms of diplomacy. It can be provocative and damaging but falls far short of being an act of war. It is pervasive, but far from uniform, spanning agents of influence, fomenting protests, political funding, shaping academia, currency manipulation and plenty more besides.

It can also be entirely fictitious; a fig leaf used by authoritarian regimes to clamp down on legitimate dissent. Russia, for example, has labelled the prominent dissident Alexei Navalny, whom it tried and failed to assassinate in 2020, as a CIA stooge. As we will see, states find it so much easier to blame external subversion than acknowledge internal disaffection.

When thinking about subversion, we must recognize its place in our world of covert competition; but we must also stay alert to the politicization of subversion. This can be a fine line. When is alleged subversion merely dissent or diplomacy? Does external assistance by a hidden hand delegitimize that dissent? These questions are difficult to answer, and subversion can be a label applied by those with vested interests. At the same time, it very much exists. Yet it is hard to know and to fully understand because it works alongside overt statecraft, because it often straddles the line between legitimate and illegitimate behaviour, and because it piggybacks off internal local actors who may well be doing this stuff anyway. Isolating the hidden hand and its effects is difficult. But the hidden hand is not going away.

For those states seeking to subvert others, the playbook is enticingly straightforward. Recruit agents of influence or simply co-opt useful idiots. Operate at the fuzzy border of internal and external activity, of the legitimate and illegitimate. Determine the divisions or fault-lines in the target society – and then crack them wide open. Shape political debate. Use propaganda and the power of the internet to create chaos, confusion and cynicism. Exploit media fragmentation to undermine trust in political authority and the media, even in truth. Detach people from their loyalties. If you get found out, accuse the target state of whipping up racial tension. Russia and China both accuse the west of racism, or inciting tensions with their local diaspora when exposed.

Do not do more than you must. The difficult aspect comes, as ever, when balancing the secrecy and scope of the subversion. Too much and it becomes obvious, potentially creating a backlash among the target state or the international community as well as an increase in defensive measures; too little and it becomes pointless. The more secrecy, the less impact. All of this gently simmers away under the surface.

Sometimes, though, states turn up the heat and bring it to the boil; instead of subtly influencing politics, they rig the elections.

5

HOW TO RIG AN ELECTION

In the hot summer of 2016, American voters would have given little thought to the prospect of covert electoral meddling. This was the summer when a terrorist attack in an Orlando nightclub hit the headlines, and when protests broke out in major cities against yet more police shootings of black men. It was the summer of the Rio Olympics and Pokémon Go. The impending election of course generated incessant round-the-clock punditry debating the improbable rise of Donald Trump, but not foreign subversion. It was simply not on the radar: the stuff of Cold War spy stories; something that happened overseas to less powerful countries, certainly not something affecting the famed land of the free. The US exported democracy to others; it did not have to worry about its own.

Unbeknown to all outside of the intelligence and security world, Russia was busily doing just that. Russian intelligence agencies were using social media accounts to spread propaganda, stealing and leaking personal emails, and even compromising local electoral systems. The Kremlin sought to manipulate the US presidential election and, if that was not enough, undermine trust in democracy itself.

In the end, Russia's favoured candidate, Donald Trump, was victorious over the experienced favourite Hillary Clinton. It sent shockwaves around the world. Even if the Russian operations ultimately made little material difference to the outcome of the election – and it is difficult to know for sure – the wider fallout was nuclear. 'Fake news' was everywhere. Amid all the talk of Putin, of manipulation, of collusion and of subversion, trust in traditional media outlets – and indeed democracy – plummeted. The fragility of America's lauded democracy was brutally exposed; it was the year that covert action went mainstream.

Covert electoral interference combines propaganda and subversive political action. It is not unique to this century; neither is it unique to the Russians. In the decades after the Second World War, for example, the British helped interfere in elections from Italy to Chile to keep the communists out. And with the empire in decline, spies and diplomats conspired to fix elections across Africa to ensure the 'least bad' nationalist was in power as colonies became independent. The French did something similar to protect their own interests in post-imperial Africa. In 1960, for example, French intelligence helped fix the presidential election in Gabon, a country on the west coast where Paris maintained extensive investments in uranium, oil and timber. Covert action ensured the victory of Léon M'ba, a president willing to cater to French interests. Seven years later, after M'ba's death, French intelligence's Africa chief hand-picked his successor.[1]

On a different scale entirely, the US and the Soviet Union, then the Russians, covertly interfered in almost eighty elections worldwide between 1945 and 2000. Some examples are infamous: the CIA's first ever major campaign targeted the Italian election in 1948. Others are more obscure. Few people know that the Soviets covertly meddled in the 1970 Costa Rican election, for instance, or in the 1973 Bangladeshi election for that matter. Electoral rigging did not stop at the end of the Cold War. The US covertly intervened in Albanian and Romanian elections in the early 1990s, and, perhaps more surprisingly, in the 1999 Israeli election. Plans were even afoot to manipulate the 2005 Iraqi election, an outrageously hypocritical scheme given that, in the absence of weapons of mass destruction, the rationale for the US being in the country became to bring free and fair democracy to the people.[2] Interestingly, and for all the talk of Russian covert operations today, there are no known examples of democracies covertly interfering in elections since 2010.[3]

Broadly speaking, intelligence services can covertly rig an election in one of three overlapping ways: through propaganda; through funding a particular party; or through directly altering votes. States use propaganda to manipulate the information environment, targeting the minds of voters in an attempt to convince them to vote for a particular candidate or even to stay at home and not vote at all. This is the easiest and cheapest to do – but has the lowest success rate.

We have already seen how states use social media and troll farms to influence audiences. This extends to influencing voting intentions. One recent example comes from Taiwan, where China spread propaganda to influence elections in 2018 and 2020. President Tsai Ing-wen was re-elected in January 2020 and her party maintained its legislative majority. This victory, a rebuke to China from the people of Taiwan, came despite much Chinese interference.

The election took place against the backdrop of protests in Hong Kong, where the deteriorating situation made Tsai – who took a firmer line with China than the opposition did – increasingly popular with the Taiwanese electorate. China had a clear incentive to manipulate Taiwanese perceptions of Hong Kong, stop Taiwanese voters from identifying with Hong Kongers, and neutralize it as an election issue. On one occasion, an account on the Chinese social media platform Weibo shared a fake notice from the Taiwanese Ministry of Justice stating that the government was deporting Hong Kong protestors who had fled to Taiwan. On another occasion, a poster supposedly from Hong Kong 'rioters' offered a bounty of HK$20 million for the murder of Hong Kong police officers. Many Taiwanese voters believed it was real.[4]

Taiwanese officials point to 'unequivocal evidence' of China using its army of trolls to spread division, while a US congressional body added that these influence campaigns had increased in scope, sophistication and intensity. One Taiwanese diplomat killed himself after falling victim to a fake news story. The operations sought not only to promote pro-China candidates but also to create a fake civil society that could subvert the entire democratic system.[5] The disinformation campaign failed this time, largely thanks an impressive legal and factchecking response from Taiwan.

On top of using troll farms and propaganda, states can steal documents or emails and leak them online to influence voters' thinking. Long ago the KGB would steal (or forge) and leak material to the press, but the cyber dimension has ramped up the scope and scale of such activity. It is now known as 'hack and leak'.

'Lock her up! Lock her up!' Trump grinned widely, conducting the crowd. Just days before the election, with the polls tightening, his supporters chanted to demand a criminal inquiry into Hillary Clinton's apparent use of private emails to conduct government business. The 2016 US presidential election offers the most famous example of 'hack and leak'. Hackers linked to Russian military intelligence got inside the computer of John Podesta, chairman of Clinton's presidential campaign. They stole thousands of emails and gave them to Wikileaks. The emails revealed gossip from inside the Clinton campaign, including one accusation that Clinton had terrible instincts, as well as a range of business and financial dealings. Trump quickly pounced on them. Worried British officials watching from afar realized that this 'hack and leak' was a 'game changer'.[6]

The following year, on the eve of the French presidential election, President Emmanuel Macron fell victim to another huge hack. This time tens of thousands of mundane emails ended up online for all to see. In late 2019, Jeremy Corbyn, the UK opposition leader, jumped on leaked documents suggesting that the National Health Service would be on the table in a post-Brexit trade deal with the US. It made big news but had little material impact on the impending general election. As with the French hack, fingers pointed towards Russian intelligence. In all three cases, troll farms and social media networks amplified the content of the leaks, repackaging the material to shape voting intentions.

Covert operations in 2016, 2017 and 2019 loomed ominously as the 2020 US presidential election approached. In the run-up to the vote, intelligence officers, politicians and the public all wondered whether Russia would repeat its tricks from four years earlier. In many ways, the mere worry of electoral influence became a form of influence in itself. Sure enough, the Kremlin did try again.

According to US intelligence, the Russians denigrated Joe Biden and the Democratic Party, supported Trump, and generally tried to undermine confidence in the electoral process and exacerbate tensions in society. Russian intelligence used contacts in Ukraine and their networks inside the US to spread propaganda in a vain attempt to bolster plausible deniability. These contacts laundered disinformation through US media organizations and prominent Americans, including some who were close to the Trump campaign. In short, the Russians relied on unwitting amplifiers, people who might once have been called useful idiots.

Although intelligence officials stopped short of publicly saying it, some commentators have pointed the finger at Rudy Giuliani as being one such useful idiot.[7] Once lionized as the mayor of New York City on 9/11, Giuliani had become a prominent member of Trump's legal team. The lasting image of him after the election was one of chaotic desperation, black hair dye running down his cheek, spreading false claims about voter fraud from the car park of a garden landscaping company bearing the same name as an upmarket hotel he seemingly thought he had booked for a press conference.[8]

Russia's propaganda narrative, amplified by the likes of Giuliani, essentially involved corrupt ties between Joe Biden, his son Hunter and Ukraine. 'Smoking gun email reveals how Hunter Biden introduced Ukrainian businessman to VP dad,' screamed an exclusive headline in the *New York Post*. It was the middle of October 2020, just weeks before the election. Trump was behind in the polls. Suddenly 'bombshell' correspondence supposedly revealed that this meeting came less than a year before Joe Biden pressured Ukrainian officials into firing a prosecutor who was investigating the very same company. Joe Biden influenced US foreign policy to help his son. Allegedly.

The exclusive details supposedly came from Hunter Biden's laptop, which someone had handed into a repair shop. The laptop also apparently contained compromising images of Hunter Biden. The shop's owner alerted the FBI but for some reason also copied the hard drive and reportedly gave it to Giuliani's lawyer. Giuliani then gave it to the *Post*.[9] Supposedly.

It was all very odd. A mysterious laptop dropped off but never collected. Smoking gun emails. A hard drive slipped to Rudy Giuliani. Many people, including former senior intelligence officials, thought it had the hallmarks of a Russian influence operation. Although no concrete evidence has emerged, it certainly fitted Russia's style and methods, and we do know that Russia had been digging for damaging material on the subject. Intriguingly, a Ukrainian politician, Adriy Derkach, sanctioned by the US Treasury for being a long-term Russian agent, had reportedly met Giuliani at least twice to discuss accusations of corruption against Biden. It was enough for former directors and deputy directors of the CIA to speak out publicly.[10]

The following year, after Biden's inauguration, the intelligence community formally assessed that Russia had launched such operations in 2020 but did not name the notorious *Post* story as an example. The assessment did, however, name Derkach as having played a prominent role in the electoral interference, by releasing telephone recordings four times in 2020 to try to implicate Biden in supposed corrupt activity in Ukraine.

Derkach and others, some with Russian intelligence connections, lobbied US officials – including those linked to Trump – to formally investigate Biden. They contacted media figures and even helped produce a documentary broadcast in January 2020. *The Ukraine Hoax*, which aired on One America News Network, amplified the Biden corruption line and accused the US of meddling in Ukrainian elections.[11]

Meanwhile, Russian operations tried to undermine Americans' confidence in the election process more broadly. During the primaries, trolls backed any candidate from either party deemed to be an outsider so as to attack the supposed establishment or cosy political elite. They later spread claims of electoral fraud. The nefarious Internet Research Agency, now renamed Lakhta Internet Research, amplified controversial domestic issues in an attempt to stoke division. As US counterintelligence closed in, the trolls worked through unwitting third countries such as Nigeria and Mexico to avoid detection.[12]

This time, Russia was not alone. Iran carried out a similar operation. Unlike Russia, it aimed to denigrate Trump rather than Biden. Like Russia, though, it also sowed confusion and undermined confidence in the US election process more broadly. This was likely authorized by the supreme leader Ayatollah Ali Khamenei himself. Iranian intelligence spread messages via social media, sent threatening emails to US citizens and amplified rumours about electoral fraud. Iran relied on cyber tools to spread its propaganda because they were cheap, accessible, deniable enough and allowed direct access to the US.

To complete the international orgy of influence, US intelligence also pointed the finger at others for conducting smaller campaigns. Lebanese Hezbollah supported efforts to undermine Trump – again largely because doing so was cheap and easy. Cuba also had a go by pushing pro-Democratic Party messages across the Latin American community. Venezuela hoped to join in as well, but probably lacked the capability to do so – or at least to make much of a difference.[13]

China was notable by its absence from the 2020 election. Beijing knew that either winner would be bad for China given the bipartisan consensus in Washington. It considered influence operations but ultimately decided against it. The risks of blowback and damage to China's image outweighed the advantages. Besides, China had a range of other means to influence US policy, such as political lobbying and economic measures. Covert action was not worth it on this occasion.[14]

Alongside propaganda, states can manipulate elections by covertly funding a particular political party and its leaders. The CIA spent vast sums of money during the Cold War funding friendly parties around the world, from Chile to Japan. Between the 1940s and 1970s, it spent around $75 million on Italy alone – a staggering almost $500 million at today's values.[15]

Massive spending continues to subvert democracy today. Russia, China, Iran and Venezuela have spent at least $300 million between them discreetly funding political parties since 2010. They have interfered in thirty-three different democracies globally on more than a hundred occasions.[16] The charge sheet against Russia is long and growing. It allegedly funnelled money to right-wing parties in Italy, France and the Netherlands. German newspapers reported covert Russian funding of the right-wing nationalist AfD party ahead of a recent election there. The scheme involved selling gold via a middleman at under-market values. The financial arrangements are so byzantine and confusing that sometimes even the party itself might not realize what is going on.[17]

Meanwhile, China has a growing track record too. It has allegedly used so-called straw donors to fund parties and politicians in Australia and New Zealand. Both China and Russia exploit various legal loopholes in electoral financing laws. Russia in particular is now much better integrated into western financial systems, thereby increasing opportunity for discreet political funding. London is awash with Russian money.[18]

Politicians are belatedly waking up to the idea that this constitutes a threat to the UK's national security. According to the British National Crime Agency, 'many hundreds of billions of pounds of international criminal money is laundered through UK banks, including their subsidiaries, each year'. Assets stored and laundered in London support Putin's campaign to subvert the international rules-based system, undermine UK allies and erode the mutually reinforcing networks that support UK foreign policy.[19]

The Russian offshore system generates so-called black cash: a slush fund to help buy influence abroad. For example, one lawyer running companies connected to Russian banks also owned companies connected to Czech politics. His employees provided over half of the total donations made to the political party of the Czech president, long considered an ally of Putin.[20]

The Kremlin enjoys massive leverage over oligarchs living overseas. Many owe their wealth to Putin.[21] According to Joe Biden before becoming president, Moscow can ask – or pressure – businesspeople 'to help finance its subversion of political processes elsewhere – by making contributions to an anti-NATO organization in Sweden, for example, or establishing anti-fracking groups in Bulgaria and Romania to fight developments that might threaten Russia's dominance of the eastern European gas market'.[22] Wouldn't it be nice, the Kremlin may say to some oligarch based in the Balkans, if you donated to this particular politician ahead of this particular election? According to Russia expert Mark Galeotti, this can be small scale enough to create the illusion that it is individual activity rather than part of a wider campaign organized by the Kremlin.[23]

Some covert political funding is definitely not legal. In 2010, Venezuela allegedly donated large sums of money to the

Eurosceptic populist Italian party, Five Star Movement, ahead of regional elections. In a move seemingly straight out of a spy novel, a suitcase stuffed with $3.5 million in cash made its way to the party via the Venezuelan consulate in Milan. Both Venezuela and the Italians deny the claims, insisting that documents incriminating them were forgeries.[24]

Bribery and blackmail constitute another shadowy tactic of covertly influencing elections. MI6 once had a top-secret slush fund for this very purpose. Its intelligence officers used bribery, including of politicians, to rig Iranian politics in the early 1950s. One target demanded a staggering £2 million, a price at which the penny-pinching British baulked. When trying to bribe Iranian politicians, one embassy official lamented: 'the wheels of Islam need more lubricating than those of other faiths'. Elsewhere, Prime Minister Clement Attlee, normally remembered for being rather mild mannered, once asked MI6 if any Albanian government officials were 'for sale'. We do not know, prime minister, came the response.[25]

There is one case we do know about, though. Julius Steiner and Leo Wagner were two conservative politicians in the West German Bundestag. Both had large debts and exploitable personal indiscretions, a penchant for women or drink. Steiner needed money to support his lavish lifestyle. Wagner, nicknamed Handsome Leo, was a confident rising star who spent thousands of deutschmarks living the high life in Bonn. In private, the story was rather different. He was saddled with debts he could ill afford and cheated on his wife with multiple women. Both men were ripe for recruitment by the East German intelligence service, the Stasi.

In 1972, these agents came in very useful indeed when the West German chancellor Willy Brandt faced a vote of confidence. The Kremlin approved of his friendly policies towards the east and wanted him to stay in power. The Soviets also worried that Brandt's impending demise would have ended the use of their best intelligence asset in West Germany: a personal aide to Brandt himself. They knew the vote, brought by the opposition leader, would be tight. And so the Stasi instructed both men to abstain, depriving the opposition of two crucial votes. It could have made all the difference between Brandt – and his policies – falling or surviving. The Stasi half bribed, half blackmailed both of them; without the money they would have been ruined. It worked. Brandt survived by exactly two votes.

Steiner later admitted that he had sold his vote for 50,000 deutschmarks; but Wagner denied it until his death. Suspicion followed him, though, especially when it turned out that an anonymous source had donated 50,000 deutschmarks into his account shortly before the vote. A fellow politician generously claimed he had lent Wagner the sum – but this was hardly convincing. Surviving Stasi documents later settled the question.[26]

The final way of influencing an election is the most direct: change the votes. Historically, states have achieved this bluntly by posting armed thugs to stand outside polling booths and intimidate voters. The Russians used strong-arm tactics to solidify power across eastern Europe after the Second World War. Alternatively, it can be done more discreetly through hacking into voter databases, manipulating registration systems and falsifying the vote count. This is the most difficult means of rigging an election. It is also the most effective.

Russia targeted Ukraine in one particularly audacious example shortly after it annexed Crimea in 2014. On the day of the presidential election, alarmed Ukrainian intelligence officers discovered a worrying intrusion which would have caused its central election commission to display inaccurate results. Russia had secretly planned to put a forged bar chart on the commission's website – just in time for the primetime news broadcasts. It knew full well that Ukrainian intelligence would quickly detect the fake election results, and so the goal was as much to sow distrust in the actual results among the already sceptical Ukrainian public by forcing the government to make a correction.[27]

Two years later, Russian hackers targeted US voter registration systems before the 2016 presidential election. They quietly probed websites in twenty-one states and successfully breached a few voter registration databases. Hackers even managed to install malware on the network of a company that made software for managing voter rolls. This gave them the potential to cause great damage by directly manipulating who could vote, creating delays at the polls, or preventing people from voting altogether.[28]

Crucially, Russia stopped short of doing so. The hackers did not alter data, and neither was there any evidence that they even intended to. It was instead a simple espionage operation. This grey area – espionage with the potential to do something destructive – created a thorny conundrum and complicated the American response. The operation was ambiguous, sitting between routine intelligence and illegitimate interference. It was hardly an act of war – even of sabotage – and so President Obama lacked the justification to respond too forcefully, but, at the same time, he knew that the Russians might be able to do real damage. He also feared provoking them into just such an action by responding too harshly. It cleverly backed the US into a corner.[29]

Reflecting on the US experience, British officials insist that the mechanics of the UK voting system are 'largely sound'.

This is because the UK uses a wonderfully archaic decentralized paper-based voting and counting system. It is impossible to hack. Sometimes antiquated British processes have their advantages. Nonetheless, GCHQ has undertaken a great deal of work to protect the online voter registration system.[30]

More recently, US intelligence assessed that neither Russia nor indeed anyone else had tried to interfere with the actual electoral processes during the 2020 election. Intelligence agencies uncovered numerous attempts to access voting systems and even to hack one of Biden's campaign advisory funds, but crucially these operations were part of broader intelligence-gathering activity rather than covert electoral interference. This is a crucial difference: the latter would have been much more controversial than the former. It is important to keep things in perspective.

Leaders choose to meddle in elections when they have both motive and means. Anyone contemplating electoral interference must first believe that another influential party in the target state is willing and able to seriously threaten their interests if it were to win. There is no point risking such a controversial measure otherwise. This provides the motive. So far so obvious. In addition, intervention requires somebody influential inside the target state who is ready and willing to be aided. This is the means. Without cooperation, or even mere passive consent, a blind eye turned, the operation becomes unfeasible. This is far from a given. Anyone being assisted by another state risks huge reputational damage if exposed. A president elected with the support of a foreign power will suffer an automatic crisis of legitimacy and forever be tainted as a puppet. A stooge.[31]

If these two conditions are met, the next choice is trickier: whether to interfere overtly or covertly. Rolling your sleeves up, puffing your chest out and openly meddling brings benefits. It allows much more extensive manipulation and a higher degree of control. The president of a wealthy state could publicly threaten to withdraw resources from, or promise trade with, a weaker state, depending on which candidate the weaker state's population vote for. Dov Levin, perhaps the world's leading expert on this activity, finds that such open interference is much more likely to succeed than covert action. On average, it swings the vote share of the supported candidate by 3 per cent more than covert interventions.[32]

Prime Minister David Cameron could barely contain his glee as he enjoyed a barbecue with President Obama in the garden of Downing Street shortly before the Brexit referendum in 2016. The UK, Obama breezily threatened afterwards, was 'going to be at the back of the queue' if it left the European Union. Of course, this was not a threat, he insisted with all the reassurance of a mafia boss; it was merely a point of view. He did, however, feel the need to justify his temerity in getting involved, knowing full well that it was a big deal in that it demolished a central argument made by the Leave campaign. There was a twist. Obama, it later turned out, had made the public intervention at Cameron's request.[33]

On the downside, this is little more than coercion. It risks a significant backlash against the bullying state and the supported party. A state would only consider this dramatic route if it had sufficient clout to get away with it.[34] Indeed, Brexit supporters screamed blackmail and demanded Obama butt out of British affairs. Cameron lost the referendum, largely as a consequence of the ill-thought-through complacency typified by his invitation to Obama to intervene.

If a leader does not have the temerity or clout to go public, then *covert* electoral interference becomes more appealing. Working in the shadows is less likely to create backlash – assuming it can remain plausibly deniable. And that is a big assumption. CIA operations targeting Italy, Chile and elsewhere during the Cold War soon became an open secret. Even if it does stay in the shadows, acting covertly has a cost. Manipulation is inevitably less extensive – in order to maintain secrecy – and so becomes less effective. Any covert funding or vote rigging must stay below a particular threshold and so is less likely to make a difference.[35] Covert action has a ceiling if it is to remain covert.

These trade-offs do not dissuade states from engaging in covert electoral interference. Leaders may prefer to bribe, bully or blackmail in the open but most lack the power to get away with it. Leaders are drawn to the relative cheapness of covert action. Secret meddling does not require the public promise of significant sums of aid. It also, theoretically at least, allows them to protect their own interests while hypocritically and virtuously promoting sovereignty, respect and international law to everyone else.[31] Covert action may be less impactful than open meddling, but there are more examples of successful covert electoral inter-ferences than overt ones – simply because there are far fewer historical cases of open meddling.[37]

It works. Sort of. More accurately, it works compared to other covert means of regime change such as overthrowing govern-ments by assassination or sponsoring insurgencies. US examples of covert success include Italy in 1948, Peru in 1962 and Bulgaria in 1991. The last known CIA operation was to meddle in Serbian elections to keep Slobodan Milošević from power in 2000 (attempts to target Iraq in 2005 were aborted). The Yugoslav president, serial human rights abuser and 'genocidal maniac', as one CIA officer involved put it, was competing for re-elec-tion. He fully expected to win. Working alongside the open – if discreet – work of US-funded non-governmental organizations, the CIA fully intended to stop him. President Clinton was on board: 'Milosevic was a stone-cold killer', and, besides, the covert action 'did not rig the vote or knowingly lie to the voters'.[38]

With the president's backing, intelligence officers busily held secret meetings with key opposition figures, providing campaign advice and plenty of cash. They might even have supported anti-Milošević street protests. Either way, the operation succeeded. Milošević was out, and, although it is difficult to isolate the key factors behind the result, incoming government officials quietly credited the CIA as having played a pivotal role. Senior CIA officers involved were certainly (if unsurprisingly) confident that they had made all the difference.[39]

The Russians have a slightly shorter and less illustrious track record of successful covert interventions, including Congo in 1960 and both Chile and Pakistan in 1970. The last known Russian attempt was the US presidential election of 2020. It failed.[40]

The reason for higher rates of success is simple: CIA officers and agents could move relatively freely in democracies, or at least in states with competitive elections. They could exploit the vulnerabilities of open societies. Freedom of the press allowed them to plant stories in newspapers; freedom to oppose governments allowed them to fund and advise opposition parties. It is harder to encourage grassroots protest when protest is banned. Compared to orchestrating coups in authoritarian regimes, the CIA enjoyed much more breathing space when meddling in democracies. As is so often the case, the greatest strengths of democracies, openness and freedom, also provide the greatest vulnerability. To change a government, it is easiest to go covert and target a democracy. The more free and fair the better.

Rather frustratingly for the budding election rigger, there is, as ever, a catch. Even if successful, electoral interference, like all forms of covert action, invariably has longer-term effects which may outweigh initial benefits. It may end up a classic short-term success and long-term failure, the preserve of politicians desperate for a quick resolution of a prickly problem.

The story of Forbes Burnham offers a prophetic warning. Burnham was a lawyer and skilled orator from British Guiana. He caught the CIA's attention back in the 1960s as a leading opponent of the left-wing prime minister, Cheddi Jagan. The Americans deemed Burnham suitably pro-western, a stark contrast to Jagan, whom, as we have seen, they considered a dangerous communist. The British worried that he was in fact dangerously anti-Europe and would be a deeply flawed leader, but as the colony inched towards independence from British rule, President Kennedy insisted that it could not have such a seemingly loose cannon as Jagan in charge. The CIA launched an extensive campaign to drive him from power by stacking pre-independence elections in favour of Burnham.

The CIA recruited an expatriate psychiatrist whose brother worked as an aide to Forbes Burnham. Joseph Smith, a CIA officer, trained him in the art of secret writing and other forms of spy tradecraft. It succeeded. Burnham was on board. The Americans now had motive and means. Next, at the start of 1964, the CIA secretly created a new political party among Jagan's own ethnic group to try to peel away support from Jagan's party. It followed this by financing campaign activities, such as leaflets and badges, as well as advising Burnham's party on tactics.

As the situation became more tense, violence broke out. The summer of 1964 saw at least five houses burned down every day and almost two hundred murders. Some were nervous in Washington. National Security Adviser McGeorge Bundy warned: 'I think it is unproven that CIA knows how to manipulate an election in British Guiana without a backfire.'[41]

Election day was 7 December. Turnout was high, but as the votes came in Jagan was doing better than expected. He ended up winning the popular vote but, given the colonial context and heavily rigged electoral system, the British offered Burnham – rather than Jagan – the chance to form a coalition. Jagan was out. There is another lesson here: covert action can only achieve so much.[42] To successfully rig an election, it helps if you control the state.

Burnham was elected prime minister in 1964 and guided British Guiana to independence shortly afterwards. Unfortunately for the US, despite all the aid, which continued over the following years, including during the 1968 election, things went horribly wrong. By the 1970s, Burnham declared his country on the road to socialism and developed ever closer relations with the Soviet Union. He pursued the very same policies which the CIA had intervened precisely to prevent. The successful operation ended up pretty unsuccessful. Kennedy's adviser on Latin America, Arthur Schlesinger, later apologized. By then, it was too late.[43]

The Burnham prophecy was not an isolated incident. CIA regime change operations – even when successfully accomplished – did not necessarily improve relations between the US and the target state; they failed to bring about long-term reliable allies.

Changing a state's foreign policy requires more than a change of leadership, not least because the new leader will face the very same problems and electoral constraints as the previous leader. And no leader wants to be seen as a puppet of the United States – or any other foreign power for that matter. Around half of all leaders installed by CIA-backed covert regime changes ended up being violently removed themselves afterwards. New leaders find themselves in a very difficult position.[44]

Recent statistical analysis makes for grim reading. US covert regime change attempts – whether by electoral interference or other means – increased the likelihood of armed conflict between the US and the target state by about six times in the decade afterwards. Even a successful regime change did not decrease the chance of conflict: it stayed the same as it would have been had the US not undertaken the operation at all. When it failed, however, the risks rose considerably. Covert regime changes also increase the risks of civil war and mass killings in the target states. Ousted governments might disperse to the countryside and launch an insurgency against the new regime. Covert electoral intervention decreases the level of democracy in the target state.[45] On the plus side, electoral meddling has brought the US higher levels of cooperation from the target country. But this is temporary, limited to relatively democratic countries, and the effects are more significant following overt rather than covert action.[46]

Meddling in elections is the easiest way to covertly remove a president or prime minister. There are plenty of ways in, from propaganda to shape voters' minds through to stuffing ballot boxes and directly altering votes. Secrecy imposes a ceiling on this activity, creating a trade-off between deniability and impact, but even so, with a willing accomplice on the inside, the chances of success are comparatively reasonable, especially when targeting a relatively open society in which you can exploit various freedoms. Turn strengths into vulnerabilities.

What comes next is quite a gamble. Quick wins can be easily wiped out by stubborn leaders trapped between covert support and domestic pressures, by more regime changes or by mass violence. Success therefore becomes a judgement call. Perhaps the short-term bounce was worth the longer-term costs? How sure can we be that it really was the regime change that led to a country's future problems, especially as the timespan between events grows? A whole host of buffeting winds might break the chain of causation. One thing is for sure: rigging elections is not the easy option, the silver bullet, that a leader hopes for.

There is a further, potentially fatal, flaw. What if there are no elections in which to meddle? Stage a coup.

6

HOW TO STAGE A COUP

On 10 January 2020, Sultan Qaboos of Oman died aged seventy-nine. He was the Arab world's longest-serving ruler, an absolute monarch, and a close ally of the United Kingdom. The prime minister, Boris Johnson, quickly exulted Qaboos as an 'exceptionally wise and respected leader who will be missed enormously'. He would, according to Johnson, 'be remembered for his devotion to the development of Oman into a stable and prosperous nation'.[1] No mention, critics pointed out, of Qaboos's autocratic grip. The very next day, Johnson arrived in Oman to offer his condolences in person. It was an incredibly senior delegation, including the defence secretary, the chief of the defence staff and even Prince Charles – reflecting the long-standing closeness of the relationship between the two royal families.

Amid all the praise and remembrance, it would have been impolite to mention that Qaboos had been put on the throne with British help some fifty years earlier in a remarkably successful covert action. Back then, Oman was waging a brutal and ineffective counterinsurgency campaign against leftist guerrillas. The sultan, Qaboos's father, was an unflinching despot who thought nothing of sealing water wells as a brutal form of collective punishment. In the background, the British quietly learnt that young Qaboos was interested in deposing his beleaguered father and, despite some hesitance in the Ministry of Defence, the British never looked back.

In July 1970, around thirty Omanis forcibly entered the palace in Salalah. It looked to all the world like local action – a classic Persian Gulf regime change – the outcome of intrigue and plotting within a ruling family.

Few knew that the coup was actually organized by the sultan's British defence secretary with the support of the Foreign Office. The Omanis were led by Ray Kane, a British officer acting on direct orders from his British commanding officer. Kane, armed with a machine gun, chased the sultan, who took refuge in a locked room. Kane then smashed the bullet-proof glass by repeatedly firing at the same spot. The sultan received four gunshot wounds, at least one of which was self-inflicted. He literally shot himself in the foot and then surrendered.

Qaboos presided over half a century of close relations with the UK. He allowed GCHQ to maintain spying facilities in his country and bought billions of pounds' worth of British weaponry and surveillance systems. As late as 2019, he received secret advice from an elite privy council including serving and former heads of MI6, Britain's national security adviser, British defence chiefs, a British foreign minister and advisers to the British royal family. They would quietly fly in once a year to brief Qaboos on what one member called 'hot topics' during midnight meetings.[2] In this sense, the covert action was a resounding success – at least from a British defence and security perspective.

*

Sometimes there are no elections in which to meddle. If the target state is not a democracy, if its elections are already rigged by a dictator, or if elections are simply too far in the future to resolve a pressing threat, then a coup d'état becomes a seductive option.

A coup involves the infiltration and seizure of a small but critical segment of the state apparatus, and then using this to displace the government from its control of the remainder.[3] Coups come in many shapes and sizes; most originate from inside the country. We are interested in those where another country offers a helping if hidden hand.

Some are inside jobs, technically called palace revolutions rather than coups. Qaboos's father lost power in just such a palace revolution where the state's bureaucracy is so closely tied to the ruling family that the overthrow must come from the inside, by a commander of the palace guard or, as in this case, a relative.[4]

The UK was particularly accomplished at engineering such coups across the Persian Gulf, where informal ties and influence discreetly shaped changes in dynastic regimes. Oman was not a one-off. Five years earlier, in 1965, British officials had helped to remove the leader of Sharjah, a small emirate in the Persian Gulf. After much agitation and plotting in London, the ruling family handed British representatives a letter saying that they wanted to depose the sheikh. As the RAF flew him away to Bahrain, British diplomats presented the whole thing as an internal family affair. A year later, the leader of Abu Dhabi met a similar fate, despite the Labour foreign secretary, Patrick Gordon Walker, needing a lot of persuading to sanction what he called a 'James Bond scheme'.

The sheikh's brother stepped forward and, once again, the ruling family offered a letter in support of the coup. On both occasions British diplomats on the ground used their close relationships with ruling families to engineer change.[5] As far as historians know, the British have not sponsored a coup since 1970.

Other coups come from outside the palace. They might be what are known as breakthrough coups, when an outsider, say a military leader, overthrows an established regime, perhaps with the help of foreign money or training. They might be veto coups, which overthrow a popularly elected government and often lead to repression and bloodshed. Or they might be less consequential guardian coups, in which, rather than fundamentally changing the structure of government, one of the usual suspects overthrows another in a game of musical chairs.[6]

Engineering a coup through covert action is certainly cheaper than despatching troops to overthrow a hostile government using conventional military force. A classic CIA-backed Cold War coup came in at a cost of tens of millions of dollars to the US government; military intervention, even a quick one such as the four-day US invasion of Grenada in 1983, cost hundreds of millions. The lengthy and unwieldy wars in Afghanistan and Iraq are on a different scale entirely.

A covertly sponsored coup brings other benefits too. Its deniability offsets the risk of inciting what would be an inevitable nationalist backlash in the case of open meddling. This advantage, of course, rests on the large assumption that it would stay deniable. Similarly, it offsets the risk of triggering wider escalation. States such as the US appear to be more risk-averse when it comes to promoting coups compared to rescuing flailing allies and so will often choose covert action rather than visible force. By contrast, they are more likely to take the risk and use open military means to rescue a friendly regime. The Eisenhower administration, back in the 1950s, used covert action in an ill-fated attempt to overthrow the Syrian government but, at around the same time, was happy to use open military intervention to rescue the Lebanese regime. This is simple psychology of loss aversion: losing ten dollars annoys us more than gaining ten dollars gratifies us.[7] Going overt is more impactful, yet more dangerous. You need the clout to get away with it, or the risk must be worth taking.

Coups may be cheap and, in theory at least, deniable, but leaders must choose their targets wisely. Certain states are riper for a coup than others. Targets need to have a modern, self-functioning bureaucracy which can be detached from the political leadership. The armed services, intelligence agencies, police and professional civil service can then continue to function in the same way as before, almost like a machine, but under new leadership. Yet if the machine is too well organized or sophisticated, with discretion to identify what is appropriate and what is not, as in the US and the UK, then a coup becomes unlikely. There is a sweet spot of just the right level of autonomy.[8]

Edward Luttwak, who wrote the classic book on coups, argues that ripe states have an apathetic population, or one which actively distrusts the government. The average citizen is economically or educationally deprived and cut off from wider politics outside of their immediate village, or is more politically literate but sees their taxes spent on the lavish lifestyle of the elite.[9] Power must be held in the centre, by elites. If it is too dispersed across different regions or corporations, a coup becomes unlikely to succeed. And, perhaps most importantly, ripe states are politically independent. It is practically impossible to stage a coup in the satellite state of another, more powerful, country, something the coup leaders in Hungary in 1956 found out the hard way after successfully seizing the state apparatus – the Soviets simply sent in tanks and troops to violently crush the uprising. When disgruntled plotters sought to overthrow the South Vietnamese leader in 1963, there is a reason why they ran it by the US embassy first.[10]

The CIA secretly sponsored at least thirteen coups during the Cold War, nine of which resulted in US-backed forces assuming power. In bad news for democracy, almost all involved military takeovers.[11]

The most famous, and perhaps the most influential, include Iran in 1953 and Guatemala the following year. In July 1953, an unassuming young CIA officer named Kermit Roosevelt completed a perilous drive across the border from Syria into Iran. Stashed in his car were several suitcases stuffed full of $100,000 in small denominations destined for a rent-a-mob. This was the culmination of nearly two years of propaganda, bribery and subversion instigated by MI6 to remove the prime minister, Mohammad Mossadeq, after he had nationalized Iranian oil. After countless appeals to President Truman had fallen on deaf ears, the British had finally managed to bring the Americans on board to stage a coup after Eisenhower became president in 1953.

The plan was simple enough: to persuade the young shah to sign a royal decree sacking Mossadeq and replacing him with a more amenable military candidate, General Zahedi, a ruthless and manipulative strongman. To soften the ground for this, the CIA and MI6 planted anti-Mossadeq propaganda across newspapers and spread rumours smearing him among the opinion formers in the bazaars. The prime minister was a corrupt communist. He was economically incompetent. Anti-Islamic. And so on. For good measure, the CIA also bribed senior politicians. This paved the way for a coup by helping to detach the army, civil servants and elites from Mossadeq, and by playing up the authority of the shah.

The oscillating shah took a lot of persuading to sign the decree. He was nervous and particularly distrustful of the British who had, in his own words, 'brought in my father' then 'threw out my father; and they can throw me out or keep me as they see fit'. MI6 and the CIA leant on his twin sister, bribing her with the finest furs.

Finally, in mid-August, the decree was ready. Unfortunately, someone leaked the plan and so Mossadeq managed to evade arrest. He had no intention of going quietly, predictably refusing to resign and instead publicly accusing the shah of collaborating with foreign powers to instigate an illegal coup against him. Crowds took to the streets. The shah fled, never quite trusting the British.

In response, the CIA and MI6 whipped up protestors of their own – including mobsters, acrobats and the clergy – to gather on the streets and demand his dismissal. They paid agents to tear down statues of the shah and drag them through the streets, in the hope that it would incite anti-Mossadeq riots. Other agents frantically circulated copies of the royal decree sacking Mossadeq. Soldiers began to switch sides and join the crowds. Zahedi delivered a radio broadcast announcing Mossadeq's arrest. After three days of confusion and riots, Mossadeq was gone. It was a successful coup. Just.

MI6 basked in the success of the 1953 Iranian coup and gave the lead American intelligence officer a VIP tour of London afterwards. He regaled an ageing Winston Churchill with tales of adventure and bravado. From his bed, Churchill, who loved this sort of thing, said that he would have gladly been involved, if only he was younger.

Equally buoyed by the success, the CIA plotted another coup the following year in Guatemala. President Jacobo Árbenz headed a democratically elected left-wing government, and many in Washington feared he was soft on communism. Perhaps more significantly, he also oversaw a series of economic reforms which hit US business interests in the country.

The coup plan involved psychological warfare, political action, subversion, and even potential assassination. As in Iran, the propaganda campaign began well before the start of the coup, softening up key targets and undermining loyalty to the president. The CIA trained and supported a ragtag paramilitary force to advance on the capital and overthrow Árbenz. A black radio station, supposedly operated independently but in fact run by the CIA, then broadcast propaganda to create the impression that the faltering rebellion was far more successful than it actually was. Guatemalan soldiers, intimidated and detached from their loyalty to Árbenz, switched sides and refused to fight. Under great psychological pressure, the government collapsed shortly afterwards. A military dictatorship took control. The final and most sinister part of the CIA plan – 'roll up Communists and collaborators' – was not needed.[12]

The success in Guatemala, hot on the heels of Iran, became legendary. It set the tone for CIA operations for the next decade.

Iran and Guatemala might be the most famous, but coups were not the sole preserve of the CIA. The Soviets enjoyed success in helping to coup-proof friendly regimes, but perhaps less so in covertly sponsoring coups themselves, especially outside of Poland, Hungary and Czechoslovakia in the late 1940s.[13] Having said that, the Kremlin believed that its covert actions did help turn various countries away from the US, especially in the 1970s. In 1974, the KGB estimated it had launched over 250 active measures targeting the CIA which led to widespread denunciations of the Americans by politicians around the world. Much of this was intangible influence work but, in the following years, a host of revolutions and coups brought more leftist or communist regimes to power, including in Ethiopia, Nicaragua, Afghanistan and South Yemen. The Soviets claimed success.[14]

Away from the superpowers, the French were particularly busy in sub-Saharan Africa, using coups to maintain post-colonial influence. Jacques Foccart, a wartime resistance fighter who later became President de Gaulle's primary Africa adviser, was a legendary figure with a remarkable rolodex of secret contacts. He would meet de Gaulle daily and formed the key link in a discreet back channel from the president, through French intelligence, to African intelligence networks. Operating from the shadows, and rarely seen in public, he is widely regarded as the instigator of many a plot, coup and countercoup using his contacts across the scattered confetti of what was once the French empire, from Cameroon to Congo, in the 1960s.[15]

No fewer than six military coups took place in francophone Africa in late 1965 and early 1966 alone. One came in Congo-Brazzaville. For a while, de Gaulle tolerated the revolutionary politics going on there, not least because it caused problems for the Americans in neighbouring Zaire. But after a while, the French president had had enough, telling Foccart, 'Let's cease this comedy and turn off the tap.' A coup inevitably followed.[16]

The following decade, in 1977, the French government secretly endorsed an attempt by mercenaries to remove the pro-Soviet leader in Benin on the west African coast. Known as Operation Shrimp, it failed miserably. When they met unexpected resistance, including from North Korean forces who happened to be protecting visiting communist dignitaries, the mercenaries noisily fled leaving behind a cache of incriminating documents. The plotters, it turned out, included leaders in Morocco and

Gabon as well as Foccart and a senior French intelligence officer, Jeannou Lacaze, a man enigmatically known as the Sphinx. The fiasco discredited France's Africa policy but did not put the Élysée off trying again elsewhere.[17]

The following year, the French president, Valéry Giscard d'Estaing, cautiously approved a coup in the Comoros, an archipelago in the Indian Ocean situated between Madagascar and the east coast of Africa. Bizarrely, the French had agreed to an earlier coup there which had removed the very same leader they now sought to put back in office. It was a covert game of musical chairs. Still, the target, Ali Soilih, was a particularly awful person, empowering a teenage militia, armed with AK-47s, to rape and kill their way across the islands.

Again, mercenaries would give French intelligence deniability. Codenamed Atlantis, the operation began with about fifty mercenaries, led by the legendary soldier of fortune Bob Denard, setting sail from Brittany. Using the cover of an expedition researching seismic activity in the region, Denard's boat sailed past the Canary Islands and around the Cape of Good Hope before finally landing on a white sandy beach north of the Comorian capital in the early hours one night in May. They quickly took control of the island and arrested the ill-fated president in his bedroom. Rumour has it he was high on marijuana watching a pornographic film with three naked girls.[18] He was shot dead shortly afterwards, supposedly trying to escape from house arrest.

In 1979, the French fomented another coup, this time targeting the Central African Republic. Operation Caban reinstated David Dacko as president, and had French fingerprints all over it from start to finish. French intelligence officers had to cajole Dacko, who feared for his personal safety, onto the plane in the first place. They made him prerecord a message announcing the coup and requesting French military assistance. Commandos, operating without insignia to ensure deniability, then secured the airport without a shot fired, partly by offering money to local troops. Dacko successfully landed and made his speech. Within minutes, French forces secured key locations across the capital.[19]

These three examples offer a mere flavour of covert action in post-imperial Africa designed to maintain French influence across the region. It made CIA intervention look like playground games. Too often these coups are omitted from Anglo-centric history books which focus on US – and to a lesser extent – British activity.

And what about elsewhere, beyond the usual suspects? So much attention on subversion and subterfuge in Latin America focuses on the apparently omnipotent US, but other countries in the region meddled closer to home. Historians associate plotting against Salvador Allende's socialist government in Chile almost exclusively with the CIA, but documents recently unearthed in local archives reveal the hidden hand of others.

Allende was elected in 1970, following a closely run contest and a string of earlier defeats. He governed for just three years, nationalizing various industries in the process, before being famously removed in a 1973 coup. General Augusto Pinochet, leading a group of military officers, seized power on 11 September. Allende committed suicide shortly afterwards.

We now know that the Brazilian military played a covert role in abetting the coup. Two years earlier, the Chilean ambassador in Brazil uncovered secret plans to instigate an insurrection against Allende. The Brazilian army had successfully infiltrated officers into Chile, posing as tourists, to gather intelligence on where guerrillas might operate during any coming uprising. The head of Brazil's military regime even visited the White House and told President Nixon directly that Brazil intended to depose Allende. Nixon, who had his own plans, hoped they would work closely together.[20]

Over the next couple of years, Brazil operated quietly in the shadows. It established back channels with dissident Chilean military officers and invited them for secret discussions about coup plotting, developed links with a violent Chilean organization determined to overthrow Allende, and offered advice gleaned from its own military coup back in 1964. Once Allende was overthrown, Brazil was the first country to recognize the new government and worked discreetly to prop it up. It acted very much in its own interests and of its own volition – not as an American puppet.[21]

It is misleading to overplay the CIA hand when thinking about covert actions. Other intelligence agencies, including those of regional powers, have hands of their own. We also know that another intelligence agency, this time from over seven thousand miles away, was involved in the Chilean coup: the Australian Secret Intelligence Service.

In the autumn of 1970, the US requested assistance and, over spring and summer the following year, Australia dutifully established a spy station in Santiago. Directly supporting CIA covert action against Allende, Australian spies quickly brought over a range of paraphernalia, such as hidden cameras. They requested a 'German, repeat German made Volkswagen Beetle' in 'light grey or fawn', and later reported back that another car had taken a 'sad beating' after being caught up in a rock fight during riots in Santiago. The windscreen was smashed. It is unclear exactly what they were up to, but they certainly drove around the city meeting agents recruited by the Americans and submitted intelligence reports back to CIA headquarters in Langley, Virginia.

The new Australian prime minister, Gough Whitlam, shut down the station in July 1973, just two months before the coup. One operative, however, stayed on. Whitlam worried about exposure. Should Australian activity come to light, there was no way he could credibly justify involvement on the other side of the world where Australia had no real interest. Unlike counterparts in Brazil, they were doing it purely to help the Americans, although no doubt intending to get something in return. Whitlam later admitted as much following just such an embarrassing leak: the Australian Secret Intelligence Service was working as a proxy of the CIA.[22]

Plenty of states covertly sponsor coups; on occasion they team up and sponsor coups in the same target country. But how useful is it as a means of covert regime change? The results are mixed.

The political scientist Lindsey O'Rourke has examined the CIA track record and offers us some statistics. Sixty-nine per cent of US-sponsored coups succeeded during the Cold War, almost all of which targeted democracies. This is a pretty decent success rate. When the US targeted authoritarian regimes, it went for dictators who governed through sheer force of personality rather than people's allegiance to their party or ideology – and succeeded three out of six times. Governments built around a single personality appeared more fragile, with better odds of generating real change if that single personality was removed. By contrast, well-established one party states proved the most difficult regimes to remove by coup. This is unsurprising: these regimes had decades of practice in self-protection, possessed entire secret services geared towards coup-proofing, and generally tended to be more stable. O'Rourke also found that CIA covert action to encourage a democratic revolution by backing pro-democracy groups enjoyed a 50 per cent success rate. However, statistics can be misleading because those that did succeed may well have done so regardless of CIA involvement. For example, by the time the US began to support the Polish Solidarity movement in the early 1980s, the organization had already amassed nine million members.[23]

We can draw a few conclusions from all of this about how states successfully foment a coup from afar. The choice of target is crucial. US experience suggests coups stand a decent chance of overthrowing a democracy. As with electoral rigging, the inherent openness and freedom within democracies create vulnerabilities which can be exploited. US experience then suggests even odds on a successful coup targeting a cult of the personality, and a poor chance against one party states. Even within those categories, some states are riper than others, depending, as we have seen, on the nature of the bureaucracy, the apathy of the population and the centralization of power.

History tells us that, to be successful, plotters require a few key ingredients. First, the target government must have a structure that lends itself to takeover by a small team. Second, a credible candidate willing to receive covert support is equally vital, yet not easy to find given the risk of being labelled a stooge if exposed. Third, and linked to this, plotters need to acquire the support of key groups, especially the military, softened up by propaganda and political action in advance. This requires outstanding intelligence on personalities, and their loyalties, hopes and fears, which then informs the line used to recruit them. In Latin America, for example, potential military conspirators were receptive to the line that the sacred trust of the armed forces requires intervention to clear up the mess made by politicians to achieve national progress.[24] In Iran, it involved protecting the integrity of the shah and Islam from Mossadeq. The line must be carefully calibrated.

Fourth, and alongside this, a coup requires the acquiescence – if not support – of the wider population, which can also be softened in advance. Indeed, time and planning are essential. Covert action in Iran began in 1951, almost two years before the coup. The CIA began an earlier – aborted – attempt to overthrow Árbenz in 1952. Coup plotting in Chile began in 1970 – three years before the coup.

Fifth, as the coup unfolds, plotters will have to move quickly and with great precision, taking key public buildings, controlling road links and arresting politicians. The message is vital; it is no coincidence that successful coups quickly capture the national broadcaster.[25] This also involves impeccable planning, and operational secrecy to prevent the chaos that happened when Mossadeq found out he was about to be arrested. Finally, as in the case of Iran in 1953, plotters need a fair bit of luck, intuition and creativity.

Such a checklist is all very well and good, but there is a deeper, more existential, issue at play. Given that coups require a credible leader, and that covert action only ever pushes history along rather than creating opposition from scratch, it is difficult to know if and when the hidden hand – and whose hidden hand – made all the difference. And there is a crucial difference between instigating a coup and turning a blind eye to a coup. This, in turn, creates problems for those wanting to know what works and what does not.

The story of the 1971 coup in Uganda, which brought Idi Amin to power, is instructive. In January of that year, Amin, the head of the armed forces, ousted the president, Milton Obote. The coup was swift and relatively peaceful, with Amin choosing to strike while Obote was overseas at a Commonwealth heads of government conference. By the very next day, life in Kampala had returned pretty much to normal. Amin went on to establish a brutal and despotic dictatorship. Hundreds of thousands of people were killed during his rule.

Historians have tended to see the neocolonial hand of the British lurking in the background of the coup. This is wrong. The historian Harriet Aldrich has recently found that Amin had planned his own coup which caught the British unawares. Any tactical external support he did receive came not from the UK but from Israel. Wanting to counter Arab influence in east Africa, Israel had been working with Amin since 1969 to funnel weapons across the Ugandan border into Sudan to rebels fighting the Arab government in Khartoum. The relationship between Uganda and Israel became fraught when President Obote began to criticize Israeli aggression in Egypt and its treatment of Palestinians. Amin, whom the Israelis had secretly helped become head of the army in 1969, was the prime candidate to step in and replace him.[26]

When Amin made his move, the Israeli attaché in Kampala, Colonel Bar-Lev, advised him closely during the coup's most critical hours. He helped disarm Obote's aircraft and even recommended whom Amin should eliminate. Before we start blaming Israel for abetting the coup, there is another twist. The enthusiastic Bar-Lev over-reached; he acted without his government's permission. He knew about the coup months in advance but seemingly did not tell Tel Aviv. When orders came on the day of the coup itself not to meddle, he promptly ignored them.[27]

To be sure, Britain was opportunistically pleased with the outcome and quickly recognized the new regime. Yet it did not sponsor the coup. UK covert action is blamed for many things, but it is not responsible for bringing the murderous Amin to power. How to stage a coup? As Bar-Lev did, mentor someone who is staging one regardless.

These coups, from Iran to Chile, may be classic twentieth-century spy stories, but they have descendants today. In autumn 2016, all eyes were on the US presidential election and the unlikely rise of Donald Trump. Russian spies moved in the shadows, meeting political advisers, opposition leaders, and even the clergy. They quietly planned a coup. If that failed, a motley bunch of mercenaries would storm the capital and assassinate the leader.

This was not Washington, D.C., but five thousand miles away in Montenegro, in southeastern Europe. It was a dramatic plot, straight out of a thriller, and the stakes were high as Montenegro was just months away from joining NATO. At the very last minute, an informant tipped off the authorities. The perpetrators included opposition leaders, a retired commander of an elite Serbian unit, a bunch of angry nationalists and, last but not least, Russian military intelligence. Police were ready and waiting. A Montenegrin court later convicted two Russian intelligence officers in absentia. British politicians deemed it 'an astonishingly bold move in a country just a few months from its accession to NATO'.[28] The chief of MI6 himself later publicly pointed the finger at Russia.[29] This was a clear-cut case worthy of the Cold War.

In April 2021, news broke of another apparent, if murkier, coup attempt, this time in Jordan – and, for once, not linked to Russian intelligence. It seems the US embassy in Amman tipped off Jordanian intelligence about a brewing plot led by allies of King Abdullah's half-brother, Prince Hamza. He had spent years courting far-flung and disaffected tribal leaders who felt increasingly overlooked by the government. Authorities began listening in on conspirators as they solicited support from tribal chiefs and former military officers: 'Our guy has made a decision to move; do you pledge allegiance?'[30]

Shortly afterwards, security services raided Hamza's residence and put him under house arrest. They arrested around twenty people for supposed plotting, including a powerful tribal leader and a confidant of the Saudi crown prince. Intercepted WhatsApp messages, including with the Saudi confidant, allegedly discussed when Hamza could bring his supporters out onto the streets to join independently planned protests calling for political reform. 'I don't want to move too quickly.'[31]

Jordan's King Abdullah spoke of his shock and pain. Details were sparse, mired in allegation and counter-allegation. Press reports suggested that Israel and Saudi Arabia, maybe even with the tacit approval of the Trump administration, supported the coup. After all, Jordan had opposed Trump's flagship Middle East peace plan, the so-called Deal of the Century, and the king had become increasingly isolated as a result. There were even suggestions of the Saudis arming southern tribes. Although Israeli intelligence quickly sent a private message to the king disavowing involvement, a Jordanian government report accused the plotters of 'conspiring with foreign agendas'.[32] Eventually, two men, another relative of the king and the Saudi confidant, were found guilty of sedition and incitement against the crown. They received fifteen years of hard labour.

This case is symptomatic of the swirling confusion surrounding contemporary covert action. It is hard enough understanding coup plots from fifty years ago using fragments of archival evidence, stitching together a story from each snippet, each piece of paper, silently suspended in slow time capturing a specific moment and a specific moment only. As we have seen in Uganda, it can be difficult to pinpoint agency and instigation. It is even more difficult when there is no archival record yet. There may have been a coup plot, there may not have been. Perhaps it was mere sedition. The protests were planned independently of Hamza; he merely (allegedly) wondered when and how to join them. It may have had foreign support; it may not. Foreign support, if it existed, might have impacted developments; it might have been utterly superfluous. It is hard to know. That Jordan chose to hold the trial in secret created more confusion and left questions unanswered.

Other twenty-first-century coups are equally unclear. They are more grey than black, existing in a murky world where soft power and diplomacy meet more discreet measures. Russia allegedly had a hand in a 2010 coup in Kyrgyzstan by encouraging opposition forces to destabilize the president. Shortly before the coup, Russia withdrew financial assistance, pushed up energy prices and used propaganda to smear the president. His days were numbered.[33]

In 2017, China seemingly attempted something similar in Zimbabwe. The Chinese had long held substantial economic interests in the country and enjoyed the political influence this bought. Despite earlier supporting President Mugabe, including covertly with weapons during his pre-independence days as a guerrilla fighter, China had grown increasingly concerned about the mercurial dictator's volatility. Shortly before the coup, Zimbabwe's military chief visited Beijing. Just days later, his forces seized control and put the ageing president under house arrest. China used a combination of economic and political pressure, combined with discreet support for a particular faction.[34]

*

Covertly sponsored coups – and allegations of covertly sponsored coups – are neither new nor rare. Thinking about recent alleged plots helps to elucidate the past, and vice versa. The ambiguity surrounding modern examples offers three important insights. First, there is clear continuity involving the need to find credible candidates, to secretly recruit allegiance among key groups, and to act covertly.

Second, the idea of state sponsorship varies immensely: in fact, it is a misleading term. There is a vast difference between turning a blind eye to something that would happen anyway, piggybacking off internal events or off allies' operations, and then endorsing, approving, sanctioning and directing. This equally applies to Cold War coups and, even though they happened decades ago, it remains difficult to label the exact level of external involvement. States calibrate their involvement carefully, if sometimes opportunistically, yet too often we lazily reduce it to sponsorship.

Third, recent plots emphasize the importance of overt action. We know that Russia and China had visible diplomatic dealings with Montenegro, Kyrgyzstan and Zimbabwe respectively, which might have outweighed the impact of any *potential* covert action. Secrecy, after all, puts a limit on what can be achieved. Although historians and the wider public remember them for their tales of subterfuge and derring-do, the classic Cold War coups were also not entirely covert. The UK put huge economic and political pressure on Mossadeq at the very same time as it secretly engineered his demise; the CIA did the same regarding Guatemala. Coups, whether today or in the Cold War, even those considered covert action, involve a combination of both open and deniable pressure. To be successful, covert action can only exist alongside overt tools of power.

Reducing these events to stories of states secretly orchestrating coups is simplistic. There will always be ambiguity, allegation and counter-allegation. How journalists, academics and, most importantly, governments represent the situation – and how they respond – is what matters most. This confusion, this interplay between the story and reality, constitutes the real grey zone.

Sometimes a coup is unfeasible or impractical in the first place, especially when targeting a well-established one party state or the satellite state of a larger power. In this case, a more violent, less surgical, use of force might be tempting. States wage secret wars.

HOW TO WAGE A SECRET WAR

'The Amazon Washington Post,' President Donald Trump angrily tweeted late one night in 2017, 'fabricated the facts on my ending massive, dangerous and wasteful payments to Syrian rebels fighting Assad…'

Outrageously undiplomatic tweets were so commonplace during the Trump presidency that they became almost routine. This one was anything but. For nearly half a decade, the CIA had been running one of its largest covert operations since the 1980s: secretly funding, arming and training rebels fighting the brutal regime in Syria. Civil unrest and protests had erupted back in early 2011 as part of the wider Arab Spring but the president, Bashar al-Assad, refused to give an inch and turned to lethal force to quash pro-democracy demonstrations. As violence intensified, different rebel factions took up arms to fight the government. They looked, among others, to the United States for support. The CIA activity soon became a $1 billion operation. Five years in, at a stroke, and seemingly on a whim, Trump publicly acknowledged it. And cancelled it.

The US covert operation was one of many in what had become an anarchic playground of proxies. Saudi Arabia, Turkey, Qatar,

Jordan, the UK and France all covertly intervened to different degrees. It was chaos. The Saudis, Turks and Qataris sponsored different rebel groups, often intent on fighting each other as much as Assad. To make matters worse, some of these groups comprised outright jihadis with a long-standing hatred of the US. On the other side, Iran, through its Lebanese proxy Hezbollah, supported the Assad regime. As did Russia.

Syria was just the latest in the series of uprisings once optimistically known as the Arab Spring. In Libya, the UK and others had supported rebel groups fighting another brutal dictator, Muammar Gaddafi, the mercurial 'mad dog of the Middle East', as President Reagan called him. Prime Minister David Cameron scrambled for ideas. He suggested dropping used Libyan banknotes worth $1 billion into the country, but his horrified attorney general quickly blocked what would have been an illegal scheme. Cameron settled instead for a few undercover officers embedded among the rebels.[1]

He also turned to E Squadron, the most shadowy arm of the British secret state. E Squadron is a small elite unit of special forces operatives working with MI6, the successor to what was known as the Increment. It operates under the command of MI6 and the director of special forces to engage in some of the more dangerous forms of covert action. It was active in Libya, and probably in Iraq and Afghanistan too, working with anti-Saddam and anti-Taliban rebels respectively.

As would happen in Syria, a confused flurry of covert units joined the subterranean fray. Special forces and intelligence teams from France, Italy, Egypt, Qatar and the UAE organized and trained the rebels, offering advice as they prepared to march on Tripoli. The French sent a team of around forty men, dressed in civilian clothes, to protect rebel leaders and deliver arms.

Their aeroplanes secretly dropped large bundles of weapons, including machine guns, anti-tank missiles and rocket-propelled grenades. The Qataris set up a training camp outside Benghazi and worked closely with French intelligence to deliver weapons.[2] Special forces facilitated – but did not control or dictate – the rebels' push on the capital.

Tripoli fell in the summer of 2011. Aided by US and French intelligence, the excitable rebels eventually found Gaddafi, blood-soaked and hiding in a drain, the following October. The mob grabbed him, beat him, and sodomized him with a bayonet. In front of a crowd of mobile phones pointing at the bewildered captive, the rebels shot him dead.[3]

The aftermath of the Libyan uprising was a tragic one, falling far short of the initial optimism and promise. Civil war continued for years with both sides attracting continued foreign support. Egypt, the UAE and Russia supported forces fighting against the recognized – but flailing – national government. By the end of the decade, hundreds of Russian mercenaries were active in the country, recruiting, training and fighting alongside militias.

These mercenaries had cut their teeth in eastern Ukraine where, in spring 2014, armed separatists stormed government buildings not long after Russian covert operatives, the so-called little green men, took over and annexed the Crimean penin-sula. Separatists then promptly declared the liberation of a new people's republic in the Donbas region in the east. Russian intelli-gence lurked in the background. The Kremlin did not necessarily instigate the insurrection, but it supported the rebels, ensuring that they survived the inevitable counterattack by the Ukrainian army. Armed volunteers arriving from Moscow in their droves cheekily dubbed it the Russian Spring. Mercenaries fought along-side the separatist rebels as the conflict dragged on.

*

Complex wars in places like Libya and Syria feature conspicuously in international politics today but sponsoring violent rebels – whether overtly or covertly – is not new. Neither did it begin with the Cold War, even if, in the popular imagination at least, this supposedly stable era of superpower standoff provided the heyday of secret wars.

States have been doing this for centuries, millennia even. The Romans supported the Mamertines, mercenaries from the shin of Italy, against Carthage in the First Punic War; Queen Elizabeth I secretly sent money and mercenaries to Protestant rebels fighting against the Spanish in the Netherlands; Cardinal Richelieu, the seventeenth-century French foreign secretary, subverted a range of foes, from the Holy Roman Empire to the Habsburgs, using an entire web of proxies. He called it *La Guerre Couverte*.[4] The chances of rebels receiving support from a foreign state have risen dramatically over the last two centuries, and with this the chances of rebel victories over incumbent governments have also grown.[5]

Given this extensive history, as long as statecraft itself, there must be good reason why covertly sponsoring rebels appeals to such a wide range of leaders. Convenience and cost offer the best answer. Presidents and prime ministers, monarchs and cardinals, have turned to covert paramilitary action when conventional military intervention is politically impossible.

Some leaders wrongly see it as a silver bullet to solve an intractable problem. A quick fix. Some hope it will prevent backlash from their publics who might be opposed to war. As one scholar of proxy wars, Geraint Hughes, put it, funding rebels offers 'a superficially seductive policy option to any state that is (to quote Alexander Pope) "[willing] to wound, and yet afraid to strike"'.[6] For President Eisenhower, it was 'the cheapest insurance in the world'.[7]

Prime Minister David Cameron turned to covert operations in Syria precisely because he was unable to intervene openly and militarily. The seemingly never-ending conflicts in Afghanistan and Iraq had made the British public incredibly wary of any more wars in the Middle East. For years, television cameras had broadcast sombre footage of coffin after coffin draped in the Union Jack returning home through the small market town of Wootton Bassett en route to yet another military funeral. People had had enough.

When Cameron allowed a parliamentary vote on whether to launch military action against Bashar al-Assad in Syria, he suffered an embarrassing defeat in the House of Commons. The legacy of Iraq audibly reverberated throughout the chamber as ministers repeatedly evoked claims of dodgy dossiers and intelligence failures. And so, Cameron turned to the hidden hand. Covertly supporting Syrian rebels, including through facilitating the transfer of weapons, allowed him to bypass domestic constraints.

President Obama faced a similar problem. In August 2012, he had publicly stated that use of chemical weapons in Syria would constitute a 'red line'. The threat was clear: if Assad used them, the US would have no choice but to intervene. The words came back to haunt Obama when, a year later, Assad did just that.

Like Cameron, Obama was unable to intervene openly. Despatching American forces was out of the question. His European allies were stalling; legacies of Iraq hung over the intelligence community, who did not want to be blamed if they were wrong in assessing that Assad was the perpetrator; and Republicans in

Congress, under pressure from constituents, warned that, however bloody, the civil war did not affect US interests. The speaker of the house insisted that military strikes would require congressional authority and warned Obama about the risks of escalation. Even Obama's own legal team had doubts. There was no real claim of self-defence and no United Nations Security Council resolution to justify action.[8] When presidents lack either a credible self-defence claim or international authorization to launch a war, they are much more likely to turn to covert paramilitary action.[9] And so, just as his predecessors had done before him, Obama reluctantly turned to the CIA. By autumn 2013, the CIA was sponsoring supposedly moderate rebels in Jordanian training camps.

This is the world of risk management, covert action as a coping mechanism.[10] As Obama vacillated over whether to support the Syrian rebels, his CIA director and secretary of state convinced him that it offered a means of managing a tricky situation. This was conflict without the risk, war on the cheap. Less than that, it would undermine Assad's authority without war or responsibility.[11]

There is still much we do not know about the decision-making process leading up to the Syrian covert action, or indeed the consequences, and so it might help to turn briefly to a historical example of covert action as risk management to shed more light on the matter: a different sponsor, different continent, different century – but the core issues are the same.

In the late 1960s, France covertly intervened in the Nigerian civil war. President de Gaulle watched with great interest as rebels from the eastern region of Biafra fought for independence from the federal government. He sensed an opportunity to reduce Anglo-Saxon influence in west Africa, a significant region for post-imperial France, and was happy to make life difficult for the

British – who wholeheartedly supported the Nigerian government against the breakaway rebels.

At the same time, though, he did not want to intervene
so directly and obviously as to sever relations with London.
Therefore, French intelligence sent paramilitary advisers and
recruited mercenaries to support the Biafran secessionists in the
break-up of Nigeria. They also used the Ivory Coast as a stalking
horse as a conduit for weapons and to do other things that the
French could not do publicly. De Gaulle knew that keeping
support indirect would cost less money, less political capital and
fewer lives compared to sending in French troops. If the Biafrans
lost in their bid for independence, which they eventually did, he
also knew that France had little to lose and could restore relations with Nigeria easily.[12]

Whether the US and Syria in the 2010s or France and Nigeria
in the 1960s, whether facing threat or opportunity, it is all about
risk management. The impact of covert action is far below that
achieved by open military intervention, but this time the trade-
off fell towards secrecy.

What about dictators who delegate violence to rebels and
terrorists? They do not have to worry quite so much about
domestic backlash, oversight or media exposure,[13] and they
might sponsor fighters for more coercive and ambitious reasons,
rather than as mere coping mechanisms.[14]

Iran, for example, not only wanted to defeat the rebels challenging Assad in Syria, but to effectively gain control of a land
corridor linking Tehran to Beirut. Unlike the US, Iran seeks
more binding relationships with its partners, in order to establish
longer-term regional dominance.[15]

Iran has a well-deserved reputation for being a sponsor of
violence. Aiming to counter Israel, contain Saudi Arabia, reduce

US presence in the Middle East and fight ISIS, Iran has developed a comprehensive strategy over recent decades of using proxies to dominate the region. Violent groups covertly receiving Iranian support can be found in Iraq, Afghanistan, Syria, Lebanon and Yemen – although it is important to remember that each enjoys its own autonomy and, as we shall see, has a different relationship with Iran.[16]

The list of groups is bewilderingly long, spanning a who's who of violent groups across the region. Iran has supported Hamas in Palestine and Hezbollah in Lebanon. In Yemen, it has partnered with Houthi rebels, an armed Shia Islamist movement, to increase pressure on the Saudis.[17] In Iraq, it has subsidized the Badr Organization, once a covert actor opposing Saddam Hussein and now an influential political party.[18] Various paramilitary groups, numbering some 100,000 fighters, have facilitated Iran's influence in the country further, influence which pre-dates the anarchic aftermath of the ill-judged 2003 invasion. Iran sponsored Shia militias inside Iraq way back during the Iran–Iraq War of the 1980s. After the invasion, Iran inserted paramilitary fighters inside Iraq, gradually scaling up activity to include training militias, smuggling improvised bombs across the border, and even sending in money and drugs. Tony Blair later blamed Iranian activity for damaging western attempts to bring democracy to Iraq.[19] In September 2018, Shia militias fired rockets at American targets in Baghdad and Basra. The US blamed Iran and condemned its sponsorship of the perpetrators.[20]

Iranian sponsorship of terrorists and insurgents extends beyond the Middle East. In early 2021, Ethiopian intelligence personnel arrested a sleeper cell planning a terrorist attack in the capital Addis Ababa. The US military claimed that Iran had masterminded the plot and had activated the network in part to attack soft targets in Africa as retribution for US and Israeli covert action against Iran, and to pile pressure on the nascent Biden administration.[21]

These terrorist groups can add value in specific areas. Hezbollah provides Iran with specialist knowledge, training camps and a proven track record of effectiveness. Elsewhere, states like Sudan have covertly sponsored terrorists in order to reduce the need for conventional military operations which might prove too expensive. Attacks by terrorist groups, especially those receiving government support, are often more aggressive than covert actions conducted by risk-averse government agencies. This could potentially increase the bargaining power and leverage of states sponsoring them.[22] Its imperial ambitions may be consigned to the ancient past, but Iran uses these covert means to expand its influence west across the Arab world, and especially among minority Shia populations. This increased following US drawdowns in Iraq and the Gulf.[23]

Despite not having to worry about media exposure or domestic oversight, Iranian covert action still involves risk management. Delegating violence increases ambiguity, if not always deniability, making it difficult for targets to respond. By contrast, going to war risks international condemnation, huge financial cost and loss of life. War with Israel or Saudi Arabia to achieve regional dominance would be too much of an ask. Israel has nuclear weapons; Saudi Arabia is much richer than its neighbour.[24] Both have close relations with the US. Covertly sponsoring others to fight on your behalf mitigates those risks.

Theoretically, at least. In Iran's case, what it sees as a pragmatic defensive response to security threats can end up feeding suspicion and hostility in others. This, in turn, might spur its rivals into some sort of action which could undermine Iranian security, as demonstrated by the killing of Soleimani and various Israeli strikes. And so, a vicious cycle of covert strikes begins.[25] It may not always work, but the core principle here is that states seek to get as much as possible out of a conflict without having to assume the burden of risk associated with actually doing the fighting themselves.[26]

How and why states wage secret wars is highly mythologized. Contrary to popular opinion, the aim is not necessarily to overthrow or defeat a target government, or liberate the supported population. The need for deniability usually precludes such stellar impact.

According to the CIA's official historian, covert paramilitary operations tend to fail more than political or influence operations.[27] When debating these options targeting Syria in 2013, President Obama commissioned an in-house CIA evaluation of its track record of covertly supporting rebel groups. The report remains classified, but newspapers reported that its conclusions made for gloomy reading.

Only two examples exist of the CIA successfully overthrowing a government by sponsoring rebels alone: in Afghanistan and Chad.[28] And even these rarities come with a catch. Both took place in the 1980s, hardly a coincidence given President Reagan's proclivity to plough huge sums of money into operations notable for their performative faux secrecy. Both relied on networks of covert international support. Both started small without initially harbouring regime change ambitions.

In 1978, the Afghan Communist Party assassinated the president and overthrew his government. The new regime quickly clamped down on Muslim traditionalists, but quickly fell into an internal power struggle. Another coup took place the following year. The Soviets sent secret units to help quell emerging rebellions. Three months later, in December 1979, the new president was assassinated in yet another communist coup – at which point the Soviets invaded the country.

Armed groups revolted against communist rule – and the US government was willing to help. It started innocuously enough. President Carter offered discreet support before the Soviets had even invaded, but the covert action fell far short of regime change. He permitted the CIA to support rebel propaganda, provide cash or non-military supplies, and work with third countries to get radios to the Afghan population. He also sanctioned propaganda to expose the despotic leadership of the Afghan government and publicize the rebels' activity, before gradually stepping up the operation by channelling funds and weapons to the rebel fighters through Pakistan.[29] Saudi Arabia matched American funding; the UK, China and Egypt also became involved.

By the middle of the 1980s, the Afghan operation had ramped up dramatically. Delighted by the discomfort that the mujahideen were causing Soviet forces, President Reagan escalated it further still. The budget trebled. The US sent heavier and more obvious weapons, including the Stinger missile which could take out Soviet helicopters. It became an open-ended and protracted conflict in which the US was determined to make the Soviets bleed, and to inflict a Vietnam-type scenario on them. According to the CIA station chief in Islamabad, 'I was the first Chief of Station ever sent abroad with this wonderful order: "Go kill Soviet soldiers". Imagine! I loved it!'[30] All Soviet forces had left by the end of the decade.

Meanwhile, in north Africa, Reagan baulked at the expansionist ambitions of Chad's neighbour Libya, where Muammar Gaddafi soon became his bête noire. Reagan thought him barbaric and intent on exporting terrorism and revolutions; the CIA knew that Gaddafi had conducted plenty of covert actions of his own, from political intrigue to sponsoring terrorism. Gaddafi had designs to the south in Chad, itself mired in a civil war.

In response, the US, alongside Egypt, Morocco, France and Sudan, covertly funnelled weapons and funds to the ruthless rebel leader Hissène Habré. A former defence minister, Habré had found himself exiled in Sudan amid bitter fighting. He was a controversial figure at the time, with even the few US politicians privy to the covert action questioning whether it was appropriate to sponsor a man already known for his involvement in massacres. The buccaneering head of the CIA did not care; he wanted to bring back the glory days of the 1950s and wondered where the agency's sense of pragmatism had gone. The international media widely reported the discovery of a mass grave near Habré's home, stuffed full of beheaded skeletons. The very same month, the US began covert action, providing Habré's fighters with training, money, arms and ammunition.[31]

After a slow start, it became a rare success, at least in terms of meeting short-term operational objectives and even then only with the help of other countries like France – although there was plenty of mistrust between them. For all the focus on the CIA, it should be remembered that France had intervened in Chad for years, treating the country almost as a laboratory for covert action, and its intelligence services had informally supported Habré long before Reagan came along. Working closely with Egypt and Sudan, and under pressure from African allies like Senegal, French intelligence sent money, machine guns and vehicles to the rebels. President Mitterrand was reluctant, though, and pulled the plug, switching support to the interim coalition government, known by the unfortunate acronym GUNT.[32] The diplomacy surrounding covert action, which was so often international, constituted a complicated business.

Interestingly, the initial US aim was merely to give Gaddafi a bloody nose – not use rebels to change a regime. Still, a year later, in 1982, Habré assumed power and quickly became a brutal dictator responsible for systematic torture and political killings. France, in another U-turn, quickly recognized the Habré regime. Gaddafi now found himself boxed in, and the enthused CIA turned its attention to sponsoring rebels elsewhere.[33]

Outside the US experience, we might look to India and the creation of Bangladesh as another example of success. In March 1971, a large revolt broke out in what was then East Pakistan. Sensing an opportunity to damage their rivals, Indian intelligence quickly supported the rebellion by training, arming and sustaining the insurgents. They established almost sixty training camps by November, through which a couple of thousand militants passed through every six weeks. One intelligence veteran has even described the rebels as the brainchild of the first head of India's foreign intelligence service, the Research and Analysis Wing. Indian intelligence complemented paramilitary covert action with a black propaganda campaign, transmitting pro-Bangladesh material and exposing brutalities committed by the Pakistani army, all from a ship anchored in Kolkata. Meanwhile, a naval special operation discreetly blocked supplies from reaching Pakistan.[34]

It was a comprehensive approach which helped facilitate Bangladeshi independence. Importantly, though, this is not merely a story of covert action succeeding in overthrowing a government. India also fought Pakistan in an open military conflict in December 1971 shortly before Pakistan surrendered, thus confirming Bangladesh's independence.

Such examples are few and far between. Sponsoring violent rebels is not necessarily about regime change; and even when it is, it often takes place on a large, implausibly deniable and international scale. Regime change only works if you are willing to cede secrecy. However, that is not necessarily the end of the story because it is simplistic to assume that states covertly sponsor rebel groups solely to turn the tide in a conflict and overthrow a government without anyone finding out. The most famous, or rather infamous, failed liberation operation was not, in fact, a liberation operation at all.

In the early Cold War, MI6 and the CIA trained and armed Albanian dissidents. Boatloads of fighters arrived on rocky beaches under the cover of darkness and made their way inland to start an insurrection against the communist regime and, so the story goes, liberate it from the Soviet bloc. It went horribly wrong. The Albanian intelligence and security forces were ready and waiting. They ambushed the rebels. Some died, while others fled across the border to Greece. Historians wrongly remember it as a classic paramilitary failure, a prototype covert action characteristic of the wider failure to roll back the Soviet bloc.

Few realize that the initial objective was not regime change at all. It started off simply as a means to disrupt supply lines running from Albania to Greek communists waging a civil war against the Greek government. The British were particularly worried that a communist regime in Greece would undermine access to the Mediterranean, and, with it, choke British trade and imperial policy. Even afterwards, the main goal in Albania was to subvert and harass the communist regime – not overthrow it.[35]

Something similar applies to much-vaunted Russian operations in eastern Ukraine. The Russians seemingly had little idea of the end game when they began sponsoring rebels in eastern

Ukraine in 2014. It was all rather improvised and opportun-istic. Russia exploited local separatist movements and general frustration with Kiev by sending volunteers and equipment to the Donbas region, and amplified this using a political warfare campaign designed to subvert the local government. A tangled clutter of pro-Russian paramilitaries, mercenaries and ideologues soon intensified the fighting. They proved difficult to control.[36]

The covert action was not enough to sustain a liberation move-ment, and so resulted in confusion, frustration and stalemate. Russia gradually distanced itself from either recognizing the separatists' independence or annexing the region as it did with Crimea, until February 2022 when, amid international tension, Putin upped the temperature by recognizing the rebel regions as independent states. Over thirteen thousand people have died. The conflict drags on.[37]

Covert paramilitary operations are about so much more than liberation. The objective is not always – or indeed is rarely – regime change. More often than not, it is about subversion: using rebels to weaken the target state's authority. Covert action can help to eliminate the presence of the state in rebel-held areas by, for example, intimidating or assassinating bureaucrats. It can create no-go zones, complete with parallel institutions, raising the cost of governance for the target state. It makes life diffi-cult, tying down their resources and armed forces. It keeps the rebels strong enough so that they do not lose, but weak enough so that they do not win. States then exploit the ensuing stalemates. Perhaps the state will gain leverage over a rival by turning off the tap in return for concessions. Perhaps it will keep the target unbalanced or distracted to make space for action elsewhere. Perhaps it will use ungoverned spaces almost as a buffer zone to protect it from the adversary.[38]

Secret conflicts between India and Pakistan offer an instructive example of covert paramilitary action as subversion. The two countries have fought four wars and many smaller skirmishes since their independence. Below this, in the famous words of one Pakistani officer, Pakistan has made India bleed by a thousand cuts. India is a huge country, too large and diverse for strong central rule throughout, allowing Pakistan to exploit the remoteness of certain regions, as well as the cultural diversity. Just as India exploited the distance and difference between East and West Pakistan before the creation of Bangladesh.[39]

Pakistan has been inflicting cuts on its larger neighbour for much of its existence. Back in the 1950s, Pakistani intelligence secretly sponsored an insurgency in the remote Nagaland region of northeast India. It is rugged terrain: mountains, deep valleys and jungles which transform into a shifting swamp during the monsoon season. The Nagas wanted independence; Pakistani intelligence was happy to help. In response, Indian army units quickly occupied parts of the region and herded thousands of civilians into internment camps where disease was rife. Many died. As Naga money, weapons and followers dried up, Pakistan set up training camps for the beleaguered rebels.

The aim was not necessarily to liberate the Naga people from India. Instead, it was subversion: preventing the Indians from being able to govern their own territory, chipping away at their authority. The gruelling insurgency tied down 30,000 Indian soldiers and, particularly pleasing to Pakistan, it publicly undermined India's human rights record.[40]

Pakistan has also supported separatist Sikh terrorists in the Indian Punjab, a territory running along the border between the two states. Its intelligence services set up training camps and smuggled small arms across the frontier. The covert action caused

India to devote large resources to hunting down the fighters and neutralizing the threat. This heavy-handed response intensified unrest and instability, which, in a vicious cycle, then demanded yet more Indian resources to counter. India even launched a full-scale military offensive to flush out Sikh fundamentalists who had taken over the sacred Golden Temple shrine in Amritsar. It caused outrage. The violence culminated in the assassination of Prime Minister Indira Gandhi in 1984. All the while, Pakistan was pleased that tying down so many forces in the Punjab prevented those very same forces from threatening Pakistan.[41]

In April 2009, violent unrest spread across Balochistan, a mountainous province in southwest Pakistan sandwiched between Iran and Afghanistan. When three nationalist leaders were brutally executed in broad daylight, the militant Baloch Republican Army retaliated by launching grenades, bombs and even rockets. Pakistan angrily accused India of quietly stoking the violence. Although India denied doing so, its own military chiefs have since openly advocated reprisal attacks against Pakistan or, as they euphemistically put it, removing a thorn with a thorn.[42]

Pakistan has long accused India of supporting the Baloch liberation movement from Afghan soil, although hard evidence is difficult to come by. This is partly because, as one former Inter-Services Intelligence chief admitted, Pakistan has an incentive to exaggerate the threat, and partly because of the difficulties in distinguishing external support from genuine internal disaffection with a repressive Pakistani regime. Any covert assistance provided by India would likely have involved money and small arms designed to cause nuisance rather than serious attempts to promote an insurgency or achieve independence from Pakistan.[43]

Covert action can be attritional; it creates stalemate. Whether this constitutes success or not depends on the goals. One thing is clear: states do not always covertly sponsor rebel groups to achieve victory in overthrowing governments – and so the bar for success is lower than we often assume. States fund rebels to put pressure on adversaries by keeping wounds open and bleeding; to undermine authority and generate ambiguity they can exploit. It is an extension of diplomacy.

If using rebels to overthrow governments or liberate countries is one myth, then secrecy is another. Secret wars do not have to be all that secret. Those waging them need not worry too much about exposure or plausible deniability.

Arming, funding and training rebels is hard to deny. At least plausibly. Although many leaders turn to such activity to save face, covert paramilitary operations, whether in Syria, Libya or Ukraine, lie towards the more overt end of the covert action spectrum. Many are implausibly deniable.

At the height of the Libyan uprising in March 2011, a helicopter landed in the middle of the night in a dusty farmyard outside the rebel stronghold of Benghazi. A British special forces team dressed in black and led by a young MI6 Middle East specialist disembarked onto the dry ground hoping to make contact with rebel leaders. It did not go to plan. The noisy landing aroused suspicion and locals quickly detained the team. The news soon leaked. 'What was our man on the Libyan farm really up to?' the *Daily Mail* asked. 'SAS bunglers had secret computer codes in pockets,' a *Sunday Times* headline breathlessly added. 'Brit held with SAS in Libya was spy,' declared *The Sun*. *The Times* predictably called it a 'James Bond blunder'.

The dramatic capture was front page news for days. It put the foreign secretary, William Hague, firmly on the back foot. The newspapers taunted him, asking whether he was still up to the job. To his credit, Hague stood up in parliament and admitted authorizing what he called a small 'diplomatic team' to build on 'initial contacts and to assess the scope for closer diplomatic dialogue'. It was a magnificent parade of euphemistic banalities. Somehow, he even managed to keep a straight face when insisting that the misadventure was not entirely a failure because the team did, after all, make contact with the rebels. They just happened to be in handcuffs at the time.[44]

Eventually, the storm blew over. The press moved on to a much bigger story a few weeks later: the killing of Osama bin Laden. Nonetheless, Hague's embarrassing episode was merely the most dramatic exposure of the covert actions in Libya, Syria and Ukraine, many of which were implausibly deniable and received plenty of press coverage.

Exposure of elephantine paramilitary operations, thudding and large, is nothing new. Anyone who thinks plausible deniability was anything more than a myth during the supposed golden age of covert action in the early Cold War is deluding themselves. As we have seen, the CIA covertly trained and sponsored a ragtag rebel army to overthrow the Guatemalan government in 1954. US involvement was such an open secret – and widely criticized around the world – that the CIA then felt it necessary to launch a follow-up covert operation shortly afterwards to convince sceptical onlookers that the regime really did pose a threat to the US. It was an attempt to rewrite history, rather fittingly codenamed PBHISTORY.[45]

A few years later, in 1961, a *New York Times* headline reported that 'Anti-Castro Units Trained to Fight at Florida Bases'. This came days *before* the failed invasion of the Bay of Pigs. In a notoriously ill-fated operation, the CIA had trained, funded and directed a rebel army to invade Cuba and overthrow Fidel Castro.

They landed in the Bay of Pigs in the southwest of the island, but quickly lost the initiative. Castro was waiting. Several mainstream American newspapers had discussed CIA training of Cuban exiles in camps in Florida and Guatemala. Plausible deniability was a collective delusion. The operation was reported in real time.[46]

There are plenty of other examples. Large-scale paramilitary operations in Laos and Angola also lacked plausible deniability. In Laos the CIA waged a remarkably relentless air campaign from 1961, dropping bombs on average once every eight minutes.[47] This staggering scale and pace could hardly go undetected. In Angola the following decade, the CIA imported some thirty thousand rifles into the country. Like many covert paramilitary theatres, the Angolan civil war soon attracted other intelligence agencies keen for a slice of the action. French intelligence, sensitive to any developments that would harm their post-colonial interests on the continent, established training camps in Morocco for guerrillas fighting the leftist government.[48] All of this was hard to keep secret, and even typically unhurried academics began picking over the affair soon afterwards.

The most famous example is the CIA's covert support of Afghan rebels in the 1980s. The operation is so famous that it has spawned a Hollywood film, *Charlie Wilson's War*, and bizarrely holds an official Guinness World Record for the most expensive covert action in history – at $2 billion. In the early days, it was still just about deniable. The CIA funnelled Second World War-era rifles and basic weapons from Egyptian, Chinese and even Soviet sources to make it difficult for anyone to prove the US hand.[49]

As the decade progressed, the US sent heavier and heavier weapons. Reagan openly hinted that America was aiding the resistance forces. Senators even engaged in proxy-war tourism along the Afghan–Pakistani border. Known as Operation

Cyclone, this was implausibly deniable covert action: decidedly apparent and barely unacknowledged.

Not that it matters too much. Even when exposed, these secret wars are unlikely to escalate into a damaging conventional conflict. This, perhaps counterintuitive, lesson from history offers another incentive for leaders wanting to manage risk by sponsoring rebels.

In early 2021, General Sir Nick Carter, the British chief of the defence staff, issued a stark warning. Covert action – or the grey zone as he called it – risked misperception, miscalculation and misunderstanding. History, he claimed, teaches us that this is a very dangerous and unstable business. It could unleash uncontrollable forces easily leading to all-out war.[50] This is a common misassumption.

Unsurprisingly, funnelling heavy conventional weapons to rebels in a civil war can – and does – dramatically increase the number of battlefield deaths and duration of the conflict.[51] The involvement of outside states increases the chances of disputes turning into some form of military exchange.[52] This is obviously bad news for those involved. Importantly, however, there is little evidence supporting claims that *covertly* backing rebels unleashes large-scale, conventional confrontations.

It is difficult to think of any examples where even the most provocative covert paramilitary operations, restlessly vibrating through volatile conflict zones, escalated to conventional warfare and dragged in the sponsoring states. One rare exception is perhaps the 1967 war between Israel and the Arab states. Syria's support for Palestinian guerrilla groups was a major factor in causing the conflict. It had sponsored cross-border attacks and provided shelter to the fighters. Israel responded with force; Syria lost the war. Even here, though, the Syrians were doing this long before and after war broke out, and without escalation.

Another exception perhaps comes from the war between Uganda and Tanzania in 1978. After Idi Amin took power in Uganda, thousands of refugees fled across the border into Tanzania from where they launched attacks against the Amin regime. Claiming that Tanzania was arming and supporting rebel forces, Uganda declared war. Tanzania won.[53]

More often, the sponsoring states get away with it. Rather than covert action spiralling into conventional warfare, it is more likely that the reverse will happen: conventional warfare simmering down to covert action. Wars between states can fizzle out or formally end but still linger on in the shadows as both sides secretly sponsor rebels. The conflict in 1999–2000 between Ethiopia and Eritrea, over their disputed border, offers a good example. The vicious interstate war transformed itself into a covert proxy conflict, with each side supporting rebel fighters across the border, until Abiy Ahmed became Ethiopian prime minister and normalized relations with Eritrea in 2018.[54]

This raises an intriguing question. How can states wage a secret war, which is not really all that secret, but which does not escalate to an open military conflict? The answer lies in non-acknowledgement.

Leaders sponsoring rebels need not acknowledge their actions, even if exposed. According to research by the political scientist Austin Carson, lack of acknowledgement reduces pressure to retaliate, which dampens the ability of hawks on either side to mobilize and escalate. Compared to an openly declared assault, going covert sends a message of restraint, thereby easing tensions and limiting war. As soon as a state acknowledges something, even if it is already exposed, the dynamics quickly change. The sponsoring state lays down the gauntlet: yes, it was us. What are you going to do about it?

Acknowledgement rather than exposure is key. Without acknowledgement both sides can hide in a blanket of fog, however thin, able, as Carson puts it, to tacitly collude in the fiction of secrecy.[55] Others call it strategic ignorance. Denials can be disproved; secrecy expires. Therefore, leaders fall back on the politically convenient fig leaf of feigned ignorance.[56]

This was true during the Cold War and holds up today. In early 2018, the media reported that US-backed forces in Syria had killed dozens of Russian mercenaries. This revelation could have been explosive, not least because American personnel were operating alongside the rebels when they came under tank fire. The US responded with a lethal airstrike. It had the potential to become a dangerous flashpoint: the deadliest clash since the Cold War amid a complex and unstable conflict in Syria.[57]

Counterintuitively, it did not escalate. The dead Russians were made to disappear. American forces did not comment on the identity of the deceased; President Putin's spokesman claimed to lack data on Russian mercenaries, and the Kremlin quickly distanced itself from the forces. For all the exposure, lack of acknowledgement on either side reduced pressure to retaliate. The US and Russia managed to step back from a crisis.[58]

Leaders waging secret wars need not worry too much about secrecy. In fact, carefully calibrated exposure in the twilight zone of quasi-secrecy can be a good thing. Secret wars are impossible to hide. And so fully hiding them is rarely the intention. States do not sponsor rebel groups in the naïve assumption that it will stay entirely secret. Covert paramilitary action is performative; it has an audience. It sends messages and shows resolve. Operations are less about deniability and more about states' willingness to accept implausible denials.

The Afghan war in the 1980s presents us with another puzzle. The covert action became utterly implausibly deniable. And yet it is widely considered successful. How can that be so? It was all about sending secret – unacknowledged – messages to various audiences. American intelligence knew that the Soviets were sending secret units to quash uprisings against the communist government in 1979 – before the Soviet invasion. The CIA also knew that subsequent changes in the level and intensity of covert involvement demonstrated growing Soviet resolve in defending the faltering Afghan regime. And Russia knew that the White House knew. Meanwhile, the Soviet covert action simultaneously communicated support to its allies in Kabul.[59]

In return, the US used its own covert action to send a targeted message to Moscow: aggression does not pay. Soviet intelligence knew what the Americans were doing and, according to one former CIA analyst, the covert action 'contributed to Soviet fears of the desire and readiness of the United States… to attempt to influence the situation in Afghanistan'.[60]

The Soviets launched secret cross-border raids into rebel camps on Pakistani soil. They also waged a secret campaign of subversion in the vast refugee camps along the Afghan–Pakistani border where militants gathered for training. Working through Afghan intelligence, the Soviets sent arms to the border tribes, spread propaganda, recruited teachers to the communist cause, and even placed bombs in bazaars. Except, once more, none of this was especially secret. The CIA and Pakistani intelligence knew full well what was going on. The US interpreted it as a deliberate attempt by the Soviets to demonstrate commitment to Afghanistan and to emphasize that Pakistani support of the rebels would not derail Russian plans. Soviet covert action was a bellwether of Soviet ambitions.[61]

Finally, the covert action also signalled to domestic audiences: Ronald Reagan boasted during his presidential campaign that he intended to 'unleash the CIA'. He wanted to look tough and exploit public desire to take the fight to the Soviets. That his covert actions in Afghanistan and Nicaragua became open secrets allowed him to do just that.

Decoding signals and messages sent via covert paramilitary action is more difficult when thinking about current examples. Government reports indicating knowledge of covert action and the inferences drawn remain highly classified. However, we can assume that something similar is going on today. Indian operations in Balochistan send a clear message to the Pakistanis, challenging Islamabad's sponsorship of terrorism in the disputed province of Kashmir. The CIA used rebels in Syria to communicate resolve to Assad. Covert action was never about acting entirely secretly, but convincing the regime that victory was impossible and encouraging them to change tack.[62] It also demonstrated resolve both to local allies and to the Russians. This is covert paramilitary action as a most curious form of diplomacy.

The same logic applies to Iran. Its covert sponsorship of terrorist groups sends a message to select audiences inside Israeli intelligence. Few people would take Tehran seriously if its leaders threatened military retaliation against every perceived Israeli aggression. Using terrorist groups is much more credible.[63] States expect the adversary's intelligence agencies to know broadly what is going on.

Covert action signals to allies as well as adversaries. David Cameron and his intelligence chiefs sat around the National Security Council table in 2012 as the Syrian uprising degenerated into a bloody civil war. They discussed options to prevent the rebels from getting obliterated by Assad's security forces. Cameron was under pressure to do something.

The intelligence chiefs warned that sponsoring Syrian rebels would have little effect on the outcome of the conflict. Cameron was not interested. He liked the idea of covert action, not necessarily because it would make material gains on the battlefield but to show allies in the Gulf, and especially the CIA, that the British were on board. Cameron used covert action to ensure skin in the game, to visibly demonstrate reliability, commitment and partnership. Covert action had an audience.

Like any means of communication, this does come with risks of misperception. Back in the 1980s, the Pakistani president had known that 'the water in Afghanistan must boil at the right temperature', while the head of Saudi intelligence, also covertly funding the rebels, recalled certain unspoken rules about what was – and what was not – acceptable.[64] What if the message is misunderstood? What if the adversary interprets the secret war as weakness not strength? What if one side understands something as a limited covert action but the other misinterprets it as an existential threat? The Cuban Missile Crisis in 1962 arose partly because the Soviets desired to make the island invasion-proof after the failed Bay of Pigs covert action the year earlier.[65]

The twilight world of quasi-secrecy brings a second advantage or opportunity beyond covert communication: exploitable ambiguity, in so far as the grey zone fogs and softens the lines between war and peace, combatant and non-combatant.

Russian volunteers and mercenaries rolled into the Donbas region of eastern Ukraine from spring 2014 to fight alongside separatist rebels. Russia had just successfully annexed Crimea and now pro-Russian nationalists declared independence of their own.[66] Exploiting the situation, Russian intelligence services and special operations forces discreetly supplied and advised these groups. They used propaganda to frame events as a humanitarian crisis that could be blamed on Kiev. For a long time Moscow denied any involvement, resorting instead to euphemistic allusions to irregular activity.[67]

Implausibly deniable Russian covert operations in Donbas were sufficient to make a difference on the ground, but not to warrant a large-scale western retaliation. Cumbersome institutions like NATO and the EU scrambled to work out if and when Russia had crossed a line. They struggled to respond. Russia could exploit this ambiguity; exposure of Russia, combined with non-acknowledgement of action, allowed the Kremlin to test western responses and, when targeting NATO members, raise questions about the utility of NATO's Article 5, the agreement that an attack against one member state is an attack against them all. Such unacknowledged exposure, prevalent in covert paramilitary operations, blurs the borders between internal disorder and external intervention, and between state and non-state activity, making it difficult for the international community to differentiate legitimate from illegitimate behaviour.[68]

Ambiguity allows the construction of powerful narratives. Knowledge of Russian activity – again without formal acknowledgement – allowed the Kremlin to cultivate an image of omnipotence. This extends not just to sponsoring rebels but to covert operations more broadly, up to and including assassination. Skittish western commentators see Russian subversion behind every gooseberry bush. They are convinced that Putin is already successfully waging a so-called hybrid war against eastern Europe, if not the whole of NATO. This has played straight into Putin's hands.[69] Quasi-secrecy and ambiguity create space for myths and fear to take hold.

*

States have been waging secret wars for millennia. This lengthy history teaches us a few lessons when it comes to sponsoring violent rebels. Covertly training and arming resistance fighters is highly unlikely to lead to the overthrow of an established government or the independence of a breakaway state. Such lofty ambitions require weapons and money on a scale which cannot remotely be plausibly deniable. It requires visibility, cooperation with plenty of other states, and perhaps even the use of conventional military force.

Sponsoring rebels to subvert a target state is much more common – and effective. Covert action can create no-go zones for the government, cleverly undermining the state's authority while also tying down its armed forces in lengthy counterinsurgency operations. Secret wars aim to make the target bleed. Even this, however, is unlikely to remain plausibly deniable. Setting up training camps and smuggling large quantities of weapons will hardly go undetected. States therefore calibrate exposure carefully, thinking about the message sent to specific audiences, all the while confident that, so long as they do not acknowledge their involvement, the secret war is unlikely to escalate into a spiralling military conflict.

This all sounds deceptively straightforward. Unfortunately for the sponsoring state, the rebels have minds of their own. They are rebels after all. Can you really trust them, let alone control them? They might turn on you, or double-cross you. They might be so abhorrently violent that you would lose domestic support if the newspapers splashed the operation across the front pages tomorrow. How to pick which rebel groups to support is one of the most difficult – and potentially deadly – decisions that leaders make.

HOW TO PICK YOUR REBELS

Laurent Kabila was a veteran Congolese revolutionary. Back in the 1960s, he had waged guerrilla war from dense jungles against President Joseph Mobutu, himself the beneficiary of American covert action. He bolstered his credentials by fighting alongside Che Guevara, although the legendary guerrilla leader dismissed Kabila as more interested in drinking scotch with beautiful women than being the vanguard of revolution. Even so, by the mid-1990s, Kabila had seen a lot of action. Insurgency warfare, kidnapping, smuggling – he had been there and done that. By this time, he had been battling the regime for decades but still enjoyed little support and could hardly compete with Mobutu and his decades of American backing. So, when neighbouring Rwanda and Uganda offered significant outside support to his cause, he gratefully accepted.

Rwanda hoped to eliminate remnants of the Hutu militias which had carried out the 1994 Rwandan genocide and which still received support inside neighbouring Zaire, as Congo was then called. It secretly helped create and sustain the rebel group known as the Alliance of Democratic Forces for the Liberation of Congo-Zaire, and putting Kabila at its head. Rwanda bolstered the group's efforts further by then sending its own troops to fight alongside them.

Uganda, a close ally of Rwanda, joined the effort to over-throw Mobutu. Its motivations were slightly different: to secure its western border. Rebel groups, including the Lord's Resistance Army, known for its widespread human rights violations and use of child soldiers, was using bases inside eastern Zaire to attack Ugandan forces. In response, Uganda quietly helped to direct Kabila's dissident fighters. According to French and Belgian intelligence, it trained around fifteen thousand of them.[1]

With the help of Rwanda and Uganda, Kabila successfully overthrew the government and became president in 1997. He certainly needed their support, having spent decades fighting and flailing in the jungle. To again quote Che Guevara, Kabila 'was an agitator who had the stuff of a leader, yet lacked serious-ness, aplomb, knowledge'. He was no Castro.

Almost immediately after his victory, Kabila turned on his patrons, Rwanda and Uganda. He hypocritically criticized both countries' influence on Congolese politics and, particu-larly treacherously, allowed rebels to launch attacks on Uganda from inside his territory. He even aligned himself with the very same Hutu rebels that he – and Rwanda – had previously been fighting. It sparked an intermittent cycle of proxy wars, drag-ging in neighbouring states both officially and unofficially, continuing to this day.[2]

Covert paramilitary activity can be incredibly controversial and counterproductive. Operations involve secret collusion with violent non-state actors: rebels, insurgents and terrorists. These can be decidedly unsavoury people with questionable records when it comes to human rights – and that is putting it mildly. Kabila's rebels committed large-scale abuses of refugees in eastern Zaire, massacring many and blocking the efforts of humanitarian agencies, leading to the deaths of many more from starvation or disease.

If a state is set on this course of action, it is therefore essential to be very careful indeed when choosing which rebels to support. This is easier said than done, for it is difficult to know precisely who the rebels are and how they would act if they were successful and did end up forming a government. Again, Rwanda found this out the hard way.

Who are these fighters? Are they able to win? Are they open to counter-bribery from your enemies? Are they trustworthy? Are they willing to die for their cause? These questions appear blunt, Machiavellian even, but there is no point in sponsoring a group and wasting valuable political capital and money if they are not able or willing to achieve the objective. Or if they would stab you in the back. Equally, do exiled groups seeking covert assistance have support back home? Famous CIA operations like assisting Cuban exiles invade the Bay of Pigs in 1961 and assisting Nicaraguan exiles in the 1980s failed partly because of a lack of domestic support for the fighters.[3]

If there is no rebel group available, sometimes states try to create one. In the 1950s, Egypt was a regular practitioner of covert action. An arid country, mostly desert, it was heavily reliant on neighbouring Ethiopia, from where the Blue Nile originates. When negotiations to secure access to the river failed, Egypt unsurprisingly turned to covert action. With no rebels to support, it used propaganda to foment rebellion among the disaffected Muslim population of Eritrea, which had recently been federated into Ethiopia. In doing so, it cultivated a rebel group which it could then sponsor to undermine Ethiopian authority and distract its government from Nile-related projects. A thirty-year war of Eritrean independence followed.[4]

The origins of the group are important. How well established are they? How organic? Rebel groups founded by intelligence services and inserted into the target state to do their bidding fail at a significantly higher rate than those which establish themselves locally. The UK and the US trained and infiltrated dissidents into Albania in the early Cold War. The US did the same in Cuba a decade or so later. None of these groups were particularly durable or effective. Many were loose-lipped and leaked secrets like a sieve. By contrast, local groups founded organically that go on to work with the CIA, Mossad, or whoever, have better security skills, better local knowledge and better long-term incentives. They have already managed to survive in a repressive environment, hunted by state intelligence agencies.[5] But who are these groups? And can they be trusted?

Answering these questions requires outstanding intelligence. States need to know the balance of power on the ground, the strength of internal security mechanisms, levels of external support for the government, and the strengths and weaknesses of each rebel group. Unfortunately, there is always a serious risk that this intelligence is flawed given that it often comes from sources within those very groups who will be biased in wanting to secure covert funding. Yes, they will say, send us a few more weapons and a lot more money and we will be able to achieve anything.

A fine line can separate moderate rebel fighters from terrorists. Much of this is about presentation or perception; very few leaders will portray their proxies as terrorists, or even as proxies for that matter. The west has partners and allies; proxies are for meddling manipulators like Iran. The language used to criticize President Trump when he was withdrawing from Syria was instructive: he abandoned and betrayed Kurdish partners. On the other hand, the governments these fighters target almost always label them as terrorists or bandits. President Assad unsurprisingly dismissed the very same Kurdish fighters as foreign-backed terrorists.[6]

The best-known and most characteristically bombastic examples come from the 1980s when President Reagan covertly supported anti-government fighters in Nicaragua, known as the contras. He enthusiastically described them as the moral equivalent of America's founding fathers. Fighting against the leftist Nicaraguan government, the contras enjoyed plenty of secret – and illegal – aid from the Reagan administration.

Far from heroic, their tactics were brutal and terroristic. One former contra admitted to terrorizing the civilian population to stop them from cooperating with the government. This amounted to killings, torture, mutilation and rape. Another boasted about assassination teams targeting teachers. Even the CIA division chief for Latin America admitted to the House Intelligence Committee that the contras had killed civilians, nurses, doctors and judges.[7] Propaganda played down such atrocities, instead presenting them as nobly fighting for freedom.

Meanwhile, the Afghan mujahideen, another beneficiary of Reagan's covert action, were similarly presented as freedom fighters. The British even launched a covert propaganda campaign to bolster this interpretation and emphasize how Moscow was intentionally violating international law by invading Afghanistan. The mujahideen were freedom fighters nobly acting in self-defence against a foreign aggressor.

More recently, Russia has sent heavy weapons to Hezbollah for use in Syria, but vehemently denies that this constitutes supporting a terrorist group. Russia has also smuggled weapons to the Taliban, but for political reasons does not appear on the

US government's state sponsors of terrorism list.[8] Terrorists are terrorists when it suits.

During the post-Arab Spring violence, Prime Minister David Cameron was widely ridiculed for insisting that an army of 70,000 moderate fighters existed in Syria, ready to receive British support. One of his Foreign Office ministers, Alan Duncan, later contradicted this, musing, 'Nobody really understands the Syrian war, and most of us are in no position to assess who are the goodies and who are the baddies'.[9] Duncan used the same simplistic – almost infantile – terms to describe the Libyan conflict, again dividing the myriad fighters with complex motivations and beliefs into two camps: goodies and baddies.[10]

Even if it is possible to divide complex groups of fighters with disparate motives into goodies and baddies, freedom fighters and terrorists, making sure covert action only helps the goodies is just as difficult. Intelligence agencies do differentiate between groups when choosing whom to sponsor. This is crucial work. Some are more extreme than others; some have wildly different values from the sponsoring state; some might only briefly align with the sponsor's interests. Importantly, though, differentiation becomes hard to achieve when faced with the brutal reality of quick decisions, messy conflicts and imperfect intelligence.

Another Foreign Office minister later had to admit that during the war against Gaddafi the British government – by which he presumably meant MI6 and special forces – was probably in contact with 'former' members of two Libyan terrorist groups: the Libyan Islamic Fighting Group and 17 February Martyrs' Brigade.[11] The head of Britain's armed forces accepted that cooperation with such terrorists was 'a grey area' and a weakness. 'The need for speed to prevent Benghazi falling,' he maintained, 'meant that we were committed to conflict in an imperfect world.'[12]

Amid the rise of proxy wars and indirect interventions, British foreign policy now strongly emphasizes the importance of supporting partners. Ambitious plans include using new forces capable of special operations to discreetly train, advise and accompany partners in high-threat environments. This is eminently sensible: it reduces the UK's footprint and costs while maintaining influence. The word 'partners' is horribly ill-defined, though. It can, of course, mean NATO allies. It can also cover a multitude of sins. When questioned, the chief of the general staff offered merely: 'regular and irregular partners and proxies'.[13]

The CIA unsurprisingly supported 'moderates' rather than 'terrorists' through its covert action in Syria. In reality, though, the Americans struggled to vet the fighters properly. Their databases of jihadists were incomplete and out of date. Over half of the recipients were likely terrorists who simply knew how to talk their way into the moderate rebel training programmes. In one case, seventy-five graduates of the Pentagon's train and equip programme defected to a terrorist group, al-Nusra, bringing weapons and ammunition with them.[14]

Even if it is possible to differentiate 'goodies' from 'baddies', arms and funding are likely to diffuse from one group to another. And even if intelligence agencies could precisely vet and approve rebel groups, they are practically powerless to prevent smaller weapons ending up in the hands of others, whether through being sold on the black market or captured in raids.[15]

These risks make for controversial activity. Exposed links between violent groups committing atrocities and states' intelligence services create political problems for presidents and prime ministers. This is partly why CIA sponsorship of rebels becomes significantly less likely during periods of divided government. When one party controls the White House and the other Congress, there is means and motive for opponents to cause trouble for the president. It is safer to scale back than risk a scandal.[16]

This form of covert action is especially controversial for liberal democracies, which pride themselves on promoting certain values and being a force for good in the world. It can be tortuously difficult to align security interests with these ill-defined values. What is appropriate? How will the public react if (or more likely when) they find out? If the covert action was splashed across the front page of the *New York Times* tomorrow, could the government look the public in the eye and justify it?

Scholars and spies alike have thought carefully about this, tying issues of whether covert action aligns with the state's values to debates about success. If it does not align, it cannot be deemed truly successful.[17] Sponsoring murderous and fanatical terrorist groups clearly does not align with American values. Sponsoring plucky freedom fighters rebelling against oppression or occupation probably does. The divide is not always so clear cut. The old, often thoughtless, cliché about one person's terrorist being another person's freedom fighter rears its head here. Evidently there are differences between groups, which intelligence agencies should – and do – assess, and terrorism is merely a tactic that can be used in pursuit of both freedom and oppression. As ever, though, perceptions are crucial.

A second cliché also springs to mind: whether the ends justify the means. Politicians and publics are more willing to sacrifice values and look the other way if the stakes are high enough. And history shows that liberal democracies have sponsored a wide array of dodgy groups over the decades.

Ironically, a rare example of morally justifiable covert paramilitary action comes from a more unlikely source: Soviet support for anti-apartheid forces in South Africa. That said, its intentions during the Cold War were hardly benign.[18] A better example might stem from Indian covert support for the African National Congress. Its overseas intelligence agency, the Research and Analysis Wing, assisted anti-apartheid struggles in both Namibia and South Africa, while also training intelligence officers in other African states.[19]

Covertly sponsoring rebels is both hard to deny and highly controversial. There is another downside: controlling them is difficult, if not impossible. They are, after all, rebels. Groups have different motivations from the state and will probably have been waging their own attacks against the target for years before the CIA or whoever came along. They are not puppets being manoeuvred by a hidden hand. It is therefore wrong to think of a state covertly controlling or coercing rebels to do its bidding. They have their own independent action and, at best, work in partnership with the sponsoring state. Boris Johnson, as foreign secretary, was characteristically evocative yet misguided when describing the Middle East situation in 2016: 'you've got the Saudis, Iran, everybody, moving in, and puppeteering and playing proxy wars'.[20]

Covert action tends to unfold against the background of long-standing conflict. The rebels funded by the CIA in Syria had been fighting Assad's regime long before the US secretly showed up. It was covert action amid a civil war. And, in Syria, just as in Afghanistan three decades earlier, there were plenty of different states and factions involved. The CIA worked alongside and through other states, including Saudi Arabia, Turkey and Qatar, each of whom had different goals and interests, and worked with different rebel factions. The US unsurprisingly found it difficult to achieve sufficient influence to make much of a difference.

Each group of fighters had their own objectives and their own preferences about which intelligence service to partner with. And each possessed their own sources and channels of intelligence entirely independently of anything shared with them by the supporting state. The Kurds preferred to partner with the US, happy to receive the boost in legitimacy it brought. The Free Syrian Army partnered with the Turks, willingly exploiting Turkey's use of covert action in a bid for neo-Ottoman influence. Meanwhile, Turkey thought ISIS posed the best chance of damaging Assad and so smuggled weapons into Syria destined for hardcore jihadists. Hezbollah was no pawn of Iran, instead partnering with Tehran to achieve mutually beneficial goals. Qatar covertly bought weapons in Libya and eastern Europe, before funnelling them to the Muslim Brotherhood and other radical groups. The Saudis created an Army of Islam and despatched money and weapons to them from eastern Europe, via Jordan. Occasionally, Jordanian intelligence sold off weapons supplied by the Saudis and the CIA on the black market. Many ended up in the hands of ISIS.[21]

It was a fast-moving and confusing situation with multiple covert agencies half cooperating and half competing. Reliant on regional partners, the US struggled to prevent weapons from reaching terrorists acting against American interests.

Syria was a mess. It is impossible to understand the covert action without understanding the goals and preferences of the rebel groups – on top of all the other states involved.

There are echoes of the large-scale covert action in 1980s Afghanistan. Popular history remembers it as a CIA operation, but Pakistan, France, China, Egypt and Saudi Arabia were all involved. Even before the Soviet invasion, Egypt was quietly funnelling arms into Afghanistan and using its intelligence officers in Pakistan to meet resistance leaders in Peshawar and Islamabad in the late 1970s. After the invasion, Egypt, like others, stepped up cooperation with the US.[22] Some of these states, notably Pakistan, supported extreme Islamists, leaving the US frustrated at having to rely too much on fundamentalist networks.

Meanwhile, MI6 officers had their own preferred rebel leader, whom they recommended to the US largely in an attempt to curry favour in what had become an increasingly asymmetric relationship. The US appreciated this partnership because it allowed them to operate outside of Pakistan's clutches. However, the CIA simultaneously developed its own independent contacts with this same rebel faction so as not to become overly dependent on the UK. Complicating matters further, the French also selected the same faction – and drew a rebuke from Pakistan in the process, with Islamabad insisting aid should be channelled through them.[23]

Alongside all this, India supported and cultivated sources among Afghan warlords to help counter growing Pakistani influence and remove any suspicion that Pakistan might go on to use the mujahideen against India.[24] This is international covert competition. Afghanistan, like Syria, was so much more than a simplistic story about the CIA sponsoring brave freedom fighters.

The relationship between the intelligence agency and the rebel group is difficult to manage. Given that it is illicit, contractual arrangements can only be informal and cannot be enforced. It is therefore tricky for the state to monitor rebels and maintain control, yet, without close observation, the rebels might shirk responsibility, take the money and run, or commit excessively violent acts. In early 1980s Nicaragua, for example, the US-backed contras initially did little effective fighting. The leftist government recorded just forty-five clashes with the guerrillas between 1981 and 1982, compared with a whopping 234 cases of cattle rustling.[25] More recently, without close monitoring US-backed fighters in Syria have misused resources, allowing money and weapons to find their way into terrorist hands. Trucks, anti-aircraft guns and even grenade launchers all likely ended up with ISIS.[26]

Rebel groups have their own agendas. They are not fighting for US interests, or anyone else's, but for their own. They are also difficult to coordinate. Working indirectly with different groups, through different intermediaries, and with different states acting as discreet facilitators, makes it incredibly challenging to coordinate covert action to maximize effectiveness and achieve results quickly and efficiently. To make matters worse, lack of oversight can lead to corruption among the rebel groups, escalation of violence, or could tip the delicate balance of power in the wrong direction, sucking in yet more of the sponsor's resources into a never-ending quagmire.[27]

This is a complex business, full of risks. History offers two pieces of advice for those considering sponsoring a rebel group. First, it is important not to dictate from Langley, London or Moscow but to generate objectives which suit both sides as a partnership. Those wielding the hidden hand would do well to mind their hubris. It makes far more sense to offer a carrot rather than a stick: to achieve mutually desired outcomes by using what economists might call a performance-based compensation model, including the ultimate prize of taking charge of government after the rebellion. This is more likely to end in success compared to dictating terms and then punishing poor performance.[28] The words of Kermit Roosevelt, who led the CIA's efforts in the Iranian coup back in 1953, are timeless: 'If you don't want something that the [indigenous] people and the army want,' he warned, 'don't give it to clandestine operations, give it to the marines.'[29]

Second, presidents and prime ministers would be wise to pick a single group rather than hedging and supporting a bunch of different rebels. These myriad forces are as likely to fight each other as they are the government, as the recent conflict in Syria aptly demonstrated. At the same time, sponsoring multiple rebel groups will create a whole host of new problems if the regime falls. They will continue to fight each other for power, potentially plunging the country into a bloody civil war.[30]

Problematic marriages of convenience are not limited to western democracies and rebel groups. The Khmer Rouge were a notoriously brutal regime. When they governed Cambodia in the 1970s, torture and summary executions, fuelled by paranoia and purges, were widespread. These atrocities culminated in the Cambodian genocide, which killed around a quarter of the country's entire population. In 1978, Vietnam invaded and overthrew the Khmer Rouge. Across the border in Thailand, the government worried about the growing Vietnamese power and the loss of Cambodia as a buffer zone protecting them. And so, Thailand covertly supported Khmer Rouge fighters.

By this time, the Khmer Rouge were a spent force and might have died out completely without Thai support. Even so, the Thais felt no affinity with the infamously awful Khmer Rouge. In fact, they loathed them: not only were they genocidal fanatics, but they were communist genocidal fanatics.

Covert action took three forms: first, the Thais allowed the Khmer Rouge to set up camps inside Thai territory along the border with Cambodia; second, they diverted aid supposedly destined for malnourished refugees to the beleaguered fighters; and then, third, they worked with China to rearm them. Thailand acted as a discreet conduit, transporting Chinese weapons and ammunition directly to the resistance groups hiding out – and recovering to full strength – in the dense jungles.

The covert action succeeded in frustrating Vietnam and preventing it from consolidating its hold on Cambodia. The conflict lingered on into the 1990s, though, with an empowered Khmer Rouge neglecting peace settlements and boycotting elections.[31]

Sometimes the rebels outgrow the initial relationship; rebels become stronger and more difficult to control. For years, Pakistani intelligence covertly sponsored militants in the disputed province of Kashmir. They had enjoyed much success tying down some 200,000 Indian troops.

In December 2001, things went wrong. One of the groups went too far and attacked the Indian parliament building in New Delhi. The outraged Indians wanted retribution and blamed the Pakistani president, Pervez Musharraf, for facilitating the attack. To diffuse tensions, Musharraf condemned the terrorists and promised to cooperate with India. The militants felt betrayed and, accusing Musharraf of treachery, turned their violence on the Pakistani government and even the president himself. Musharraf survived numerous assassination attempts over the following years.[32]

To make matters worse, the terrorists gradually developed a broader Islamist agenda beyond Pakistan's limited aims in Kashmir, and developed links with other fundamentalist groups such as al-Qaeda. It is not just the cessation of state funding that ends covert relationships. Sometimes, the rebels' growth and autonomy can do it instead.[33]

Another equally important example is Iran's relationship with Hezbollah. Iran helped to establish Hezbollah among tired and marginalized Shia fighters in Lebanon in the 1980s. It has supported the group ever since, sponsoring terrorist attacks against Israel and building its military strength as a means to exert Iranian influence in the Middle East. It has provided huge sums of money to the group, up to $700 million a year, alongside weapons, training and technical assistance. In return, Hezbollah has worked tirelessly to further Iranian interests.

Over the course of a remarkably long forty-year relationship, Hezbollah outgrew its proxy status. It has morphed into a large political and military force in its own right; it is the world's best-armed non-state actor having amassed around 130,000 rockets and missiles. Hezbollah now even works with proxies of its own. As it became less a puppet and more of a partner, Iran has had to manage the relationship carefully, giving more autonomy over the group's activities. This is not only the case regarding domestic politics in Lebanon, where Hezbollah is now a political party, but also in terms of allowing it to stockpile and pass on heavy weapons.[34] Proxies are not puppets, and the relationship must be managed carefully.

If a rebel group does not exist, cannot be created, or is simply too risky or repugnant to support, states have another option: mercenaries. Impecunious leaders have been outsourcing fighting for years, millennia even. The Romans recruited barbarian tribes to fight as far afield as modern-day Germany.[35] During the Cold War and the era of decolonization, French mercenaries were notorious across Africa. The most emblematic was Bob Denard, the dapper, self-proclaimed pirate of the republic. Denard was involved in a string of coups, including in the Comoros and Benin, as well as various insurrections and intrigues across the continent.

Meanwhile, the US also saw advantages in using mercenaries. In places like Congo, Angola and Nicaragua, mercenaries helped lead and direct inept local forces. In the mid-1960s, President Johnson's White House helped raise – and bankrolled – a force of a thousand European and South African mercenaries to quash a supposedly pro-communist rebellion in Congo. American security advisers feared another Vietnam scenario and predicted that, without help, the Congolese forces would drop their weapons and be thrashed by 'pygmies carrying spears and machetes'. Given the ongoing difficulties in Vietnam, open military assistance was out of the question, while a small number of CIA officers would not have been sufficient to make a difference. In stepped the mercenaries. Offering quick wins, they made an impact while maximizing deniability.[36]

Given the long history of states using private military contractors, there is no reason to think they have stopped doing so today. The Wagner group is perhaps the best-known example. A private mercenary group with close links to the Russian government, it has been active from Ukraine to Syria, from the Central African Republic to Mozambique, where it fought a short-lived and ill-fated offensive against Islamist insurgents.

The group seems massive, with up to ten thousand people having undertaken at least one short-term contract over the last few years. Emanating from over fifteen different countries, although most are Russian, Wagner fighters include former military personnel, civilians and criminals. Their average age is forty. Most are in it for the pay cheque, seeking to escape deprivation. Unfortunately for them, according to a Moldovan intelligence officer tracking the mercenaries, the reality of life in Wagner does not live up to expectation. When the money drops – or stops altogether – disillusionment becomes rife among the recruits. Some are now being investigated for war crimes, including torture and extrajudicial killing.[37]

Wagner cut its teeth in 2014 during the annexation of Crimea and then in eastern Ukraine, where some of its operatives who fought and died even posthumously received the Russian military Medal for Courage in Death. In Syria, its mercenaries apparently took on elite infantry duties in support of Assad. They reportedly played a key role in helping to take the city of Palmyra back from ISIS in 2016. Since then, Russian personnel have discreetly begun training security forces and guarding mines in Sudan and the Central African Republic.[38]

In 2020, a dusty tablet computer with a cracked screen belonging to a Wagner operative was recovered from a Libyan battlefield. Offering a rare insight into the group's activities, its contents included maps; manuals on building bombs; diagrams of Russian and Soviet mines; e-books, including *Mein Kampf* and *A Game of Thrones*; and even a guide to making wine. Libyan intelligence also uncovered a Wagner shopping list of such remarkable extravagance – including tanks, mortars and even the latest radar technology – that a state must have been supporting them.[39] It all added to the mythology.

Wagner is difficult to pin down as it does not legally exist, further complicating matters of deniability and punishment. There is probably no official company called Wagner; instead the name refers to a network of overlapping businesses, groups and interests. Operatives apply for short-term contracts with shell companies. However, talk of a mysterious single Wagner creates a sense of ethereal ubiquity and omnipotence which makes its operations difficult to counter. Whenever accused of sponsoring covert paramilitary operations, Russia simply responds that Wagner does not legally exist and that mercenaryism is illegal under Russian law. Both statements are true, making accountability difficult.[40]

Outsourcing to mercenaries brings benefits. It increases deni-ability, or, at the very least, increases confusion and blurs the line between state activity and that of private companies. It also reduces the cost of training specialized units and, according to US intelligence, provides manpower for countries with declining populations and resources.[41] And, in a post-War on Terror world of weary publics, as one professor of contemporary warfare bluntly points out, 'There are no repatriation ceremonies for dead private military contractors, no flag-draped coffins, no public recrimination at fatalities.'[42]

It also has some serious drawbacks. American use of merce-naries during the Cold War attracted considerable media attention, and, although multiple newspaper stories did not probe the links to the US government too heavily, they did raise questions about plausible deniability. More problemati-cally, revelations about mercenaries were a propaganda gift for the adversary. Officials in the State Department despaired that communist and non-aligned states around the world were having a field day tarring the US as being in bed with 'blood-merchant' mercenaries, as one Egyptian newspaper put it.[43]

Over time, criticism grew at home too, especially in the aftermath of Watergate and various intelligence scandals in the mid-1970s. Congress became increasingly critical of an emerging mercenary industry on US soil. Many turned out to be difficult to control and went renegade or became whistle-blowers, causing much tension with Congress and the public more widely.[44]

The same applies to Wagner today. Plausible deniability is diminished, while knowledge – and rumours – of Wagner's activities create a propaganda gift for Russia's adversaries. Perhaps more importantly, the corrupt web of informal networks surrounding Russia and groups like Wagner risks embroiling the Kremlin in reputational and physical risks. Keeping them illegal and unacknowledged allows Russia to crack down on them if desired, but informal corrupt networks are also more difficult to keep in line.[45]

Supporting violent rebels is a complex and controversial form of covert action. It is hard to keep secret and denials ring hollow. Myths, stories and signals fill the gap between exposure and acknowledgement. These operations involve multiple countries, cooperating and competing with each other, and partnering with multiple violent factions, each with their own goals, preferences and intelligence. It is not a strictly hierarchical relationship. Proxies are not puppets. Some factions are more violent or extreme than others, but governments will never portray their proxies as terrorists and, even if they are sponsoring 'goodies', weapons can still easily end up in terrorist hands. In short, covert paramilitary action is distinctly difficult and untidy.

Intelligence services stand a better chance of success when working with organically created resistance groups, rather than trying to create dissidence from scratch. They need to decipher which groups are most reliable, trustworthy and capable. This is easier said than done in a fluid and fast-moving environment. And they then need to ensure that any weapons stay within the target group and do not end up in the hands of terrorists, perhaps by manipulating weapons to make them inoperable after a set period of time.

Leaders wrongly see covert paramilitary action as a cheap option to resolve an intractable problem. It is certainly not cost-free and is not even particularly low-risk. Some groups might rebel against the hand that feeds them; others might be utterly despicable genocidal maniacs. A marriage of convenience only succeeds so far and can cause serious political and physical blowback. No liberal democracy would want to be seen supporting groups committing human rights abuses. To make matters worse, rebel groups cannot be controlled, and sometimes outgrow their relationships, causing all sorts of problems for the supporting state.

How to pick your rebels? They are not your rebels. The relationship needs careful managing, all the while recognizing the interests and leverage of the non-state actor. If sponsoring rebels is too difficult, states sometimes raise mercenary forces instead. This also comes with significant risk of reputational damage. Control is the key variable here. States outsource to increase secrecy, but this reduces control. Loss of control can cause political blowback and less impact on the course of the conflict as rebels lack the resources and skills of a state. It is a balance.

Perhaps it would be easier not to covertly sponsor armed groups at all. Perhaps secret wars are a step too far: too exposed, too controversial, too difficult. In this case, presidents and prime ministers might be tempted by a shorter, sharper and more direct use of force. Sabotage.

HOW TO SABOTAGE

I n 1985, when a French diver, Jean-Luc Kister, attached a limpet mine to the hull of Greenpeace's flagship vessel, he did not intend to kill anyone. The top-secret mission sought only to sabotage the *Rainbow Warrior*, moored in Auckland, and prevent it from sailing onwards to disrupt French nuclear tests in the South Pacific.

It never arrived. The mine exploded shortly before midnight, ripping a hole in the hull. A second mine exploded soon afterwards, killing a Portuguese photographer on board. He drowned in his cabin. The forty-metre-long shipwreck, covered in rainbow-coloured anemones, has since become a prime scuba diving location, perhaps making it the only underwater covert action exhibit in the world.[1]

Amid global uproar, the French denied all knowledge. They insisted it was a terrorist attack, before changing their story to incriminate MI6. French officials privately briefed anyone who would listen that it was actually MI6 who had sunk the ship in a brazen attempt to discredit France. Or, at the very least, British intelligence had possessed advance knowledge. Britain was furious.[2]

MI6 was not involved on this occasion. That said, Britain's secret services are no strangers to peacetime sabotage. Shortly after the Second World War, MI6 conducted a maritime sabotage operation of its own. The aim, coming from the very top of government, was to disrupt illegal immigration to Palestine. A team of saboteurs zipped around the Mediterranean armed with limpet mines and timers. They planted them on five ships waiting in French and Italian ports to carry Jewish refugees to Palestine. Three were badly damaged. This was classic sabotage rather than an assassination mission: nobody was on board the ships at the time. Even so, it was high stakes activity and particularly controversial given the unimaginable horrors inflicted on Europe's Jewish communities just months before. At least Britain, unlike the French, then had the faux decency to create a fake terrorist group to shoulder the blame.

Sabotage continued throughout the Cold War. In the 1960s, the Americans approved operations to blow up a Cuban railway bridge, petroleum storage facilities, a power plant, and a floating crane in a Cuban harbour.[3] The Soviets ran sabotage schools to train liberation movements in these arcane arts. In 1980, members of the armed wing of the African National Congress, extensively trained by Moscow, launched four attacks on oil storage tanks and a refinery in South Africa. The huge fire burned for a week.[4] By the 1990s, things had become slightly more hi-tech; sabotage now included spraying abrasive dust inside computers to destroy floppy disks.

Advances in technology brought ever more opportunities for hi-tech sabotage by the new millennium. In 2009, baffled Iranian nuclear scientists could not work out why their centrifuges, integral to the enrichment of uranium, kept failing. To make matters worse, their computers kept mysteriously crashing and rebooting as well. It was not a coincidence. American and Israeli intelligence had successfully unleashed malware, known as Stuxnet, to degrade the Iranian nuclear programme. Many hailed it as a game changer; the first known example of a real-world cyberattack causing physical sabotage.[5] Attacks then came thick and fast.

ISIS terrorists were equally confused in the 2010s. They had successfully exploited the messy quagmire in eastern Syria and western Iraq to develop a worryingly large proto-state. Here, their puritanical regime ruled through brutal violence and fear. And they used this safe haven to plan terror attacks abroad.

All of a sudden, ISIS drones would not fly. Its communications kept failing at critical moments. Sometimes commanders gave incorrect directions, sending the terrorist foot soldiers in the wrong direction – occasionally to their deaths. They even struggled to get into their computers. Those who succeeded found their files inexplicably corrupted and propaganda deleted. Morale was evaporating. This was no mere technology failure. GCHQ had launched an offensive cyber-sabotage operation targeting terrorists' laptops and mobile phones. It disrupted, degraded and spread distrust within ISIS. This hampered terrorists' abilities to coordinate attacks.

In late 2020, amid the coronavirus pandemic, ministers instructed GCHQ to 'take out anti-vaxxers online and on social media', according to one source. Methods apparently included hacking into systems to remove disinformation about the virus and disrupt adversaries' propaganda operations. GCHQ encrypted targets' data to prevent access and blocked them from communicating with each other. The techniques were similar to those deployed against ISIS.[6]

We tend to associate sabotage with two different – seemingly unrelated – things. It is either modern-day cyberattacks of the type outlined above, or it is Lawrence of Arabia blowing up rail-ways to cut Turkish supply routes during the First World War, or the legendary Special Operations Executive saboteurs para-chuting into southern Norway during the Second World War, trekking cross-country on skis, to blow up a Nazi heavy water plant. This is all part of the same thing. The means may have changed, but sabotage is sabotage. Whether targeting emigrant ships in the 1940s or Iranian nuclear plants today, the aims are the same: to disrupt, delay and degrade. To frustrate the adversary.

Cyberattacks may have generated much recent attention, but states deploy sabotage both online and offline. Much cyber sabotage – or cybotage in horribly neophiliac jargon – is still sabotage. The number of states quietly conducting this activity is growing, and includes the US, the UK, France, Australia, Israel, Russia, China, North Korea and Iran. Canada has nascent capabilities too and, like the UK, has used offensive cyber to disrupt terrorists.[7]

Amid the excitement, we need to remember one thing: breath-lessly inserting the cyber prefix on any and all twenty-first-century activities does not make them revolutionary. Equally importantly, the line between cyber sabotage and what we might call old-school physical or analogue sabotage is blurred. Old-fashioned blowing up of underwater internet cables would obviously have cyber effects (and states have been sabotaging underwater cables to disrupt communications for well over a century), while cyber operations sometimes rely on human agents.

Many operations can now be conducted remotely. This reduces the risk of capture or death to those involved, especially when compared to the brave saboteurs operating behind enemy lines in the Second World War. Britain's wartime operatives had somehow to plant explosives, hidden inside fake horse droppings or dead rats, within a factory or beneath a well-guarded bridge, and then get out again in one piece. The work was so dangerous that many of them carried cyanide pills with them, concealed inside a pen or pair of spectacles, to be ingested if caught. By contrast, much cyber sabotage can be conducted remotely.

We should not oversimplify this distinction, though, since cyber sabotage can still be dangerous work. It may be informed by a well-placed human source risking his or her life inside the terrorist organization or nuclear weapons plant. Alternatively, a human agent might insert an infected file into the target network to bring about the sabotage.

Human agents were integral to the famous Stuxnet operation. The CIA and Mossad worked with Dutch intelligence to recruit an engineer inside the Iranian nuclear plant. The agent posed as a mechanic working for a front company and not only provided valuable intelligence about the various systems and how to infect them, but – even more crucially – helped ensure delivery of the worm using a flash drive (although it should be pointed out that the actual delivery was more complex than someone inserting a dodgy USB stick into a computer, like in a Hollywood film).[8] It is important not to overplay the hermeticism of cyber operations; sabotage is not necessarily a case of either online or real-world.

In spring 2021, sabotage damaged the electricity grid at Iran's main nuclear facility, Natanz, causing a widespread blackout. The Iranians cried terrorism, while many commentators speculated that the explosion was caused by a cyberattack or a human agent. Or both. Mossad operatives had reportedly recruited up to ten Iranian scientists to carry out the sabotage – although the scientists supposedly wrongly believed they were working for some sort of international dissident group rather than Israel.

According to press reports, which, as ever, should be taken with a pinch of salt, Mossad reportedly delivered some of the bombs to the scientists via drone and others hidden inside boxes of food in the back of a delivery lorry. The explosions demolished most of the centrifuges in the plant, apparently delaying Iranian nuclear plans by up to nine months.[9]

This act of sabotage was sandwiched between two other attacks. In summer 2020, another explosion took out Iranian centrifuges. This time, Mossad had patiently and audaciously managed to smuggle explosives inside the marble foundation which supported the centrifuges as the facility was being built. When the time was right, they detonated them.[10] A year later, Israel managed to smuggle an armed drone, piece by piece, into Iran. Mossad then used it to launch attacks on another nuclear facility, this time in the north of the country.[11]

Sabotage and demolition in the shadow war between Israel and Iran extend beyond the nuclear weapons programme. They also target commercial interests, often bluntly and noisily. In July 2020, as thick smoke billowed up from seven burning ships in the southern Iranian port city of Bushehr, it dawned on Iranian officials that their country was suffering an unusually large number of fires and explosions. In recent weeks, military installations, nuclear facilities, an aluminium factory, power plants and a petrochemical plant had all been damaged. Meanwhile, as summer turned to autumn, wildfires swept for miles through woodland. The weather could be blamed for some of this – but other damage could perhaps be traced back to saboteurs. Without clear evidence, though, Iran struggled to respond.[12]

Two years earlier, a spate of attacks began to target oil tankers in the narrow Straits of Hormuz in the Persian Gulf, through which 20 per cent of the world's oil reserves passes. These vast vessels, bottle necked in busy shipping lanes, have become slow-moving targets for saboteurs armed with explosives. On one Sunday in May 2019 alone, four tankers were sabotaged off the world's largest bunkering hub on the coast of the UAE. The ships suffered substantial hull damage, but there were no casualties or oil spills. Although details remain sparse, the Saudi government warned that sabotage sought to disrupt the flow of traffic.[13]

Many of these attacks, involving sea mines and speed boats loaded with explosives, can be traced back to groups supported by Iran.[14] US intelligence analysts assessed that Tehran was using economic sabotage to drive up the price of oil, to hurt the Trump administration, and to increase uncertainty and insurance costs in the region.[15]

As the shadow war intensified, Israel engaged in tit-for-tat sabotage of Iranian ships, opening up a new front in the eastern Mediterranean and the Red Sea. Most were carrying oil; some carried military equipment; others allegedly acted as hubs for Iranian-backed saboteurs. Israel's aim was to curb Iranian military influence in the region, especially by disrupting the transport of supplies reaching Syria and Hezbollah, and to prevent Iran from circumventing American oil sanctions.[16]

In June 2021, the biggest ship in the Iranian navy sank after an unexplained fire in its engine room. The following month, a suspected drone attack on an oil tanker managed by an Israeli tycoon killed two people, a Briton and a Romanian; a reminder that even shadow wars cost lives.[17]

Once more, this is not a case of either/or. This shadow war at sea contains a substantial cyber dimension alongside the physical sabotage. For example, Israel, in addition to sinking ships, allegedly used a cyberattack to disrupt shipping and cargo in the Iranian port of Shahid Rajaei, one of the country's key logistics hubs. The Iranian government downplayed the damage, but satellite imagery showed extensive delays at the container terminals.[18]

Effective saboteurs nimbly manoeuvre between the online and offline worlds, combining their complementary means to wreak damage. Cyber may be new – and offer new opportunities – but it goes hand in hand with physical sabotage. It is imperative to recognize the interplay between the two.

Sabotage is commercial, economic and technological. It is about degrading capabilities to cripple the adversary before they can do harm themselves. Alongside the more famous, indeed infamous, cyberattacks on its reactors, western intelligence agencies have also infiltrated the supply chain underpinning Iran's nuclear programme.

The sheer number of sanctions and restrictions in place has forced Tehran to rely on just a few – sometimes black market – channels to acquire the necessary technology. This smallish network presents a rare opportunity; indeed, some of the channels used may even be front companies run by western intelligence. Sabotaged power units, discreetly inserted into the supply chain in around 2006, ultimately managed to take out about fifty centrifuges in the Natanz nuclear facility. And this was on top of other mysterious fires in European warehouses which just happened to store material destined for the Iranian nuclear programme.[19] It did not end there; over a decade later, newspaper reports suggested that the Trump administration was still exploiting logistics channels to disrupt the Iranian programme.[20]

This is remarkably reminiscent of a Cold War operation which supposedly caused the largest non-nuclear explosion in history. In 1982, the CIA manipulated a Soviet supply line by inserting faulty software which seemingly ended up triggering a huge explosion in a Siberian natural gas pipeline. The aim was to stop the Russians from exporting gas to western Europe. The fire could be seen from space.[21]

Historians debate whether this spectacular explosion really happened, but the broader covert action certainly did. French intelligence had an outstanding agent codenamed FAREWELL inside the section of the KGB tasked with stealing high-end technology from US companies. Their shopping list included anything from radar systems to warplanes: the crown jewels.

Rather than shutting down the Soviet operation, US intelligence went on the counteroffensive. It used FAREWELL to modify products which would then disrupt and sabotage Soviet designs. Dodgy computer chips ended up inside Soviet military equipment; the Pentagon inserted wrong information into designs for stealth aircraft and space defence. It was subtle enough to go undetected but faulty enough to sabotage the Soviet effort. President Reagan, an enthusiastic supporter of covert action, was delighted.[22]

There are plenty of other historical examples of economic sabotage conducted in this manner. Twenty years before FAREWELL, the CIA bribed European manufacturers to produce faulty equipment for Cuba, including a German manufacturer which shipped off-centre ball bearings to the island. These measures caused economic damage but perhaps more importantly forced the Cubans to divert scarce resources to surveillance and counterintelligence. On the downside, it produced an unintended consequence by making Cuba more dependent on the Soviets for industry and supplies. Economic covert action is particularly risky: it can push the target further into the arms of an adversary.[23]

Such sabotage is more difficult today. Modern supply chains are not as centralized as the Soviets' channels, which FAREWELL manipulated so effectively, while Iran's are abnormal in so far as they are comparatively constrained, given the few options available to Tehran, and so can be subverted or sabotaged in a more predictable manner.

Still, sabotage can be economic in other ways. For example, states can – hypothetically – interfere with bank accounts. In the late 1990s, the CIA targeted Slobodan Milošević, the Yugoslav president charged with war crimes for his role in the horrors inflicted during the Balkan wars. It was part of a multipronged approach to undermine Milošević and then prevent him from winning the next election in Serbia. As we have seen, it formed one of the last known cases of US covert electoral interference.

The financial side was more controversial. In the words of one US official, plans involved hacking into foreign banks to 'diddle with Milošević's bank accounts'.[24] Intelligence suggested that he had hidden millions of dollars in Greek, Cypriot and Russian banks. Targeting Greece and Cyprus proved especially controversial, though, as it would have involved covertly accessing banks in friendly countries, breaching national sovereignty in the process. It could also have paved the way for retaliatory Russian intrusions into American banks. Most importantly, it risked undermining confidence in the world banking system.[25] There is a big difference between an operation planned and an operation executed: fiddling with leaders' finances was a red line then and remains a red line now.

It was this latter reason which convinced the Bush administration to block similar proposals the following decade. In the mid-2000s, the CIA allegedly pushed for an operation to empty the bank accounts of Mexican drug cartels. Intelligence officers thought that financial sabotage would disrupt the drugs trade, but the Treasury ultimately convinced the White House to veto the plan: it would damage confidence in the global banking system.[26] Similar arguments constrain more recent suggestions to 'diddle' with the bank accounts of Putin and various Russian oligarchs.

Sabotage attacks a wide range of commercial, industrial and scientific targets to disrupt adversaries. Its consequences need to be properly controlled, and this is difficult in the modern age, but it can certainly have impact. To paraphrase Lawrence of Arabia, the death of technology or money or means can be much more effective than the death of an enemy soldier in battle.

We live in an age of disruption. States use covert operations to disrupt and degrade the adversary. Sabotage keeps the enemy off balance or, as Alex Younger, former chief of MI6, recently put it, in 'their half of the pitch, not ours'. Launching the UK's new National Cyber Force, General Sir Patrick Sanders, commander of strategic command, stressed the importance of offensive disruption. 'You can't hide behind digital walls, you can't hide behind a digital fortress, you've got to be able to get at threats at source'. He continued, 'It's easier to get at the archer than it is at the arrows.'[27]

Recent UK defence, security and foreign policy reviews emphasize the disruptive power of the hidden hand. They foreground secret intelligence, special forces and offensive cyber. These assets will, in the repeated words of officials, deny, degrade, disrupt, deceive and destroy. All are tools of force multiplication; the power of the hidden hand will allow Britain to do more with less.[28]

Sabotage helps to manage risks in the short term. It can, in theory at least, avert speculative scenarios. Leaders like the idea of anticipatory self-defence; of action before proof of harm.[29] It is necessary in countering terrorism. Rather than ambitiously seeking to rebuild nations and install democracy abroad, disruptive sabotage operations offer a light footprint, obviate the burdens of victory, and disrupt hostile actors before they can attack.

Our globalized world has put intelligence services and special forces on the front line against a range of elusive but troublesome opponents.[30] The French have used offensive cyber operations to disrupt terrorists in the Sahel and Sahara. The proportion of its personnel working on such activity is only expected to grow and, despite strict secrecy, observers assume that it has conducted plenty more sabotage we do not know about. It will continue to do so.[31]

Sabotage can prevent an attack, or even something as small scale as stopping somebody from boarding a plane. It can disrupt terrorist communications, degrade their equipment, bewilder their bombers. It can frustrate the adversary, even preventing a terrorist from printing a ticket.

This is covert action at the micro-tactical level, a far cry from orchestrating coups or training rebel armies. Spy chiefs like it because it is easier to control in today's increasingly uncontrollable world. Ours is a networked planet in which traditional political authority carries less agency than fifty years ago. In an era of mass communication, social movements and grassroots change, there are more variables to control than ever. Multiple interconnected actors make it far harder to affect manageable change.[32] Disruptive sabotage, seemingly so simple and effective, therefore becomes appealing.

In addition to keeping the enemy in their half of the pitch and away from our goal line, sabotage at the tactical level has an added benefit. It allows spy chiefs to quantify successes for bean-counting politicians keen on metrics and managerialism. Politicians want results and value for money. It is far easier to prove that attempts to prevent a terrorist from boarding a plane worked, say, 90 per cent of the time than it is to quantify the impact of planting disinformation in social media.

All of this has pushed secret operatives towards becoming hunters rather than mere gatherers. They go out into the world to disrupt instead of sitting back and passively watching or listening.[33] This is certainly a trend which has accelerated recently; however, it would be wrong to overplay its novelty. Much of Britain's approach since 1945 involved disrupting rather than trying to defeat the Soviets: small-scale operations known as pinpricks rather than sponsoring coup after coup. Alex Younger's football analogy is remarkably similar to comments made by Prime Minister Harold Macmillan half a century earlier. He emphasized the importance of disrupting threats at source – long before the attack could reach Britain.

Indeed, states have a long track record of sabotaging terrorists to both disrupt their activities and send them a message. For example, the conflict between Israel and Palestinian militants intensified in the late 1970s, leading to more brutal terrorist attacks on Israeli military personnel – and their families. During one particularly horrendous attack, terrorists murdered a 4-year-old girl whom they had taken hostage by dashing her head against a rock until she died.

In response, Israel created a new unit to engage in sabotage and assassination in south Lebanon, using techniques such as explosives hidden in oil cans. The order was simple: 'to intimidate, to deter, to make it clear that Israel would be aggressive on offense, not merely reactive on defense'. These operations were intended to cause chaos and give the enemy 'the feeling that they were constantly under attack'. Israel sought to 'instil them with a sense of insecurity'.[34]

Other states have used sabotage similarly when confronting terrorists and insurgents. The UK wielded it alongside other covert paramilitary activity to intimidate and deter – as well as disrupt – terrorists during its war against the IRA. On a far greater scale, France turned to sabotage, known as Arma operations in French intelligence jargon,[35] during its murky war against Algeria in the 1950s.

In October 1958, French operatives attached explosives to the hull of a West German cargo ship, *Atlas*, as it sat in a Hamburg port. A few months later, another bomb exploded on another German ship, this time outside Bremen. Both were en route to North Africa, allegedly carrying weapons to insurgents. These attacks were just two of a series of unexplained explosions and bombs targeting West Germany between 1956 and 1961. On another occasion, a businessman with links to North Africa died in a car bombing in Frankfurt. Shortly afterwards, one of his associates opened a parcel delivered to his hotel room, also in Frankfurt. It contained a bomb, which promptly exploded and badly maimed him.[36]

The foremost aim of the sabotage – which the French denied and instead blamed on a mysterious vigilante counterterrorism group called *La Main Rouge* (the Red Hand) – was disruption. It aimed to prevent arms from reaching the insurgents fighting French occupation in Algeria. Interestingly, this disruption was psychological as much as physical, for impeding the flow of arms would have been a huge blow to the rebels' morale. It also sent signals to the West Germans. The French foreign ministry repeatedly told Bonn to stop facilitating arms. At one point the French even warned their West German counterparts that they might resort to 'illegal measures'. When these diplomatic interventions resulted in little effect, French intelligence turned to sabotage to get their attention. This sent a more credible, resolute message. The sabotage also sought to intimidate businesses into stopping collusion with the rebels.[37]

The disruption successfully reduced arms sales from West Germany. It was, however, a short-term victory for the French saboteurs because the rebels' stocks continued to rise regardless. Unfortunately, the supposedly successful sabotage forced the insurgents to turn to the Soviet bloc for aid instead; and it was much more difficult to track and disrupt this sort of activity behind the Iron Curtain.[38]

Fast forward over half a century and similarities exist to recent Russian sabotage. In 2014, an explosion ripped through an arms depot in a forest in the east of the Czech Republic. It blew out the windows of nearby buildings. Although initially considered an accident, fingers later pointed at the Russian military intelligence unit responsible for sabotage and assassination operations across Europe, including the Salisbury poisonings a few years later. It was a sophisticated operation involving six undercover GRU officers, including the rare personal involvement of the unit's senior commander.[39]

According to European intelligence agencies and investigative journalists, the depot was used by a Bulgarian businessman trafficking arms to countries, perhaps including Ukraine, against Russia's wishes. The explosion therefore was not only an attempt to disrupt the activity, but also an intimidating warning shot.[40]

Each of these examples shows states using sabotage to disrupt enemy activity and also to send a stark message. They reveal mixed results. The French enjoyed some – short-lived – success regarding West Germany, while British historians disagree over the impact of the intelligence war on the Good Friday Agreement that helped bring peace to Northern Ireland,[41] and the bombing of the Czech arms depot cannot have affected the target's behaviour because a few months later the same Russian unit tried to poison him.

Sabotage will not deliver a decisive blow; it is unlikely to make a difference on its own. Instead, it is disruptive and subversive, wearing down the enemy by persistently targeting key vulnerabilities or symbolic targets. Sabotage – and even just the constant threat of sabotage – lowers morale. Stealthy raids from nowhere frustrate the enemy, looking around for an attacker that has vanished; wondering where the next strike will come from. It induces paranoia and encourages mistakes. Western sabotage of ISIS equipment offers a recent example, or before that, the French strikes in West Germany during the Algerian war.[42]

As we have seen, covert action in 1980s Afghanistan is remembered for the elaborate arms-smuggling pipeline through which a network of anti-Soviet states discreetly equipped local warlords. Less famously, the covert action also involved sabotage and demolition, which had almost as big an effect as the rebels' use of heavy weaponry such as the fabled Stinger missiles. Conducted with the help of British special forces (recently retired, of course, to enhance deniability), the aim was to sabotage fuel supplies so as to degrade military equipment.

Teams of two men would sneak up to a heavily guarded pipeline under cover of darkness. They clamped it, drilled a hole into it, and injected boron carbide powder supplied by MI6. A small amount of this chemical, noted for its hard properties and now used in abrasives and bullet-proof vests, ruined a lot of fuel.

They also disguised boron carbide as charcoal and passed it to Afghans who worked inside Soviet bases and would insert it into fuel tanks.

The chemical caused engines to overheat, generating spectacular results when targeting helicopters. Their engines seized up; aircraft simply dropped out of the sky. Some of the mujahideen enjoyed more success using this method than using the Stinger missiles. Indeed, according to the then head of Saudi intelligence, sabotage, alongside other attacks on airbases, did more to destroy helicopters and aircraft than the missiles – while simultaneously decimating Soviet morale. Sabotage formed only a small part of the covert action, and wider insurgency, but it served as a force multiplier physically and psychologically.[43]

Sabotage softens the ground to allow friendly forces to do their jobs more efficiently. Russia used covert sabotage teams to lay the groundwork before military operations targeting Georgia and Ukraine. Four years before the war between Russia and Georgia over the breakaway region of South Ossetia in 2008, Georgian counterintelligence reported that a Russian GRU colonel had moved to South Ossetia and established a secretive unit, consisting of 120 men tasked with carrying out sabotage inside Georgia.[44] Something comparable happened in Ukraine. As recently as 2021, Ukrainian intelligence arrested a man accused of heading a similar sabotage group operating in the east of the country. They claimed he had been there since the start of hostilities in 2014.[45]

Using sabotage to support a wider offensive is, of course, nothing new. The success of the D-Day landings in June 1944 came down not only to the famous deception operation which hoodwinked Hitler into thinking the invasion would take place at Calais rather than Normandy, but also because of preparatory sabotage by the equally famous Special Operations Executive (SOE). The Nazis had planned to push the Allies back towards the sea, but SOE saboteurs destroyed the rail transport system, blew up bridges, knocked down trees and mined roads. The 450-mile journey to Normandy should have taken the German army three days; as a result of the sabotage, it took seventeen.[46] The rest, as they say, is history.

Sabotage, used judiciously, puts the enemy in an uncomfortable dilemma. Do you ignore it and run the risk of a blow to critical infrastructure or national morale, if some prestigious symbol, say parliament, is attacked? Or do you take the threat seriously and send forces to guard every bridge, every shipping port, every underwater internet cable? This will protect from sabotage but will spread forces out too thinly and distract from the threat of a conventional strike.[47]

While the advent of the internet has created ample opportunities for states to disrupt each other's infrastructure, this is an extension of a form of covert action that has existed for decades, even centuries and millennia.

Sabotage can be used in and through cyberspace, sometimes with the involvement of human agents, but it is not limited to the cyber realm. Bangs and bombs still exist. Likewise, sabotage is broader than we often recognize. It is more than the lionized SOE exploits of yesteryear and it is more than disrupting the Iranian nuclear weapons programme today. Sabotage attacks economic and commercial targets. As Lawrence of Arabia said, the minerals not the military. Sabotage also has psychological functions. It can sow divisions, lower morale and frustrate adversaries.

A longer and wider perspective on sabotage throws up some interesting insights from history. First, it is important not to obsess over the novelty of cyber; it works hand in hand with the physical, human domain. They need to be considered together, and we can only understand contemporary sabotage by understanding where it came from. Second, sabotage cannot annihilate the enemy. It can only do so much given that secrecy limits impact and deniability decreases control. Instead, it is a disrupter. It degrades, buys time, softens up. It is attritional, a temporary paralysis. Accordingly, it complements other tools of statecraft, both overt and covert. It will achieve little in isolation.

Third, sabotage and propaganda are two sides of the same coin. The psychological impact is crucial; the paranoia it can induce; the morale it can sap.

It is important to keep cyber sabotage in perspective and not succumb to the shock of the new. That said, the internet has transformed the way we live and, with it, has created an entire new range of vulnerabilities. For two decades, political leaders have warned about the potentially devastating effects of 'cyberwar' or a 'cyber 9/11'. The effects of a 'cyber Pearl Harbor' would dwarf those of disruptive sabotage. The reality is very different from the myth.

10

HOW TO CYBERATTACK

magine the chaos. Anonymous hackers take down entire networks across a city. The financial sector is wiped out, losing billions of dollars in an instant. Traffic light outages cause multiple pile-ups; lorries ram into buildings. Air traffic control is sabotaged; planes fall from the sky. The media is off air or plays sinister ransom messages on a loop. Electricity grids are down; people are freezing. Hackers send surplus natural gas to overwhelm a power plant, causing a devastating explosion.

If this doomsday scenario all sounds a bit Hollywood, it should. Most of it happened in *Die Hard 4.0*. Even so, senior politicians and generals have been bracing us for a digital apocalypse for decades. In 2012, US Defense Secretary Leon Panetta famously warned of a 'cyber Pearl Harbor that would cause physical destruction and the loss of life, an attack that would paralyze and shock the nation'. An FBI director cautioned that cyberattacks would become 'the number one threat' to the USA. A chairman of the joint chiefs of staff even called it 'an existential threat'. President Obama himself, exercising more restraint, still deemed it 'one of the most serious economic and security challenges' that the country faced.[1]

Cyberattacks can certainly do great damage. Excitable commentators heralded a new dawn in spring 2007 when distributed denial-of-service attacks practically shut down the Estonian government's online services. Hackers disrupted websites of ministries, banks, political parties, media outlets and the parliamentary email server. All of a sudden, citizens in one of the most connected countries on earth could not access the news or even withdraw money from cash machines. The attack was large, disruptive, confusing and, crucially, below the level of warfare. Russia denied involvement and Estonia lacked public proof. The ambiguity tested NATO's ability to respond and questioned the utility of its Article 5. At the same time, and despite dramatic media headlines, the attack was reversible: services were fixed within days; nothing was irredeemably broken. As security practitioners well knew.

Three years later, pundits hailed another new dawn upon discovery of the Stuxnet worm used to degrade the Iranian nuclear programme. Michael Hayden, a highly respected former director of both the CIA and the National Security Agency, declared it the first time a cyberattack had caused major physical destruction. The worm had successfully managed to control the speed of the centrifuges, damaging around one thousand of them. Once inside, US and Israeli intelligence then created further iterations of Stuxnet, updating and reprogramming it to attack different parts of the nuclear facility.[2]

The dangerous potential of cyberattacks has increased in recent years as tools become more sophisticated. In 2015, attacks on the power grid cut off electricity to thousands of western Ukrainians. Inside the control centre, operators watched aghast as the cursor appeared to move of its own accord taking each station offline. Ukrainian intelligence swiftly blamed Russia.[3]

Five years later, amid a desert heatwave, Israel accused Iran of sabotaging a water treatment facility. Hackers attempted to increase chlorine levels in the country's drinking water. They came dangerously close to succeeding and making hundreds of people sick. They could also have overwhelmed the pump and cut off the water supply altogether, with potentially devastating consequences in the summer heat.[4]

In October 2020, the head of MI5 issued a sober warning of his own. States were racing for vaccines to provide immunity from COVID-19. Populations were desperate for a way out of the pandemic and international reputations were on the line. In a rare public speech, Ken McCallum warned that hostile powers were trying to steal and sabotage British research. He said that MI5 was working hard to protect adversaries from 'potentially fiddling with the data'.[5] The psychological stress and economic turmoil of lockdowns created incredibly high stakes. Sabotaging an effective vaccine by destroying data and tampering with scientists' ability to communicate with each other or to roll out the programme would have been hugely consequential. Beyond COVID, a former head of GCHQ's National Cyber Security Centre recently admitted that he lay awake at night worrying about the damage which a rogue actor, whether a state or criminal group, could inflict with a cyber tool that they did not fully understand.[6]

It certainly feels like the scale of attacks has increased in recent years. In the US, President Trump reportedly issued a blanket authorization allowing the CIA to undertake more operations against Iran, Russia, China and North Korea. This included greater freedom to sabotage critical infrastructure targets such as petrochemical plants. Trump's intervention dramatically sped up the process, cutting approval times down to weeks. Under Obama, it had taken up to a year to gain authorization. Such tardiness had reduced the number of covert actions undertaken. By the time the approval came, the operation may well have become redundant. There is a trade-off, though: speed decreases scrutiny.[7]

On the other side, the spring and summer of 2021 saw an epidemic of ransomware activity targeting the US. Gangs of hackers, often based in China, Russia and former Soviet countries, encrypted and stole private data for ransom. They disrupted schools, hospitals, food supplies and even a major pipeline, choking the supply of oil to the eastern US. Although any link between the criminals and foreign states was unclear, it quickly became a national security issue. President Biden accused Russia of, at best, turning a blind eye to hacker groups and accused China of deliberately fostering them. By the summer, the US army's *Cyber Defense Review* was arguing that the cyber Pearl Harbor had finally arrived. Thousands of cybersecurity professionals rolled their eyes in unison.

Although cyberattacks can be destructive and have serious consequences, fearmongering is misplaced. The over-hyped 'cyber 9/11' or 'cyber Pearl Harbor' analogy is flawed for three reasons.

First, any such devastating sabotage would not be a single out-of-the-blue attack. There is no big red cyber button that hostile states can press and wreak apocalyptic damage. A president cannot dramatically demand: 'Unleash the malware!' Attacks like Stuxnet require years of preparation. At the same time, we might wonder why presidents would even want to 'unleash the malware' given the complexities involved, the difficulties in generating sufficient harm to render a cyberattack anything more than an adjunct to physical force, and the difficulties in

controlling what they have created. Why not use a more direct –
and physical – means to sabotage instead?[8]

Second, governments have little incentive to advertise the
lethal effects of such attacks. In late 2020, a woman died in a
German hospital many miles away from her hometown of
Düsseldorf. The local hospital had reluctantly – and fatally –
turned her ambulance away after suffering a ransomware attack.
It was the first known case of a cyberattack killing someone –
but even then prosecutors could not prove causation. Six months
later, another attack targeted the Irish health system. Hackers
believed to be based in Russia massively disrupted hospital
appointments on a scale that the head of the health service
described as 'catastrophic'. It is unclear whether anyone died
as a direct or indirect result. Even if they did, leaders would be
unlikely to admit it given the repercussions; prosecutors would
be unable to prove it.

Third, the probability of a successful attack against a target
big enough to cause a cyber 9/11 or Pearl Harbor is quite low.
As experts Erik Gartzke and Jon Lindsay explain, 'High-reward
targets pose greater risks and costs to those that attack them.'
This is partly because attribution, especially in private, is not as
difficult as many assume, partly because of serious protective
measures in place, and partly because of the consequences of
clever deception operations designed to mislead and unsettle
the attacker. If the attacker cannot be sure that his anonymity
is secure, or doubts whether her malware will work as intended,
or worries that resources may be wasted, then the benefits of
attacking a high-value target substantially decrease.[9]

Defenders are working hard on devious ploys to manipulate the hackers' virtual world, inducing fear and paranoia, by,
for example, feeding false information to throw them off the

scent. This is twentieth-century deception, redesigned for the cyber world. The bigger the target, the more likely you are to get caught.

Equally, cyberattacks are unlikely to escalate into something more dramatic and dangerous. Surveys show that, if hit by a cyberattack, the American public would be less willing to respond with aggressive military force than when hit by other, more traditional, attacks. This is even the case when they consider the magnitude of the cyberattack as comparable to those other types of attacks.[10] Perhaps the public do not subscribe to the cyber Pearl Harbor harbingers of doom. Perhaps they fear the consequences and collateral damage. Cyber sabotage might be more reversible and transitory than old-school sabotage, through, say, a system reboot, but it is less controllable and predictable compared to the constrained psychical destruction wrought via a bomb hidden in a dead rat, SOE-style.[11] States, publics and businesses are proving surprisingly tolerant.[12]

Likewise, the British approach sees offensive cyber as de-escalatory; it can provide an exit ramp. Risk-averse governments like the UK and the US end up showing restraint when considering cyberattacks.[13] Similarly, these governments also refrain from outsourcing such activity to hacker groups. Fear of being held to account by voters when these operations spiral, go wrong and become exposed forms a powerful constraint.[14]

Excitable headlines screaming 'cyber Pearl Harbor' or 'cyberwar' are therefore highly problematic. They make us underestimate the real purpose and danger of cyberattacks: persistent subversion.

Cyberattacks are not about launching lethal, devastating or paralysing blows. They are not apocalyptic. Instead, they are a form of political warfare, persistently exploiting vulnerabilities to undermine authorities from within. They are subversive.

Attacks exploit weaknesses and manipulate targets. They destabilize targets, undermining their ability to function as intended. Cyberattacks subvert computer systems to orchestrate political, physical and economic effects.[15] Removing cyberattacks from the hype of the neophiles and instead considering them in the wider historical context of covert action reveals something crucial: cyber conflict is intelligence conflict.[16]

Using cyberattacks as a form of political warfare – to subvert and sabotage – creates a psychological impact. As people wait for a cyber Pearl Harbor, they worry about the what-if scenario. Our reliance on computer systems for pretty much all of modern life, combined with excitable headlines screaming cyberwar, creates uncertainty, paranoia and fear. Like terrorism, fear of an attack affects audiences far beyond the immediate target. For this reason, it is all the more important to keep cyberattacks in perspective. Cyber intrusions and attacks are a great deal messier and more complex than the spectacular Hollywood-style apocalypse once predicted. Focusing too much on the latter can mislead the public about the vaguer sense of unease and anxiety created by the reality of this type of covert action.

The same is true of cyber sabotage in the economic sphere. Here, even persistent intrusions designed merely to spy rather than anything more damaging can have a disruptive psychological impact. The principal threat becomes wider loss of market confidence. Again, it is vital to keep hostile activity in perspective and manage the narrative carefully so as to avoid negative psychological repercussions.[17]

States using cyberattacks as part of an intelligence conflict or wider grey zone competition must learn to embrace ambiguity.

The intangible nature of cyberspace, mysterious to many, and the way operations pan out erode the borders between espionage and sabotage, between offence and defence. All the while, states neither confirm nor deny responsibility, keen to manipulate their rivals' perceptions of their capabilities and intent.[18]

Intelligence agencies hack into adversaries' systems for many reasons: to gather intelligence; to defend against impending attacks; to deceive, mislead and ensnare aggressors; to do preparatory work well in advance of any potential sabotage; to generate options in case they eventually do want to conduct the sabotage; and finally to actually do the sabotage.[19] Ambiguity abounds.

If detected, it is sometimes impossible to know whether the intrusion was preparation for imminent sabotage, merely run-of-the-mill espionage, or something else entirely.[20] It becomes a game of perceptions, an optical illusion in which one person sees espionage and another sees an attack. But these perceptions and interpretations have important real-world consequences.

The success of the Stuxnet worm did not happen overnight. It, and other cyberattacks against Iran, relied on excellent intelligence about the various uranium enrichment facilities. Long before the centrifuges started failing, the operation began by inserting spyware into the nuclear plant at Natanz to learn more about the target. Eventually, the Iranians did discover that malicious data-mining software, known as Flame, had been extracting intelligence from their computer systems for years in preparation for the sabotage, including Stuxnet. By that time, it was too late.[21] If Iran had detected the virus in advance, there would have been no way of knowing whether this was a mere intelligence-gathering operation or if, as turned out to be the case, it formed the precursor to a damaging attack.

Chinese approaches similarly blur espionage and attack. Its military emphasizes the importance of secret reconnaissance to access, monitor and identify weaknesses in enemy systems. The requirements necessary to achieve this are very similar to those for sabotage, allowing the Chinese to switch seamlessly from espionage to attack when the moment is right. Chinese military and intelligence actors have successfully penetrated US government networks on multiple occasions, deploying malware to steal classified information. Presumably, they could use similar channels to disrupt or attack.[22] This all takes place beneath the level of active conflict but, worryingly, targets can easily interpret any intrusion as offensive and assume it is the precursor to an imminent attack.[23] The media's tendency to hype all intrusions as cyberattacks does not help.

It may be difficult to tell them apart, especially amid excitable press coverage, but espionage is different from an attack. Espionage is certainly not an act of war. Despite this, senior politicians – people who should know better – have recently made some garish claims to the contrary.

In spring 2020, thousands of US companies and federal agencies updated their computer software. This was routine; they had done so many times before. They had no idea that Russian intelligence had inserted malicious code into the update in a successful attempt to access American systems. Discovered towards the end of the year, the so-called SolarWinds intrusion was one of the largest known breaches in history, eventually spreading to countries worldwide. Although it ended up actively targeting only a small number of systems, the intrusion spawned heated debate about whether the Russians were gathering information or preparing for sabotage.

'This is virtually a declaration of war,' protested one senior Democratic Party politician. For Mitt Romney, former presidential candidate and a senior Republican, it was akin to Russian bombers 'flying undetected over the entire country'.[24] Fortunately, cooler heads prevailed. Although the media quickly dubbed it an attack, there was no publicly available evidence that Russia sought to sabotage, degrade or destroy anything. It was merely an espionage 'fishing trip' in the words of one former intelligence official. This is exactly the kind of activity at which the US excels, and so it seems myopic, hypocritical and counterproductive for US leaders to call for condemnation and retaliation.[25] SolarWinds was not sabotage, but it could easily be misinterpreted as activity leading to sabotage.

The ambiguity is reminiscent of the 2016 presidential election when, as we have seen, Russian intelligence successfully penetrated various electoral systems. This left President Obama unsure as to whether Putin was passively spying or preparing for something much more aggressive and controversial: sabotaging the election by altering the databases and votes directly. This ambiguity complicated the response. The potential for sabotage deterred Obama from taking a tough line against the espionage in case Putin escalated. At the same time, espionage did not warrant a disproportionately harsh response given that, at the time, there was no evidence of sabotage.[26] Complicating matters further, the simultaneous Russian 'hack and leak' did constitute a covert influence operation, and debates about how to respond involved discussion of whether Russia would retaliate against other US targets, for example through electoral interference.[27] All of this put Obama in a difficult position.

The ambiguity between espionage and attack, between offence and defence, could have real consequences. It is all the more dangerous because ambiguity increases paranoia. In some ways it does not matter whether Russia intended espionage or sabotage: if

the Washington establishment declares that the intrusion constituted an act of war, then the impact could be drastic.[28] All this
cyber sabre-rattling is dangerous, provocative and irresponsible.

Still, this is an opportune moment for the tweed-wearing,
elbow-patched historian inside all of us to rear our heads and
smugly caution against the newness of all of this. Cyberattacks
must be understood within the historical context of subversion
and wider covert activity.

First off, the novelty and mystique of cyber exaggerates this
sense of uncertainty. Indeed, according to one former senior
GCHQ officer, states have been able to confidently identify perpetrators of attacks for some time. They just sometimes choose not
to make those attributions public so as to protect sensitive intelligence sources or because they think dealing with the adversary
privately is more beneficial. France, in particular, prefers tackling
perpetrators directly rather than publicly attributing blame.[29] At
the same time, Russia and China have an incentive in playing up
the mystique and perpetuating the idea that attribution is virtually
impossible. Doing so helps to sow doubt about the provenance of
their operations and exaggerate their capabilities.

Second, in many ways this ambiguity between espionage
and sabotage existed in classic covert actions of the twentieth
century. Sabotage in an analogue world required the CIA, KGB
or whoever to infiltrate agents in order to gather intelligence
on the layout of a factory before the attack could take place. A
human agent is inevitably ambiguous. Is he or she passively gathering intelligence or aggressively preparing sabotage?

The story of John Darling, a British businessman travelling to
Egypt way back in May 1951, illustrates this analogue ambiguity
nicely. These were dangerous times, when nationalism began
to seriously threaten the old imperial order, while across the

Egyptian border, the young and insecure state of Israel worried about its large Arab neighbour. Darling moved freely, setting up plenty of business meetings.

Except John Darling did not actually exist. It was the cover identity of Avraham Dar, an Israeli intelligence officer. He recruited a network of Egyptian Jews to form sleeper cells in Cairo and Alexandria. They would live normal lives but strike when the time was right.

Dar's undercover agents slept for three years. Then, in the summer of 1954, they heard a codeword broadcast across an army radio channel and awoke, posting letter bombs to various addresses in the cities of Alexandria and Cairo. Shortly afterwards, small explosions rang out at American cultural centres, including libraries and cinemas. Israel hoped to blame the attacks on the Muslim Brotherhood, local communists or nationalists and ultimately to prevent British withdrawal from the Suez Canal zone.

For three years, the human agents were ambiguous. If the Egyptians had discovered the sleeper cell before the attacks, they would not have known whether they were spying on Egypt or, as was the case, lying in wait to attack.[30] They were the human equivalent of a hack or intrusion.

The biggest difference is one of scale rather than concept. The potential of a single human agent of influence is small compared to implanted malware. The latter can potentially self-replicate and go global, whereas Darling ran a small network in two cities. Human agent networks will never be as widespread as digital intrusions. The infamous Cold War Soviet spy network inside the British establishment was the Cambridge five, not the Cambridge five thousand.

This is a fair point, but even old-school intrusions could be scaled up. Let us turn to another, more remarkable, and only recently uncovered twentieth-century spy story. From 1970, American and West German intelligence owned and controlled a Swiss encryption company, Crypto AG. The company sold encryption equipment to over 120 countries worldwide, including Egypt, India, Pakistan, Libya and Argentina. These machines allowed politicians and intelligence agencies to communicate in secret.

Or so they thought. In fact, for decades the US and West Germans had rigged the devices allowing their intelligence services to eavesdrop on multiple governments and, in a double victory, make handsome profits selling the devices in the first place. The Germans sold their shares to the CIA in the 1990s, but the Americans seemed to continue the massive operation well into the twenty-first century. It was only exposed in 2020; the Swiss intelligence chief resigned within a year.[31]

The Crypto AG scandal demonstrates how rigging a supply chain can pay huge global intelligence dividends. It was like Bletchley Park on steroids. There was still some ambiguity, though, because this was about espionage: cryptologic enablement, or fiddling the machines, to gather intelligence. These early machine defects could not disable communications.[32] Yet it also helped to degrade the capability of the machines, thus blurring the line with covert action.[33] At heart, though, and like SolarWinds, it was a fishing expedition on a massive scale.

If cyberattacks are essentially subversive, designed to exploit vulnerabilities and undermine authority, then how should states use them? What can they achieve? The UK's new offensive National Cyber Force is, according to those running it, 'a potent national capability to deter our adversaries'.[34] Similarly, the US Cyber Command seeks to undermine adversaries by proactively and relentlessly going after them.[35] American strategy invokes offensive operations to impose costs on would-be attackers. This involves, as one public document puts it, the 'assertive defence of national interests, defending "forward", pre-empting attack and competing daily by way of persistent engagement'.[36]

The aim is to allow states with more sophisticated capabilities but higher constraints, such as the US and the UK, to better compete with those, such as China and Russia, who, like a drunk with a sword, deploy less sophisticated capabilities in an unrestrained manner.[37] This does come with risks, though, as one scholar put it: 'Fighting fire with fire might be viscerally satisfying but can be self-defeating if everyone is covered in gasoline and standing in the same knee-deep dry grass.'[38]

Another risk is that nobody gets burned at all. Hiding behind the wall of secrecy to make vague threats lacks credibility. When ministers don their grave national security faces and threaten consequences for cyberattacks, but then insist they cannot tell us what those consequences will be, it all becomes a bit meaningless.

Low-level disruption operations conducted online have only a limited effect – even when they successfully hack into their target. These low-cost and low-risk ways of signalling displeasure lack credibility and so are not especially likely to achieve immediate change in the target's behaviour.[39]

More aggressive operations, aiming to degrade or sabotage an adversary's computer system, stand a better chance, especially if they target government rather than civilian networks. Sabotage is blunter, more expensive and more sophisticated than mere disruption – and it is also difficult to pull off. It is therefore more credible and demonstrates greater resolve, all while showing restraint by operating below the level of open conflict and by targeting government over civilian computers.

According to a recent study by scholars Brandon Valeriano, Benjamin Jensen and Ryan Maness, such activity evoked concessions around a third of the time between 2000 and 2014. In stark contrast, the low-level disruption operations did not achieve a single concession.[40]

In truth, it is difficult to know – and more so to quantify – how far cyber-sabotage operations succeed. Intentions might well be unclear. As we have seen, disruptive propaganda, espionage and sabotage, offence and defence all blur. Effects might swirl beyond extracting concessions or changing behaviour. It can all become rather Kafkaesque.

The US National Security Agency seems to have enjoyed the most success, especially against the Chinese. In the second half of the 2000s, one degradation campaign, Cisco Raider, helped disrupt the spread of counterfeit Cisco software by degrading Chinese systems. Between 2008 and 2010, another campaign, known as Boxing Rumble, responded to Chinese attempts to penetrate US military networks by either sending bogus information back to the Chinese, which the Chinese assumed was genuine intelligence, or by sabotaging the hackers' systems altogether.[41] On the downside, though, this apparent success falls into the whack-a-mole trap: Chinese intelligence regroups and then moves on to the next US target.

What about Russia? For all its disruptive operations, and there was a notable uptick in the summer of 2021, Russian activity has seemingly failed to induce meaningful policy change. It failed to gain concessions from Estonia despite successfully attacking websites back in 2007 or when defacing websites in Georgia and Ukraine in the years afterwards. Cyberattacks played no notable role in Russian military action in eastern Ukraine from 2014; neither did they contribute much to the annexation of Crimea.[42]

In December 2015, Russia successfully caused a power outage in western Ukraine by remotely disconnecting around thirty power substations and then inundating support centres with phone calls to disrupt attempts to fix them. However, this attack affected less than 1 per cent of the population and was neutralized within six hours. A year later, Russia targeted the power grid in Kiev. This time, authorities fixed it within just seventy-five minutes.[43]

Importantly, though, goals can vary wildly and include separate propaganda value by spreading confusion and undermining trust. Russian operations have enjoyed success in disrupting, framing narratives, signalling displeasure and projecting power. The effects spill beyond the immediate country targeted.

Meanwhile, China failed to draw concessions from Japan when attacking the website of a national war memorial in 2005. It failed again five years later when targeting Japan over the East China Sea dispute. Once more, however, these operations were driven by complex domestic motivations alongside a desire to signal commitments to various other actors. It would therefore be simplistic to say categorically that they failed.[44]

Other operations might not achieve an immediate impact but still enjoy indirect success. The best-known North Korean example came in 2014. Sony Pictures made a controversial comedy film, *The Interview*, which parodied North Korean dictator Kim Jong-un. It portrayed him as a pathetic frat boy character with daddy issues who had successfully convinced his public that he was some sort of god who did not defecate. The film culminated with Kim being killed as he attempted to launch nuclear weapons on the US. The North Koreans successfully hacked Sony Pictures and released confidential emails including executives' salaries and details of forthcoming films.

The operation failed to achieve concessions from Sony – the film was released via Netflix after President Obama stepped in. Crucially, however, while the hack did not derail *The Interview*'s release, there have been no Hollywood films ridiculing President Kim since.

Iran has launched some of the largest cyber-sabotage operations. In 2012, Saudi Aramco, one of the world's largest oil companies, was hit by a virus which infected up to thirty thousand of its computers. The damage took almost two weeks to repair. Just a fortnight later, Iranian hackers struck again, this time knocking the Qatari RasGas company offline. Both were destructive attacks and on one level appear successful; but neither drew concessions from Saudi Arabia and Qatar.[45] But then how far was this the aim, compared to, say, shaping the wider use of sanctions? And what was the benchmark for success?

Iran allegedly attacked over eighty Israeli companies in retaliation for the assassination of a leading nuclear scientist in November 2020, including hacking the systems of Israel's largest defence contractor and leaking its data.[46] Although a response to Israeli covert action, it is unlikely that such activity will deter the Israelis from future operations. Impact and success are difficult to measure. Narratives become important.

The sabotage of Iran's nuclear weapons programme offers an instructive example. In many ways it was successful: it hit the target and made an impact. But this is not the full story – and outsiders still do not know all the details. Critics insist that the operation failed to delay the programme in any meaningful sense and that, worse, it may have deepened mutual suspicion between the US and Iran, thereby making diplomacy more difficult. It may have turbocharged Iran's own offensive cyber capabilities; empowered extreme elements within the regime to exploit the climate of fear and anger; and hardened Iranian resolve to gain nuclear weapons and reduce cooperation with inspectors.[47]

Supporters of the covert action disagree. Criticism perhaps focuses too narrowly on one specific variant of the malware and does not consider the longer campaign, which perhaps included as yet unknown operations. The covert action generated uncertainty which, in turn, delayed Iranian attempts to build and operate various systems. It forced the Iranians to divert precious energy and resources into protecting the nuclear programme and its supply chain; it increased paranoia among officials; and it arguably gave the US more influence at the negotiating table. Sabotaging Iran's most closely guarded secrets demonstrated US power – and bought it leverage.[48] And there were other aims to consider as well. The covert action successfully prevented the Israelis going alone and launching a dangerous military strike.

Complicating matters further still, it is difficult to know the specific impact of the cyber sabotage, not least because the US and Israelis complemented it with intense economic pressure. Iran's economy shrank 9 per cent every year between 2012 and 2015. How did this, as opposed to cyberattacks, shape Iranian behaviour? The exact contribution of covert action to the 2015 nuclear agreement is perhaps unknowable.[49]

Amid swirling arguments, counterarguments, secrecy and uncertainty, it ultimately becomes a matter of narrative – and the dominant one here is success. Initial reports eulogized sabotage for setting back the Iranian nuclear programme by three to five years.[50] Senior figures such as John Sawers, the head of MI6, put the figure at more like six.[51] Serious US broadsheets quoted unnamed sources from high up in the Obama administration saying that Stuxnet was an American–Israeli operation, allowing the two countries to showcase their great cyber power status and benefit from reputational gains.[52] Popular accounts, swept up in the novelty of it all, breathlessly echoed this story.

Only later did reports revise the headline number down to a delay of mere months. The International Atomic Energy Agency even suggested that Iran had actually increased its production of low-enriched uranium during the period when Stuxnet was active.[53] It remains hotly debated. Some scholars now think that the sabotage was 'either more costly than initially purported or had limited effects'.[54] By then, though, the story of the powerful Stuxnet worm had itself gone viral.

Leaders using cyberattacks face trade-offs and tough decisions. First, secrecy is important because if the attack is inadvertently exposed, the target can delete computer viruses or patch vulnerabilities. Yet secrecy and the need to be indirect put a ceiling on activity, while also limiting speed. It takes a long time and a lot of reconnaissance to target a system before launching a cyberattack.

Second, increasing the scale of attacks decreases the speed, the secrecy and control. The wider the scope of targets and the bigger the scale of the attack, the more likely you are to be detected. The more control, the less deniability.

Third, being more indirect, and thus more secret, leads to less control. Outsourcing to private hackers risks them doing unauthorized things. Even computer viruses can go rogue.[55] Whether they are planning assassination, plotting coups or launching cyberattacks, states cannot escape this limitation. Cyber is not unique; this is the same dilemma that constrains other forms of covert action.

Cyberattacks can only achieve so much. There is too much ambiguity to credibly signal to adversaries; old-fashioned theories of nuclear deterrence are difficult to apply to the uncertain world of cyber.[56] Disruption is the aim of the game, and, perhaps over time, the cumulative effects of multiple disruptions will shape adversary behaviour. It is too soon to tell. We need to remember that, although covert operations are often the most eye-catching measures when exposed, they exist within an arsenal of more mundane weapons from diplomacy to economic sanctions. Cyberattacks form part of a broader plan and should not exist in isolation. Sometimes those involved forget this. In the case of Stuxnet, as the covert action wore on, delay and disruption had seemingly become an aim in itself.[57] The means must align with the ends. How to cyberattack? Disrupt, disrupt, disrupt; do not expect too much; ensure integration with other levers of policy. There is little new here.

A false promise lies at the heart of excitable debates about what offensive cyber can achieve. As one recent British report put it, 'There will doubtless be a temptation in some quarters – both political and military – to assume that the NCF [National Cyber Force] will be able to do things it simply cannot.' Covert action 'should not be perceived as a technological fix to problems that offensive cyber operations are ill-suited to addressing'. It is easy to imagine an impulsive prime minister demanding that some long-suffering manager at GCHQ sabotage this or degrade that. Covert action can deny, disrupt and degrade adversaries in a targeted fashion. It can subvert and undermine authority, but this always comes with limitations. As experts on offensive cyber put it, 'it will not win a war – metaphorical or actual – on its own'.[58]

HOW TO WIELD THE HIDDEN HAND

'You will be a cog in a very large machine whose smooth functioning depends on each separate cog carrying out its part efficiently.' Disguise is essential when operating undercover in a foreign country. To disguise your appearance, you could comb charcoal through your hair. If you have distinctively large eyes, you could use soot, grease and a red pencil as improvised makeup to give the impression of a bagged half-closed eye. Put two small metal nuts up your nose to alter its appearance into a more squashed look while still being able to breathe. 'Never come out of character.'

Sometimes you will need to break into a property. 'Burglary with subversive intent is best not carried out by [the] leader himself but by subordinates – preferably local people who, if caught, can use the cover of "normal burglary". (Where necessary objects of value may be removed to substantiate this cover.)' The maximum number of people to be involved in such operations is three. Two is said to be best. If a dog is set on you, do not run. 'Imitate the owner and repeat what he says to encourage the dog to search for the third party.'[1]

Manuals for covert operations exist. The above instructions come from a Special Operations Executive syllabus written during the Second World War, which covered security, intelligence gathering, sabotage, secret armies and coordinating uprisings behind enemy lines.

Much of this operates at the tactical level: how to recruit, infiltrate and escape. There is no training manual – or at least one that has been declassified – for prime ministers and presidents. And for good reason. Any attempt to come up with a list of golden rules to ensure covert action success would be futile. As we have seen, covert action encompasses a broad range of activities conducted by a broad range of actors in a broad range of circumstances. Our journey through the grey zone has taken us from assassination through to cyberattacks, via coups, electoral rigging, and much else besides. Success in any of these fields is highly subjective: often a political label wielded rather than an obvious and objective outcome. Still, experience reveals a few insights that can give those wielding the hidden hand the best possible chance of subverting, disrupting – or even overthrowing.

Clarity comes first. In a world in which spies and special forces are romantically mythologized and covert action poorly understood, we need to be clear what we are talking about. We have seen how different countries interpret covert action differently. Universally applying the clinically bureaucratic approach of the Americans risks misunderstanding the more fluid thinking of the Russians – or even the British for that matter.

British intelligence officers and Whitehall mandarins have used a ridiculous – if somewhat endearing – range of euphemisms for various forms of covert action over the years. Personal highlights include nocturnal activity, quietism, discreet operations, direct action, pinpricks, peculiar illegal activities, and even Machiavellian schemes. This may pander to Victorian

sensibilities and help mask polite discomfort at engaging in the
dark arts of international statecraft, rather like a gentleman
visiting the little boy's room or a lady going to powder her nose,
but it is no grounds for sensible policymaking.

The British have historically used the terms covert and clandestine operations interchangeably. This imprecision, while
seemingly innocuous, is misleading and has caused confusion
when working with US colleagues. Given the importance of alli-
ances and joint activity, both sides need to know what the other
is talking about.[2]

To be sure, it helps to be flexible, nimble, and, at times, free
from the constraints of arduous definitions worn like millstones
around the neck of practitioners. Yet these definitions have real-
world implications beyond professorial pontification designed to
torment unfortunate undergraduates. Precision – or lack thereof
– has implications for cooperation and oversight; secrecy and
deniability; and intelligence and action. Define your terms.

Precision extends to knowing what you want to achieve.
And how. Formulating clear and realistic goals, which comple-
ment broader foreign policy, is easier said than done; planning
necessarily involves small groups, those dukes of dark corners
hidden away in secret rooms, working on sensitive topics in great
secrecy. It can become emotive, leading to poor decisions and
ever-expanding scope.[3]

Secrecy can be seductive, covert action never-ending. For
insider turned scholar Gregory Treverton, covert action is 'both
secret and emotional' and so it is 'too seldom the subject of hard
thought'. Secretive and emotive, covert actions start small but
grow. The operational necessities to achieve impact push them
to become bigger and bolder: more CIA officers, more money,
more weapons. This inevitably decreases secrecy and can lead

to the gradual expansion of the mission beyond what was initially agreed. Once committed to a small and secret operation, leaders are more likely to take the next step than pull back and admit failure.[4] Personal attachment pushes actions further still; simply preserving existing operations does not make for great strategy.[5]

What do leaders want to achieve using covert action? Covert tools, whether influence or sabotage, should not drive strategy. Secrecy, money and weapons need to be aligned to the goals. Objectives need to be feasible. Covert action is much hyped, and so policymakers and politicians need to be realistic about what it can and cannot achieve. It, alone, does not win wars. It, alone, does not overthrow governments. Sabotage of Iranian nuclear facilities at best delays Iranian ambitions or pushes Iran towards the negotiation table. It will remove neither the threat nor the regime. Disruption operations will not force an occupier to leave a country.

The sorry lesson of Egypt after the Second World War provides an excellent example. Under President Nasser, the country deployed one of the most aggressive covert action programmes in the entire world, targeting pretty much every neighbouring monarchy as well as the old imperial powers of France and the UK. It spectacularly failed partly because Nasser's expectations were too high. He wrongly assumed that subversion and sabotage would buy influence at little cost and without committing the army. He achieved some tactical victories but fell well short of his ambitious goals for the region.[6] It is crucial to calibrate covert resources with the end goal.

Covert action cannot be a silver bullet, a magic fix for some intractable problem, authorized by an excited politician with access to a mythical big red cyber button or a direct phoneline to trained killers. Leaders are under pressure to do something – supposedly in secret – and without thinking about longer-term consequences. Covert action, as a foster-child of impotence and ambition (or frustration), then becomes alluring.[7] President Nixon demanded the CIA sort out Chile – and quickly – back in 1970. His successor, President Ford, put pressure on the CIA against the agency's better judgement when wanting to sort out Angola shortly afterwards. More recently, as we have seen, Trump pressured the CIA to move more quickly on cyberattacks against countries like Iran and removed various bureaucratic hurdles to enable it. According to one senior official, the White House wanted the CIA to 'move move move'.[8] Similarly, modern counterterrorism operations have, according to one scholar, 'essentially been put on autopilot with default secretive, aggressive and heavily kinetic direct action missions substituting for a comprehensive strategy'.[9]

This can be dangerous. Objectives should be the result of negotiations between various layers of the CIA, including lawyers, and the White House.[10] Presidents should not turn to the hidden hand simply because it is available.

The next insight is to calibrate secrecy. As we have seen, covert action is so much more than hidden sponsorship. Secrecy is not binary, and there are multiple levels of exposure and audiences. The same operation might be untraceable to one audience but implausibly deniable to another. Allies, adversaries and domestic publics may well be aware of 'secret' activity, creating a unique form of dramatic irony. Covert action might even be thought of as a kind of secret theatre.

For all its strict delineation of covert action, US planners have not grappled with the issue of 'unsecrecy' all that successfully.

According to American terminology, covert action is that which is intended to be unapparent and unacknowledged. The CIA and the White House have consistently emphasized the fig leaf of plausible deniability.

The Russians have thought more carefully. The Kremlin recognizes degrees of secrecy and acknowledgement; covert methods overlap with their overt counterparts, making them difficult to conceptualize and counter.[11]

Russian denials of various covert operations, especially the Salisbury poisonings, were almost comical, turning the secret theatre into a farce of Shakespearean proportions – think a *Comedy of Errors* set in Wiltshire. It was not a standalone performance, and the list of implausible Russian excuses grows by the year. In spring 2021, the head of the Russian foreign intelligence service brazenly denied any involvement in the SolarWinds cyber intrusion, one of the largest and most sophisticated operations ever targeting the US. Instead, he implausibly claimed western intelligence services were behind it.[12]

A few weeks later, ten Russians were detained in northern Chad, in a remote location where the Chadian army just happened to be battling a rebel invasion from Libya. Bizarrely, they insisted that they were mere tourists visiting the Sahara Desert: 'Usually world travellers do not visit the Republic of Chad because it's not the normal route in Africa, but I checked and saw Chad is very rich in natural sites.'[13]

The British have also thought carefully along these lines. Back in the mid-1960s, the chief of MI6, contemplating the rise of oxymoronic secret wars, distinguished between 'untraceable' and 'deniable' operations. Untraceable operations were those in which the British hand 'at best will not even be suspected and at worst cannot be proved'. Likewise, black operations, as defined by the Foreign Office, had 'no evidence of Western inspiration', even if, as with all covert actions, the outcome was visible.

Deniable operations were larger-scale paramilitary operations. MI6's characterization of such an operation was striking: a covert action which 'if, in spite of the probability that [Her Majesty's Government] connived its execution and in spite of some tenable arguable evidence that H.M.G. was officially involved, H.M.G. considers it politically feasible to deny complicity in public statements e.g. in the House of Commons or the United Nations'.[14] In short, the government could get away with lying to parliament. These were *im*plausibly deniable and included not-so-secret wars in places like Yemen and Indonesia. We can only wonder if a similar line exists today.

Leaders need to work out from whom they are keeping secrets and why. A nuanced approach to secrecy, embracing its degrees of exposure and acknowledgement and calibrating who knows what and why, is crucial. This allows greater understanding of the trade-offs and limitations inherent in covert action. The more deniability, the less control; the less visibility, the lower the scope and impact. You cannot have it all. Spy chiefs and politicians have found time and again that if they want something to remain untraceable or genuinely deniable, they have to sacrifice control and scale. They cannot go beyond a certain limit. Operations may be scaled back, and effective weaponry eschewed in order to reduce the chances of detection.[15] Secrecy has a ceiling.

Do not equate exposure with failure. An exposed operation is not necessarily one that has failed. As we have seen, covert paramilitary action can send a message to friends and foes alike. It might have some sort of diplomatic value. Even fakes and forgeries can be exposed and still be successful. Sometimes a propaganda operation is deemed successful simply if it preoccupies the adversary's security authorities with laborious investigations to uncover the source – even if it was intercepted before reaching its intended recipients. Sometimes an operation is deemed successful if, despite having no influence on an event, readers might assume that it had. Knowledge of fakes and forgeries floating around the information ecosystem can spread confusion or undermine trust in the media more broadly.

Sometimes exposure is positive because it provokes the target into a denial. Recently declassified British files give a fascinating insight into such thinking, whereby a Foreign Office forgery cleverly backed the Soviets into a corner. Would they ignore the forgery and risk it gaining traction? Or would they expose the forgery, deny it was them, but then risk drawing attention to their own position on a sensitive issue?

The story dates from 1974. Aleksandr Solzhenitsyn was a Russian novelist and famous dissident whose writings exposed the horrific conditions inside Soviet gulags as well as the wider excesses of the repressive regime. They infuriated the communist leadership, who revoked his citizenship in 1974, following the publication of his damning three-volume work on labour camps, *The Gulag Archipelago*. The World Peace Council, the Soviet front organization with offices worldwide, had deliberately stayed quiet on the issue for fear of contradicting its purported stance of defending human rights and intellectual freedom. British propagandists came up with a cunning plan.

They forged a statement, in English and French, supposedly written by the WPC, all about Solzhenitsyn. To keep it credible, the forgery did not criticize Moscow but rather – more subtly – tried to dismiss worldwide protests in favour of Solzhenitsyn as irrelevant and dangerous to the recent thawing in east–west relations. They posted 504 copies to WPC affiliates, liberal literary types who supported the organization, and selected newspapers worldwide.

Just as the British had hoped, the forgery provoked the WPC to issue a denial, correctly claiming it was a western ploy. Crucially, the denial explicitly drew attention to the very fact that the WPC had failed to pronounce on the Solzhenitsyn case – a significant and revealing admission in itself. The British were even more delighted when the denial reached a wider audience than the forgery.[16] Success comes in many guises.

The hidden hand may be hidden, but it is still attached to a body. It is not some detachable extremity, like a prop from a dodgy horror film. Covert action should be synchronized with other parts of statecraft. Like secret intelligence more broadly, it is, in the words of one former practitioner, a 'critical lever of foreign policy'.[17] It needs to be properly integrated into wider decision-making to ensure that operations are thoroughly scrutinized, that they do not undercut other government activity, and that the aftermath can be effectively managed to prevent a longer-term policy failure that looks to the critical eye like a covert action failure, as happened when the US abandoned Afghanistan after the Soviet withdrawal in 1989. The vacuum and rise of violent Islamism was not a failure of the CIA, but of politicians to consider what came after.

Organizations compete. Covert action needs to be authorized by ministers and not emerge as the half-baked result of bureaucratic pressures and infighting between rival departments. In the UK, constant competition and sniping between diplomats and the military impeded a coherent approach to covert action during the Cold War. Bizarrely, at one point the Foreign Office created a planning committee simply as a harmless forum in which the military could vent their frustrations, while diplomats took the real decisions in secret elsewhere.

Similar questions remain today surrounding the joint nature of the UK National Cyber Force. Its requirements and objectives need to be decided together and coordinated by ministers, not generated by competition between GCHQ, MI6 and the Ministry of Defence. It is no secret that there have been tensions between GCHQ and the military about ownership of offensive cyber capabilities. Senior ministerial leadership is therefore essential.[18] Unfortunately, the National Security Council, under Boris Johnson, met infrequently.

The same applies to the US Cyber Command, which enjoys increased flexibility and freedom of action, but risks becoming somewhat disconnected from other organs of government. This is positive in ensuring that operations do not get strangled by red tape, but could lead to tactics and capabilities driving strategy; poor communication with more defensive actors like the Department of Homeland Security and the FBI; and it could create a damaging situation in which Cyber Command conducts operations against rivals without other parts of the state being aware of what is going on, and so would be left unprepared when those rivals complain or retaliate. Coordination ensures that states use covert action because they should; not because they can.[19]

Sometimes lack of coordination can be fatal. Sometimes use of the hidden hand can undercut military or diplomatic measures – with dangerous consequences. It appears, for example, that during the messy war in the Balkans in the late 1990s, French intelligence operatives were secretly working with Kosovan nationalists to drive out the Serbs. Unfortunately, the very same nationalists simultaneously clashed with the French military also operating in the region, thereby creating the possibility of French-on-French casualties. One commander reacted with horror upon finding out: it was 'incompréhensible'.[20]

On a similar note, despite them being secret, successful covert actions require adequate resources and bipartisan political support; the two go hand in hand. Lack of congressional support for CIA operations in Nicaragua in the 1980s caused the Reagan administration to bypass Congress and break the law. It also deprived the CIA of adequate resources, thereby necessitating the illegal arms sales to Iran to raise money for the rebels. It inevitably ended in scandal, bringing down intelligence officers and almost the entire presidency, and lies in stark contrast to the more successful operation in Afghanistan at the same time. Reagan enjoyed both bipartisan support and adequate resources when aiding the Afghan mujahideen against the Soviets.[21] It is perhaps little wonder that covert actions decline during periods of divided government in the US.[22]

Russia, China and Iran take a whole of government approach, in which warfare is unrestrained and poorly demarcated (although, to be fair, they need to worry less about bipartisan support). China uses all means, including economics, politics, immigration and culture, to achieve objectives, leaving people surprised at the extent to which ordinary things can become weaponized.[23] Similarly, Iranian operations targeting the 2020 US presidential election were very much a whole of government approach – going right up to the supreme leader himself.

Russia seeks to seamlessly meld disinformation, subversion, offensive cyber operations and conventional military force.[24] This is not to exaggerate the success of Russia's approach, though. Putin is no chess grandmaster, deviously manoeuvring his pieces across a global board. Russia's intelligence agencies compete with each other; covert action is the outcome of bureaucratic infighting. They might take on dangerously risky operations simply to outdo each other; they might encroach on each other's turf; they might tell Putin what he wants to hear simply to curry favour. As one former Russian intelligence officer put it: 'You do not bring bad news to the tsar's table.'[25]

Covert action, especially today, is all about agile networks of intelligence officers, policymakers, and agents on the ground. Formal hierarchies are probably a relic of the Cold War. States require a comprehensive networked approach, deploying a variety of means, methods and actors nimbly but in a coordinated manner.[26]

To be successful, leaders must remember that propaganda, subversion and sabotage are simply one part of a broader strategy. Assassination of Iranian nuclear scientists, sabotage of its nuclear supply chains and cyberattacks against its infrastructure form just one strand of the US and Israeli campaign to prevent Iranian acquisition of nuclear weapons. At the same time, economic sanctions target Iran's oil exports, international trade and financial transactions. Its oil exports fell by more than half and the unemployment rate rose to 20 per cent. The question, as one scholar of non-proliferation aptly put it, is thus 'whether and how covert action can contribute to policy outcomes, not whether they achieve these outcomes alone'.[27] Looking at the success of covert action in isolation is meaningless and entirely misses the point.

The key lesson here is that covert action has inherent limitations. It can only achieve so much on its own and so must be properly integrated with more conventional measures. It softens up and prepares the ground for diplomatic manoeuvres or a military strike.

*

Covert action constitutes some of the most sensitive activity states undertake. Counterintuitively, though, nimble networks extend beyond single governments and, to complicate things further, often have an alliance dimension. It is therefore essential to consider not only coordination within government but across other states. Although normally ignored by historians writing about particular countries, the international dimension of covert action is crucial. So many of the examples discussed here involved multiple countries cooperating and competing, from 1980s Afghanistan to 2010s Syria. This is diplomacy at its most delicate and discreet; covert action as a perpetual ballet. At times, it even becomes transnational, shaped by the transfer of knowledge, people and ideas across borders.[28]

Working with allies brings tangible benefits. They might have better knowledge of the situation; closer proximity to the theatre; more money; or weaker oversight. The Americans were keen to work with the British on Afghanistan in the 1980s because of Britain's longer-standing expertise and agent networks in the country and because congressional scrutiny of the CIA was particularly tight post-Watergate. In the words of one CIA official involved in the programme, the UK took care of the 'how to kill people department'.[29] More recently, and as we have seen, the Netherlands played a key role in the Stuxnet operation by recruiting the agent who inserted the malware. It might seem random, but the US and Mossad worked with the Netherlands for a very good reason: the centrifuges used by the Iranians were based on designs stolen from a Dutch company back in the 1970s.[30]

More cynically, covert cooperation can increase plausible deniability by allowing another state to take the blame. We have seen how the Stasi worked in the shadows behind the larger KGB when spreading disinformation about AIDS in the 1980s. The British have a long track record here, particularly when working with and hiding behind the CIA. As early as 1953, the CIA knew full well that if the coup to remove the Iranian prime minister backfired, it would be the Americans who shouldered the blame. And they were right: today the coup is remembered predominantly as a CIA operation even though it was the British who set the ball rolling, frantically encouraged the Americans to come on board, and then provided much of the agent infrastructure on the ground. And it was not just the US. Three years later, MI6 worked with Iraq to overthrow the Syrian government in 1956. It went horribly wrong but, to British relief, the ill-fated operation became forever remembered as the Iraq Plot.

Cooperation is also important for political reasons. David Cameron supported covert action in Syria in part because he wanted to look tough to his US and Gulf allies – to look like he was doing something, *anything*, after parliament refused to sanction the use of military force against the Assad regime in 2013. It was not a one-way street; the Americans agreed to some unpopular covert actions in South Yemen in the 1970s, blowing up bridges and the like, to keep the Brits on board elsewhere.

Achieving cooperation is tricky; even states with supposed special relationships will only tell each other the minimum. Anglo-American cooperation in covert action has long been pragmatic at best. An ill-fated flirtation with formal partnership collapsed back in the 1960s because of too much distrust and too little intelligence sharing. At the same time, though, and at a more informal level, covert action was shaped by transatlantic networks of ideas and people, of friends and drinking buddies who had served together during the Second World War or who shared the same political viewpoints. Beneath the political level, much covert action is not necessarily transactional but transnational.[31]

Trust and alignment of interests are important, but achieving these, of course, is easier said than done. Spy chiefs around the world know that it is difficult to meet a partner's expectations while protecting your own methods and sources.[32] States also want to know how the covert cooperation will be used. They may be unwilling to share the location of, for example, a terrorist suspect if that intelligence would be used to illegally assassinate him or her.

As such, relationships can be schizophrenic, involving freely circulated ideas in one area but competition in another. It is unsurprising that covert action involving more than one state takes place bilaterally rather than through larger international organizations. NATO adopted a strategy to counter hybrid threats in 2015 and member states have been broadening their toolkit ever since, but much of this involves monitoring, exposing disinformation, improving cyber defence and building resilience. NATO acts as more of a hub of expertise, supporting individual states. Its members are reluctant to share political warfare capabilities or special forces with others because this sensitive information is effectively shared to the most open country's rules. NATO special operations and offensive cyber are therefore subcontracted to a single nation, making it difficult to disentangle member state activity from that of NATO, and intelligence from action. As ever, covert action is difficult to pin down.[33]

When wielding the hidden hand, it helps to look beyond national intelligence organizations and consider a more transnational approach. As political scientists would say, it helps to decentre the reified state. The CIA has long held a reputation, at least in the popular imagination, of being the mighty Wurlitzer of

Cold War covert action, playing the tune to which everyone else danced; of coordinating a unified anti-communist campaign. As we have seen, though, often the CIA was, and remains, one actor among many – and not just state intelligence agencies. Indeed, historians are increasingly realizing that, while the CIA was undeniably important, shadowy networks existed beyond the boundaries of governments. These range from fundamentalist religious groups to ideologically driven private actors. We still know very little about them.

The galaxy of covert action involves a constellation of actors, orbiting each other, gravitating towards each other – and occasionally colliding. The transnational World Anti-Communist League, for example, provided a direct channel to finance guerrillas in Cambodia, Laos, Vietnam, Angola, Mozambique and Afghanistan in the 1980s.[34] Meanwhile, Christian networks coordinated bible-smuggling rings, and, more formally, worked through transnational organizations such as the fundamentalist Protestant International Council of Christian Churches to counter communism.[35]

A particularly shadowy group was Le Cercle. Founded as a Franco-German endeavour back in the 1950s, it expanded to include representatives from Spain, Portugal, Switzerland, the UK, the US and, later, South Africa. It consisted of right-wingers, cold warriors and plenty of retired intelligence officers, meeting behind closed doors and putting the world to rights over cigar smoke and brandy fumes. In the late 1970s, members promoted a network to attack the Soviet Union and, the following decade, tried to facilitate the overthrow of socialist regimes worldwide. Le Cercle agitated against Namibian independence, supported rebels fighting the Mozambican government, and liaised with anti-Soviet guerrillas in the Angolan civil war.[36] None of this appears in the vast majority of history books. Le Cercle still exists today.

It may appear counterintuitive when thinking about such sensitive state activity, but it is important to recognize this transnational dimension. Leaders should think about the purpose and consequences of exposure to friendly audiences as much as to adversaries, should coordinate with government partners, should embrace and harness private networks as appropriate, all while avoiding too much dependence and setting realistic expectations. This forms part of the leader's calculation of balancing control, secrecy and impact.

Covert action works best when intelligence officers harness existing forces rather than trying to establish something from scratch. Even then, successful covert action requires more than a spark. Too many senior policymakers have unrealistically assumed a single spark would ignite a revolution or a coup. Success requires plenty of groundwork.[37]

When it comes to propaganda, exploiting *existing* schisms and polarizing *existing* debates is key. These might include issues of immigration, race, police violence and so-called wokeness. Propagandists then work through networks on the ground by using *existing* unwitting idiots to amplify narratives. Successful propaganda not only spreads confusion, but nudges audiences who already hold certain views to strengthen them further.[38] Sputnik, the Russian state-owned news agency, gives a platform to a wide and seemingly incoherent range of guests including conspiracy theorists, climate change deniers and anti-NATO/ EU activists. At first glance, it appears utterly confused but they all have something in common: they harden *pre-existing* anti-establishment attitudes.[39]

Likewise, it is far more effective to work through local forces when promoting rebellion using covert paramilitary action. Successful operations exploit grievances and support existing resistance movements. As we have seen, picking rebel groups to back is particularly difficult given that interests might only temporarily align and given ethical constraints against supporting violent non-state actors who might have committed human rights abuses. Still, doing so is essential. Dissidents groups created and trained by foreign intelligence services and then infiltrated into a country stand a far higher chance of being quickly wiped out by internal security forces. As we have seen, working with existing forces, whether in propaganda or paramilitary operations, requires outstanding intelligence. What are the fault-lines? Who are the idiots? Where are the rebels?

Success is more than achieving some foreign policy objective. States must get away with it. For liberal democracies, this means that reputations need to remain intact if and when the operation is exposed. Covert action should not be a dirty word. It is not an inherently bad thing but is a potentially important tool in a state's arsenal. It is, however, inherently sensitive. Therefore, and setting democracies apart from non-democracies, regardless of whether the target is disrupted, subverted or violently overthrown, to be truly successful, covert action must pass what is sometimes known as the *Washington Post* or *New York Times* test, as set out by William Webster.[40] Director of the CIA at the end of the Cold War, Webster had to navigate the changing international climate created by the demise of the Soviet threat which had dominated the American intelligence agenda for decades and had justified hundreds of covert actions.

For Webster, a successful covert action meets three criteria. First, it has to be legal and constitutional: authorized by the president in the interest of US national security and sanctioned through proper channels. Oversight is essential. If an elected president explicitly authorizes an operation and a handful of politicians scrutinize those decisions, then covert action can be compatible with liberal democracy. Plausible deniability, if it exists at all, must take place at the state level: in which the state as a whole seeks to deny involvement.

Things become more problematic and undemocratic if the president admits state involvement but claims that he knew nothing about it, instead blaming rogue actors and bad apples.[41] This was common in the US during the early Cold War, when the CIA would speak about assassination in vague euphemisms such as knocking off, removing and eliminating targets partly to ensure that the president would not get caught with his finger on the trigger. In the US, this presidential deniability became more difficult after reforms tightening up the approval process in the mid-1970s.

More difficult, but not perfect. When controversy about the Iran–Contra scandal belatedly hit, President Reagan dodged recrimination by exploiting the grey zone between visibility and secrecy; acknowledgement and non-acknowledgement; responsibility and innocence. He trotted out the go-to managerial line: 'It happened on my watch.' In doing so, he cleverly straddled that permeable border between public display and covert action. He managed to highlight his position as commander-in-chief while simultaneously being a passive spectator, distancing himself from those who actually engaged in the covert action.[42] This lithe linguistic wriggling is not compatible with democracy.

Other democracies were slower off the mark. In France, at the turn of the millennium, President Jacques Chirac preferred not to talk about covert actions, and even not to know about them, for fear of incriminating himself. According to a former director of French intelligence, Chirac wanted presidential deniability.[43] This was highly problematic. Oversight not only ensures compatibility with democracy, but it is also essential in identifying failures and improving performance. It is integral to success.

Second, according to Webster, to be successful covert action must align with US values. Secretly sponsoring fundamentalist terrorist groups to commit atrocities would clearly fall short here. Covert action can align with liberal democratic values when it is proportionate, properly authorized, and executed only in the face of a lack of viable authorities.[44] It might seek to protect democracy and rights abroad; indeed, the US has historically interfered covertly against other democracies, such as Iran and Chile, only when policymakers in Washington believed those democracies to be in decline.[45] Others have argued that it can be ethical to subvert a democracy's elections 'as a means to thwart citizens from voting for grievously unjust policies', so long as it is a proportionate response.[46] US interference in the Serbian election of 2000 to remove the genocidal war criminal Slobodan Milošević from power offers a case in point.

Third, covert action must be sufficiently popular so that if exposed it would not cause so much political controversy that any achievements would be wiped out by domestic criticism. To ensure this, covert action must form part of a broader acknowledged foreign policy. It is a means of executing policy, whether that is countering terrorism or containing a dictator, which should have public support. The dramatic killing of Osama bin Laden formed part of a wider open policy; so too did, say, French paramilitary activity in post-Gaddafi Libya or British sabotage of ISIS communications. Covert action must also be subject to well-informed public debate in order to ensure what one recent report called 'political licence to operate'. This requires more openness about capabilities and the circumstances under which states deploy the hidden hand.[47]

In short, if a covert action appeared on the front page of the *Washington Post* tomorrow, would the president be able to look the people in the eye and defend it? This test is all the more important in the twenty-first century given the likely exposure of covert operations if not tomorrow then sometime soon.

The UK talks a good game when it comes to being a so-called responsible cyber power. It is committed to operating legally, ethically and responsibly. When newspapers broke the story about recent cyberattacks against COVID disinformation, a source told *The Times* that GCHQ only had authorization to go after hostile states when disrupting anti-vaccine propaganda. It could not sabotage cranks and conspiracy theorists: 'People have a right to say batshit stuff online.'[48] The British government deliberately frames such activity as counterattack, and the GCHQ director pointed out in late 2020, when the National Cyber Force emerged from the shadows, that it operates 'in a legal, ethical and proportionate way to help defend the nation and counter the full range of national security threats'. The foreign secretary unsurprisingly described it as a 'world leading force for good'.[49]

These operations certainly passed the Webster test. Most people shrugged and thought 'good'. There is a problem, though. Covert action – especially when conducted online – has unpredictable effects. In our interconnected world, a proportionate and just operation directed against a foreign target could find its way back into our own media ecosystem and deceive our own citizens. The Americans judge each operation on intent and so would argue that it did not intend to influence domestic targets but even rumours of disinformation can undermine trust in, and the legitimacy of, democratic institutions. Given this unpredictability and the lasting effects, it is difficult to measure the ethical criteria of proportionality etc., let alone to ensure they are met.[50]

Alternatively, the covert action might interfere with operations run by other agencies and even other countries. How do we know the target of an online covert action is not actually an alias being used by French or US intelligence? If US Cyber Command has greater freedom of action to launch offensive operations, what prevents it from unwittingly attacking a target which US intelligence is simultaneously monitoring? Other agencies may be occupying the same space, leading to a waste of time and resources – or worse.

No blueprint for covert action success exists. Activities are too varied, ranging from propaganda to assassination, and too dependent on individual circumstances. Claims of success and failure are far too subjective in the first place and often wielded as a political weapon.

That said, it is possible to distil some broad insights from history about what works and what does not. Presidents and prime ministers need to know what they are talking about in the first place, have clear objectives which align with the resources, and then calibrate secrecy accordingly. This includes thinking carefully about the level of cooperation with allies and even transnational networks. They should weigh up the relationship between secrecy, impact and control. Be under no illusions: an increase in one is a decrease in the others. Covert action should be a national asset, drawing nimbly on a variety of instruments, to support broader foreign policy. It works best when sponsoring existing rebels or polarizing existing grievances, rather than trying to establish something from scratch. It must be justifiable to the public, proportionate and with proper oversight. This is what marks democratic states out from the others. Whether subverting, disrupting, cyberattacking or staging a coup, covert actioneers should bear these principles in mind.

All these things will only take leaders so far. The secrecy, myths and sheer difficulty in pinning down covert action complicate confident assertions of success. Narratives, stories and perceptions become crucial in wielding – and defending against – the hidden hand.

CONCLUSION:
DEFENCE AGAINST THE DARK ARTS

I n spring 2021, three months after taking office, President Biden published a trove of material exposing malicious Russian intelligence activities. These declassified documents, rich in detail, named and shamed individual front companies, news agencies and IT firms which the US government accused of supporting Russian intelligence. The FBI even created a wanted poster for one political consultant suspected of interfering in the 2016 and 2020 elections.[1] At roughly the same time, 4,000 miles across the Atlantic, the Czech government went public with details of how a Russian military intelligence unit had blown up an arms warehouse seven years earlier. Meanwhile, the Netherlands declared public exposure to be a cornerstone of its defence against cyberattacks.

Many western countries are calling out plots with ever more verve and vigour. Many, but not all: France is an exception. Its leaders are not as keen on exposure as the US and other NATO allies, instead preferring forthright conversations behind closed doors or, as one commentator put it, preferring 'red phones over the megaphone'.[2]

There are many ways states can defend against covert action. Unfortunately, none are quick or easy. Options span the life cycle of an operation, from deterring or preventing the adversary in the first place, through detecting and disrupting covert actions, through to longer-term attempts to build societal resilience and educate publics.

States might try deterrence by denial, using attacks of its own to make the target's covert action infeasible. This might involve launching cyberattacks on troll farms or on the communications networks of intelligence agencies sponsoring terrorists. They can degrade and disrupt hostile operations at source. Alternatively, or in addition, states might try deterrence by punishing the target using sanctions, expulsions or prosecution. Implementing such visibly tough responses requires some sort of exposure to justify them. States need to go public with evidence of meddling and manipulation to validate diplomatic expulsions, sanctions or whatever they deem an appropriate public punishment. Biden's dramatic exposé of subversion coincided with new and tougher sanctions targeting Russia. The US expelled ten Russians from the embassy in Washington, D.C., including representatives of the intelligence services, in a classic move reminiscent of Cold War spy games.[3] Expulsion may resemble tit-for-tat political point scoring, but it can make a difference in blunting intelligence activity. The Soviets struggled to recover after the UK famously expelled 105 intelligence officers in 1971.

Exposure is not enough. It may form the linchpin of states' defences against hostile covert action, but, alone, it will not work. Shining a light on Russian disinformation, for example, will not offer a quick fix. Exposure is not a switch. States cannot simply decide to reveal something and then expect people to sit up and take note. Even when it comes to exposing serious domestic issues – from US involvement in torture post-9/11 to the Edward Snowden leaks about mass surveillance – simply releasing information into the ether does not guarantee scandal or public response. It is often inconsequential – or even counterproductive.[4]

Revelation needs to follow: a collective recognition that something has happened.[5] This is all the more important given that many covert actions are already exposed; they are hidden in plain sight and owe their invisibility not to secrecy but to political amnesia, selective blindness or wilful ignorance.[6] Disclosure therefore needs to be accompanied by some sort of sustained response from influential actors, such as frontbench politicians, or sustained interest by widely read newspapers.[7] We have to sit up and take notice.

Too often when it comes to Russian covert action, passive publics either shrug or, worse still, shake their heads in resignation and say something along the lines of 'well, everybody lies. I just don't know who to believe anymore.' Or they play the whataboutism card. Everyone is as bad as each other; the US hardly has clean hands itself. Yet this is the exact goal of foreign subversion: to undermine trust in truth and authority.

Exposing individual operations or even individual pieces of propaganda is akin to the fable about the frog slowly being boiled alive. On their own they might appear inconsequential; individual actions do not seem to cross a red line and so draw little reaction. Strikingly, a CNN poll in December 2018 found 40 per cent of Americans did not consider Russia's interference in the US election 'a serious matter that should be fully investigated'.[8] Together, though, such activities can be highly damaging. Exposure may not lead to revelation until it is too late to jump out of the boiling water.

In today's politically charged and post-truth world, publishing incriminating cables or taking a photograph of some paramilitary activity – whether Russian operatives in Crimea or American ones in Syria – will not necessarily have the expected impact. Pictures circulating on social media are more than a pure and unmediated record of events. They function as performances themselves, attempting to break free from the ocean of other images also circulating online. Their impact depends on the viewer's perspective and how the picture relates to his or her understanding of the surrounding politics.[9]

Western leaders' reliance on a modernist assumption that truth can be exposed and speak for itself is flawed. Clinging to this outdated idea will not defend against today's covert action when the adversary will just strike back with denials, obfuscation and a blitz of other narratives. Russia screams Russophobia; Iran accuses the west of deploying a false flag, softening up international opinion in advance of an attack on the country. Those disclosing covert actions must recognize the complexity of how images circulate. In a different context, local activists moved away from using images to highlight President Assad's brutality in the Syrian conflict, instead turning towards text, photoshopped memes and dark humour.[10] Factchecking is not enough; it must cut through.

Even if exposure does gain traction, it still brings risks. Publicizing the hostile activity of others might unwittingly reveal your own secret sources and methods. The intelligence services of the target state will wonder how you found out and then change their codes and toughen up internal security accordingly.[11]

This is a dilemma today when publicizing cyberattacks or publicly preempting Russian covert operations, but it is nothing new: public use of secret information has been a thorny area for centuries. The howls of cryptographers undone by an excitable and loose-lipped monarch haunt the pages of many a history book. Way back in the seventeenth century, English intelligence uncovered a secret French attempt to draw England into a war with Poland. King William III gleefully disclosed the subversion in an attempt to publicly embarrass his French counterpart. Predictably, the French changed their codes, and, at a stroke, the jobs of British cryptographers became much more difficult.

How leaders publicly use intelligence creates a second risk beyond sources and methods. In late 2020, nine senior American military commanders urgently pleaded for more material on hostile Russian and Chinese operations to be declassified. Extending beyond influence activity, the generals wanted to share satellite intelligence revealing adversaries' bad behaviour. Excessive secrecy, they argued, was holding them back in their efforts to bolster support from US allies, encourage more partners to come forward with evidence of their own, and, ultimately, win in the grey zone without having to fire shots.[12]

This was risky because the generals wanted the material for ammunition. They effectively sought to weaponize selectively edited bits of intelligence to influence foreign audiences – and inevitably the US public too. This brings a real danger of cherry-picking the more alarming material to justify a more confrontational stance. Declassifying selective intelligence to bolster a preconceived policy is fraught with problems.[13]

Exposure can backfire. It might increase tensions, especially given the foggy lines between defensive and offensive covert activity, confusion around intent, and unintended consequences. Going public and wrongly claiming that a cyberespionage operation constitutes an attack could be highly problematic. And sometimes these revelations have broader international audiences beyond the target state. Some have argued that Iran ramped up its own online disinformation activities because of widespread attention to Russian operations.[14]

It might provoke the adversary into doubling down on its covert action. If disinformation or funding rebels becomes public knowledge, the motivation for secrecy vanishes. States have less to lose and so might as well resolutely crack on; they will suffer the criticism anyway.[15]

It is a gamble. As the Arab Spring failed to live up to early expectations, it soon became common knowledge that Iran was secretly sending arms shipments to bolster President Assad's forces, in contravention of a weapons export ban, and was backing Shia militants on the ground. The US State Department publicly condemned this covert action and the United Nations published a report. Unfortunately, this merely caused the Iranians to double down. Shortly afterwards, Iran sent more of its own troops to Syria and stepped up its efforts coordinating fighters. Persistent reporting of Iran's covert action only led to Iran becoming more defiant.[16]

These risks undermine a core aspect of states' defence against foreign subversion. Leaders must calibrate their exposure carefully. A significant covert attack might warrant an authoritative public condemnation, whereas less serious threats might warrant something more discreet. As a US practitioner recently recommended, the state might reveal multiple operations at once, and so diffuse the attention given to each individual one, or focus exposure on the actor rather than the narrative.[17]

Alternatively, leaders might discreetly reveal a covert action through briefing private industry or through diplomatic channels back to the sponsoring government. The former would have the added benefit of increasing private sector and academic analysis of the operation, while also warning those who are at risk of being targeted. Sometimes exposure is best coming from government and sometimes best from private industry; both have benefits and drawbacks. Governments give credibility – unless the covert action is politically charged or evidence unforthcoming, in which case governments can look too partisan. The private sector is more discreet and independent, but less reliable.[18]

Leaders should treat exposure as a complex process, laden with trade-offs. Although intelligence services may well know who was behind a particular covert action, the actual process of public attribution is highly complex and involves all sorts of dilemmas. Whether or not it is the best option depends on what leaders want to achieve: are they disclosing to make a point about acceptable and unacceptable behaviour? Or to deter the target? Or to compel the target to change its behaviour? Is exposure intended to disrupt the adversary by tying down their intelligence services in costly leak investigations? Or is it designed to encourage allies to improve their defences?[19] Is it designed to justify punishment? When the US National Security Agency exposed a malicious Russian cyber espionage campaign called Brute Force in summer 2021, it explicitly stated that the aim was 'to warn network defenders of nation state threats'.[20] But this might not always be the case. Leaders should therefore use this tool thoughtfully, appropriately and in a tailored manner. It is the flipside of carefully calibrating secrecy when launching covert actions of their own.

One of the biggest challenges for defenders is charting a difficult course between the Scylla of downplaying covert action and the Charybdis of overplaying it.

In autumn 2020, the outgoing chief of MI6, Alex Younger, gave a rare interview in which he warned against 'bigging up' Russian successes. The head of MI5, Ken McCallum, agrees that doing so simply does their dirty work for them. Hype can turn inconsequential second-rate operations into virulent successes.[21]

When the aim of propaganda and political action is to spread confusion and undermine trust in democracy, then success counterintuitively thrives on the oxygen of publicity. Discussion of the Russian hidden hand in the United States has perhaps undermined trust in US democracy more than the operations themselves could ever have hoped to achieve and puts governments in the difficult defensive position of constantly having to disprove lies and insinuations or prove the negative.[22] Exposure can make the adversary look more powerful than it actually is, transforming Putin into some sort of darkly omnipotent genius rather than a huckster peddling confidence tricks. So often it works simply because we think it works; believing in success is to affirm success.

If the US interprets recent Russian espionage as successful influence activity, then that is exactly what it becomes. If the US interprets it as an act of war, then, worryingly, that is what it becomes. How politicians and pundits discuss covert action is crucial in determining success or failure. Interpreting the covert action can be as significant as the covert action itself.

When publicly discussing covert action, states should emphasize its weaknesses and failings; they should publicize its impotence. Unfortunately, this is easier said than done. Both sides – Russians and Americans – have incentives to collude in the idea of impact and success. For many Americans, Russian meddling provides a convenient explanation as to why such an ill-qualified, unsuitable and unstable candidate won the 2016 presidential election. The formidable potency of foreign subversion creates a useful scapegoat to mask internal policy failures and an angrily polarized society. US politicians replace their own domestic failures with external bogeymen.[23]

Moreover, bigging up Russia delegitimizes domestic voices and bottom-up concerns, diminishing the agency of the audience.[24] Suddenly, organic protests around, say, Black Lives Matter can be dismissed as foreign-sponsored subversion. This then causes further societal division: a vicious cycle.

For many Russians, on the other side, covert operations provide a comforting sense of power and prestige. Putin gets to look tough domestically and cultivate an impression of influence, pushing back against the US and punishing Washington's encroachment on Russian interests. They will naturally assume that their operations made a difference. No proof is needed and to think otherwise is to admit impotence.

This unspoken collusion in the comfort blanket of potency is far from a new phenomenon.[25] It goes back over three quarters of a century. The CIA's intervention in the 1948 Italian election to keep the communists out was a famous success. However, even CIA historians with full access to classified records still argue about whether the meddling actually made the crucial difference – or whether the communists would have lost regardless. In some senses, though, this does not matter: 'In Washington's collective imagination, the CIA had rescued Italy's democracy.' As the historian David Shimer notes, 'No proof was needed. America's preferred party had won.'[26] Importantly, even the targets were happy to collude in that story of potency. CIA success created a convenient scapegoat allowing the Italian left to explain away successive election defeats and, in the words of another historian, has 'played a prominent role in left-wing attempts to construct identities of resistance and narratives of national independence'.[27]

Five years later, the CIA successfully removed Prime Minister Mossadeq from power in the 1953 Iranian coup. Plenty of Iranians, from Muslim fundamentalists to secular nationalists who vehemently disagree over most things, found themselves united on the dark omnipotence of American influence.[28]

This remains the case today: successful sabotage of Iranian nuclear proliferation allows the US to appear powerful and able to shape events; the Iranians get to blame the US and Israel for a dysfunctional nuclear programme and continue the national psyche of having long suffered at the hands of manipulative foreign interventions. It can create a rally-round-the-flag effect.

Most famously of all, the CIA successfully overthrew the Guatemalan leader Jacobo Árbenz in a 1954 paramilitary coup. Success here was especially mythologized given that in reality the operation was flailing. 'Just as the entire operation seemed beyond saving,' the official history admits, 'the Guatemalan Government suddenly, inexplicably collapsed. The Agency never found out why.' Crucially, CIA officers replaced these failings with the legend that Árbenz 'lost his nerve' thanks to American covert action falsely amplifying the power of the advancing rebel army.[29] For Árbenz, mere knowledge of US involvement – however ineffective – was a critical factor persuading him to give in.[30]

For many in the CIA and beyond, Guatemala nurtured a sense of ease and complacency. Senior policymakers and intelligence officers were enormously pleased and revived its techniques during subsequent missions in Brazil, Bolivia, Chile and elsewhere.[31] The American role in the Guatemalan coup therefore became a success not simply because it definitively succeeded in overthrowing the regime, but because enough people – on both sides – bought into the CIA story.

Experience of charting this difficult path between recognizing but not overplaying covert action teaches us two things about defending against subversion today. First, do not breathe excessive oxygen into the adversary's activity. Doing so may give life to otherwise dead operations, allowing them to rise up like zombies. Second, when exposing or even merely discussing covert action do not overplay success; do not allow external subversion to become a scapegoat of internal divisions. Both lessons essentially involve mature and sober management of the narrative. At the same time, it also teaches us not to misread the past when justifying or proposing covert actions of our own.

All of this raises a rather postmodern problem. How do we really know this shadowy strand of international politics? Has the CIA's reputation been shaped by Soviet propaganda and forgeries over the years? Has the UK's reputation been shaped by Bond myths? Covert action is a battle to influence audiences – but afterwards it becomes a battle for the narrative about the covert action itself. Winning in the grey zone requires perceived success on both levels: influencing audiences to shape developments and then influencing wider audiences that this was successful; or, conversely, convincing wider audiences that your adversary failed. Covert action is what states make of it.

If those wanting to wield the hidden hand must learn to cooperate with others, then those seeking to defend must do the same. This time, though, states must work with altogether more powerful and, in many ways, shadier actors: the big technology companies. This is essential given that so much subversion is channelled through social media platforms. These companies have an important role in detecting influence operations and making life difficult for those behind them.

Between 2017 and the summer of 2021, Facebook took down 150 covert influence campaigns originating from fifty different countries. These ranged from Azerbaijani attempts to manipulate their own citizens to Egyptian operations targeting audiences in Somalia, Yemen and Tunisia. The largest was an Indonesian campaign involving a whopping 800 Facebook accounts, 546 Facebook pages and 208 Instagram accounts.[32]

Facebook now claims to find and block millions of fake accounts every single day, many within minutes of being created. It tries to make life more difficult for those misusing its site by, for example, tightening the rules about who can run political adverts. Alongside other social media giants, it works with academics and organizations specializing in countering online influence operations to de-platform, ban links and generally degrade hostile actors. This can disrupt covert action and, if conducted early enough, can even prevent it in the first place.[33] Social media companies, like governments, think that exposure will raise costs and gradually change behaviour.[34]

In August 2021, Twitter belatedly formed a partnership with Reuters to factcheck claims on its platform, while both Twitter and Facebook label content as government sponsored or disputed. The success of this remains to be seen. Many users do not seem too bothered about being told something is misleading or linked to a foreign government. Take attempts to label pro-Trump material as such. Supporters simply shrugged and assumed Facebook and Twitter were part of a conspiracy to elect Joe Biden.

A post by Reuters as part of its factchecking service offers just one example among thousands. As Kabul fell in August 2021, Reuters factchecked a doctored photo that had gone viral: 'A photo of three women walking in chains has been described online as showing Afghanistan in 2021. However, the original image was captured in Iraq in 2003 – and it has been digitally altered to add chains.'[35] Unfortunately, users were not grateful to Twitter for exposing the inaccuracy. Indignant responses included: 'Why are you supporting the Taliban, Reuters?' 'You worry about the photo being correct?... American civilians were left behind.' 'The chains were metaphors. With or without physical chains women are still enslaved by religious men.' And so it went on.

Both companies purge fake accounts, while Facebook additionally publishes pieces debunking disinformation. Neither, however, want to take on the role of arbiter of truth. Meanwhile, search engines Google and Bing promote genuine content and try to downgrade misleading pages on their search results.[36]

We also need to remember that Facebook and Twitter, while huge, are not the only social media platforms. Successful defence must not ignore the smaller companies. Platforms like 4chan and Reddit, as we have seen, can serve as testing grounds for bigger operations or even host campaigns outright while lacking the resources or political will to counter subversion. The same goes for local platforms outside the US and Europe; in Taiwan, for example, a bulletin-board forum called PTT is a key vector for Chinese activity.

Governments must harness industry, but without delegating the fight.[37] Cooperation with private companies is essential to make life that bit harder for those weaponizing social media. States should leverage this power but not outsource responsibility or rely too much on private companies. Critics accuse Facebook and Twitter of doing too little too late and, after all, we should remember that these are businesses trying to boost user confidence to boost profits – not to protect liberal democracy.[38] They are beholden to shareholders first and foremost.

Defence is about raising costs. This might be through exposing operations, through working with Silicon Valley to make life difficult for hostile actors, or by threatening a counterattack of one's own. The hope is that this will make targets think twice before launching covert actions. But what does deterring covert action and raising costs actually mean?

Some experts describe it as nothing more than a weak slogan repeated as mantra by successive political leaders for over half a decade. 'It purveys purpose and authority, without saying anything in detail,' according to Ciaran Martin, former head of cyber security at GCHQ. Imposing costs means whatever the state wants it to mean and simply forms another part of the battle for narratives. Impose costs, claim success. Thanks to secrecy, the government has not even got to prove it responded at all – let alone prove that it made any material difference. It can hint that it is using some mythologized covert capabilities and leave it at that.[39]

The British government provided an excellent example of this bluster in July 2021. James Cleverly, a foreign minister, updated parliament on the UK's response to Chinese and Russian cyberattacks: 'I am not necessarily going to go into details here and now about what further measures we might take, because to do so might undermine their effectiveness… the Chinese Government should expect to be held to account if they do not come back into compliance with norms of behaviour.'[40] Just days later, the British were at it again, this time figuring out how to respond to Iranian sabotage which killed a British security guard on board an oil tanker in the Gulf. An anonymous source briefed *The Sun* that the UK was mulling a retaliatory cyberattack against Iran, which would have serious consequences but which nobody back home would see.[41] Both threats were characteristically illusory and vague.

Perhaps the threats about raised costs are empty rhetoric because the UK and the US are risk-averse societies. Risk aversion makes it difficult to impose meaningful costs in response to covert action. Obama's sanctions supremo admitted the response to Russian interference in the 2016 election was inadequate. Former Director of National Intelligence James Clapper thought it incommensurate with the threat. Another official accused the US of choking.[42] Since Biden was elected in 2020, his administration has issued a litany of puffed-up verbal threats to Russia about imposing consequences. These may or may not be combined with some retaliatory covert action. But still the Russian cyber intrusions and attacks come thick and fast. Warnings and threats are not working.[43] Western states hope the cumulative effect of their own cyberattacks will gradually shape adversaries' behaviour, but it is too soon to tell if this is happening.

In the meantime, instead of blustering about raising costs and generating consequences through sabotage of their own (but you will have to trust us because it is secret); instead of crying war when a covert action – or more likely espionage – is uncovered; and instead of hypocritically condemning the outrageousness of something the US also does (the main difference being restraint and responsibility rather than anything technical), western leaders might try to develop more precise global norms as part of their defence against covert action. These include, as various experts have recently suggested, properly testing tools before using them, avoiding indiscriminate targeting, constraining automation so as to ensure operations remain controllable, preventing criminals from using their access points into systems, and ensuring proper oversight.[44]

At the same time, changing acceptable behaviour can only go so far because the existing legal framework, so central to states' responses, is not fit for purpose. Built around war and peace, not the grey zone in between, existing international law does not sufficiently recognize covert action as deserving of strong punishment. Legal ambiguities paralyse responses, as western leaders struggle to interpret the law. When the US considered using cyber operations to punish North Korea for the Sony Pictures hack, its lawyers, according to the director of national intelligence, 'went nuts'. States might therefore think not only about reforming laws and standards of behaviour, but also about how best to punish hostile actions.[45] Counterattacks form one part of a state's defence. They can disrupt, but we should not expect too much from them on their own.

The best defence is preventative and longer-term: for states to sort out their own internal divisions. This would deny adversaries the ripe and exploitable grievances necessary for successful covert action. Division and inequality create a breeding ground for foreign subversion, exacerbated by culture wars and toxic public discourse. The inability to have a thoughtful and nuanced debate about, say, Brexit or mask wearing during the COVID-19 pandemic in the UK or so-called Critical Race Theory in the US can end up having national security consequences. Whipping up of phoney division to score cheap political points does not square with the British government's countersubversion strategy.

As one distinguished former CIA officer, Ray Cline, put it, the most that can be expected from covert action is to give events a nudge in a particular direction – not determine outcomes. Russia seems to have learnt that lesson well. The Kremlin specifically conducts 'nudge propaganda' designed to strengthen the target's pre-existing grievances.[46] Addressing these grievances – and the way they are polemicized – is not only a matter of economic, public health or education policy but it protects against hostile adversaries. It protects sovereignty: hidden hands exploit and polarize existing tensions. The best defence starts at home.

At the same time, citizens need to be able to spot disinformation and critically engage with sources, recognizing bias and clickbait. Attacks on the arts and humanities by the UK government, alongside the wider culture war in which they are subsumed, could again end up having national security consequences. Media literacy education is vital in enabling young people to spot fake news;[47] yet media studies is perhaps the most maligned and ridiculed of all academic disciplines: the archetypal Mickey Mouse degree.

Importantly, though, academics must be careful of espousing incipient relativism among their students. The idea that there is no such thing as truth and that every perspective, every personalized truth, is valid can be easily bastardized and misappropriated; it is also a caricature. We need to be sceptical but neither cynical nor universally pessimistic, otherwise we play into propagandists' hands.[48] Cynicism breeds conspiracism. We therefore need not adopt an anything goes approach to truth, but should examine how particular ideas take hold as common-sense facts. This intellectual inquiry can help defend against covert action, in particular disinformation.[49]

A whole of government approach, even a whole of society approach, is necessary to enhance resilience against all forms of covert action. Some see wider societal resilience as part of modern deterrence, for situations in which threats of military punishment are inappropriate.[50] We all need to take cyber security more seriously. Electoral funding laws need to be tightened to prevent opaque money from reaching political parties. Loopholes protecting agents secretly working for foreign governments need to be shut down. Governments could brief industry far more regularly on the threat of covert action and political warfare, just as they do about the threat of terrorism and kidnapping. Nordic countries are ahead of the curve in trying to bolster societal resilience to state aggression, bringing together the private sector, government and citizens. Denmark emphasizes collaboration between civil society, universities, think tanks and businesses. Baltic countries are following suit.[51] According to a recent Canadian government report, 'We all have a role to play in protecting Canada's security.'[52]

If a whole of government approach is essential, it is unfortunate that the US response has so far been incoherent and uncoordinated. It is not even clear who is responsible for combating foreign disinformation on social media, and how they measure their effectiveness beyond trumpeting the number of initiatives under way.[53] The US, the UK and other long-established democracies of the west would do well to ditch the hubris and humbly learn the lessons of others who have been dealing with Russian subversion for a decade or more. While the US and the UK want a quick fix, states in central and eastern Europe have been playing a longer game – one that is still ongoing.

Russia has been targeting these countries for years. Georgia, for example, learnt the hard way that subversion does not simply take place online and it is wrong to obsess over cyber to the detriment of everything else. Its leaders were slow to recognize and counter the spread of influence through religious and cultural organizations such as the Orthodox Church. The Church peddled pro-Russian and anti-Europe narratives, opposing government attempts to integrate more closely with the west. Across the Black Sea, Ukraine learnt the hard way that successful defence requires more than good public relations. Besides, government narratives and persistent factchecking often fail to correct disinformation – worse, they can cause audiences to double down.[54]

Polish experience shows that when governments spread their own fearmongering and conspiracy theories for short-term gain, it leads to longer-term polarization and decline in trust. This can then be exploited by adversaries. Conspiracy theories flourished further still in Poland after the ruling party decimated, and imposed editorial control over, the public broadcaster.[55] The UK Conservative Party would do well to watch and learn, especially after recent research suggested it spread disinformation with impunity during the 2019 general election. At one point, it misleadingly renamed its Twitter feed @FactCheckUK during a leaders' debate. Indeed, 88 per cent of the party's most shared online adverts in the penultimate week of campaigning contained suspect information.[56] Its itching to dismantle the BBC is similarly worrisome given Poland's experience. For a government obsessed with protecting British sovereignty, to a frankly delusional degree, it seems bizarre that in every attempt to stoke culture wars and division, the UK government is effectively inviting foreign interference.

To the north, Sweden has created its own Psychological Defence Agency. It seeks to identify and prevent influence operations targeting Swedish interests at home and abroad, including attempts to both undermine Swedish resilience and manipulate people's behaviour. Consisting of around forty-five members of staff, it offers longer-term capacity building alongside more operational analysis.

Neighbouring Finland has developed a particularly impressive reputation in building resilience to propaganda. Unsurprisingly, this is largely because few countries can match Finland's long experience of defending against Soviet and Russian subversion. It can teach us that government and civil society need to offer pre-emptive and well-coordinated responses to prevent disinformation from gaining traction and going viral. It is important to fight back and call out lies before they fester. This will not change the liar's mind, but it might influence the audience.[57] Likewise, offering a coherent and compelling narrative is more effective than simply refuting false claims. It is vital to encourage civic media literacy and critical engagement with new media platforms. This is long-term and generational: the Finnish Ministry for Education and Culture is promoting children's media skills. Finns trust their media, in part because it is less heavily partisan compared to other countries.[58]

It is important not to be too universalist here. Countering disinformation, for example, depends on the media ecosystem of the specific country, on the sociopolitical and socio-economic models of news consumption. The cases cited above come from the global north, and we cannot make sense of fake news in sub-Saharan Africa, for example, without understanding the production and consumption of news in that region. At the same time, though, we must not dismiss the global south as inherently different or alternative, but should learn from other countries, to work together, to widen our reference points and examine multiple experiences.[59]

It is safe to say that defending against covert action is a lengthy and difficult process. Three things are essential. First, exposure must be done thoughtfully, in line with objectives, and in full consideration of the trade-offs. It is not enough on its own. Likewise, rampant factchecking, flatly denying falsehoods and tagging social media content as government sponsored or misleading is unlikely to cut through and make an impact in a world in which people cling to their personal truths and alternative facts.

Second, states should manage the narrative carefully. Empty slogans around raising costs are unhelpful. Subversion is very real and needs to be taken seriously but without breathing new life into operations by giving them excessive airtime, and without blindly assuming success or ascribing too much power to external actors. Hidden hands must not be allowed to become a scapegoat to cover internal problems and divisions. At the same time, states must heal those internal divisions and soothe toxic polarized discourse, for they serve as a Petri dish for an adversary's covert action. We have seen how various forms of covert action have a better success rate against democracies. It is vital to strike an effective balance, in which democratic freedoms and values cannot be exploited to do us harm, while at the same time protecting those very same freedoms and values. This dilemma is not easy to resolve.[60]

Third, and addressing the dilemma, defence requires a proactive and well-coordinated response bringing together multiple governments, public broadcasting, industry, civil society and universities. It should involve attempts to disrupt the adversary at every stage in the covert action life cycle. Education, especially in fields which British ministers myopically deem 'dead end', is vital; so too are operations of our own. Covert action is what states make of it; in an age of populism, pettiness and enemies of the people, we have ourselves to blame when adversaries penetrate our sovereignty.

EPILOGUE

Sabotage, subversion and secret statecraft are as old as states themselves. From classical Greece to the Cold War, history is crammed with unacknowledged interventions staged by hidden hands. The present, or whatever we end up calling our post-War on Terror era, is the same: packed full of propaganda and proxies. The future will follow suit. Suggestions that covert action peaked in the Cold War are wrong, as are claims that the decline of state secrecy will bring about the demise of secret statecraft.

The next decades will witness more, not fewer, covert actions. As hidden hands become less hidden, these covert actions will rely on confusion, disruption, ambiguity and cynicism; they will reflect our age of formlessness. This prediction might seem odd, though, because secrecy is dwindling. Intelligence officers and special forces need more than a fake passport to operate undercover in our digital era. Biometric data such as fingerprint scanners and facial recognition pose a potentially existential threat to the arts of human intelligence. Crossing borders and checking into hotels undercover is now incredibly difficult.[1] And that is to say nothing of the wider digital dust we all scatter across the internet as part of our daily existence.

Meanwhile, the remarkable rise of special forces after 9/11 makes deniability more difficult still. There are just so many of them: by late 2020, US special forces consisted of around twenty thousand personnel. They even have their own university.[2] As operations become noisier and surveillance easier, more people are listening and tracking. Affordable real-time coverage provided by global internet access allows citizens to communicate and collect evidence. It allows them to compromise plausible deniability. Suddenly, anyone with a mobile phone is a citizen journalist. Locals on the ground in places like Libya and Syria were taking photos of suspicious foreigners operating alongside rebel fighters and uploading them online for others to pore over in real time.

Access to commercial mapping and space imagery systems undercuts plausible deniability further. Groups like Bellingcat, the open-source forensic investigative journalists, use unclassified information very skilfully to undermine Russian secrecy. They are able to expose activity which western intelligence services cannot. It was Bellingcat that uncovered the scale of Russian activity in eastern Ukraine; the Russian shooting down of a civilian plane over Ukraine; and the Russian attempted murders of dissident Sergei Skripal and opposition leader Alexey Navalny. And it was Bellingcat that offered evidence of Syrian chemical weapons attacks during the civil war. Their skills and efforts, combing dark corners of the internet, make secrecy much more difficult to achieve. Governments, of course, do the same. The UK Foreign Office has an open-source unit, described by Alan Duncan, a former Conservative foreign minister, as 'a team of enthusiastic young techies' who had 'identified no end of interference by states in other states, and of course us'.[3]

Secrecy is challenged further still by a globalized civil society, bringing increased contact between armies of investigative journalists, human rights lawyers and whistle-blowers. With so many state employees and private contractors having security clearance, it is easier than ever before to steal and leak vast amounts of classified material. Tens of thousands of documents can fit on a small USB stick, as Edward Snowden notably demonstrated back in 2013. He was just one of an eye-watering 1.4 million Americans with top-secret clearance.[4] As of 2019, 4.2 million Americans – or about 3 per cent of the workforce – were eligible to access classified information.

This erosion of secrecy creates a puzzle: why is covert action still thriving, and why is it likely to do so into the future? Three recent trends offer an answer but also indicate that covert action will become more confusing and more divisive. Authoritarian regimes will use it to undermine trust in democratic authority, even in truth itself. For democracies, it will confuse, disrupt and divide its targets.

Reports of the death of human espionage are premature. People have been talking about the death of secrecy for decades,[5] but, as we have seen, plenty of covert action has taken place regardless. Intelligence agencies are adapting to manage the rise of electronic and biometric surveillance. This might involve reverting to old-fashioned, lower tech, methods to avoid detection, like the classic Cold War-style brush past, in which spies exchanged information quickly and discreetly. It might involve meeting operatives and agents in third countries with less sophisticated biometric systems. It might involve hiding in plain sight.[6]

The CIA has apparently tried recruiting foreign nationals to work almost as subcontracted intelligence officers in uncompromising countries where it is difficult to send undercover Americans. These men and women have even received some clandestine training. Elsewhere, the CIA has reportedly recruited people already working for a particular company and, with the permission of a select few company executives, transferred them onto the CIA payroll. It looks to all outsiders as if they still work for that company, rather than the CIA. Alternatively, some CIA officers live out their cover, and actually work as the engineer or businesswoman they pretend to be, even living under their real names.[7]

For those operatives needing fake personas, a lot of work goes on behind the scenes as intelligence agencies plough millions into generating electronic cover stories. Clever people are developing hi-tech gadgetry designed to evade detection at border control, including ultra-realistic fingerprint sleeves and methods of compromising foreign biometrics databases. It is possible to make it look like someone's mobile phone is in a different location. And, of course, the internet creates new possibilities to recruit and run agents online. To be sure, computers and data are closing in and do pose a real threat to tradecraft, but life always finds a way.

Secrecy may be eroding, but plausible deniability has long been a myth anyway. The idea of a golden age of state secrecy where intelligence agencies could operate with impunity is exaggerated. Even many influence operations – the least visible form of covert action – in the late 1940s and 1950s quickly became common knowledge. The first book on the CIA's covert actions in eastern Europe, *The Cloak and Dollar War*, was published in 1953.

Today, as in the past, many covert actions are exposed but not acknowledged – hidden in plain sight. As we have seen, *implausible* deniability brings benefits of covert communication and exploitable ambiguity. However, states will also mask imperfect secrecy by generating a vast background noise of conflicting narratives in order to create a surfeit of information. They will create bigger haystacks in which to hide their needle. This conceals their own real operations but also creates confusion, which is often a goal in its own right.[8] Moreover, secrecy is about political amnesia and selective blindness as well as about things actually being hidden. The US role in the Yemeni civil war, for example, has gone almost unnoticed despite taking place in a supposed age of unsecrecy.[9]

Some covert actions will become more precise and tactical, designed to disrupt a particular terrorist attack, or to sow distrust among a specific terrorist group. Others, such as those done by Russia, will become less of a precision instrument and rely more on spreading confusion and multiple conflicting accounts to disrupt and undermine trust, to induce cynicism. They will exploit people's lack of trust in authority and experts. New technologies such as AI targeted messages and deepfakes will create further confusion and further subvert reality. This is already happening: in spring 2021, Russia managed to trick senior politicians across Europe using deepfake technology on video calls imitating a Russian opposition leader.[10]

This is less about total secrecy, and more about spreading too much information to create and inflame corrosive social anxiety and political division, exacerbating distrust in democracy.[11] According to US intelligence forecasts, 'Real-time, manufactured or synthetic media could further distort truth and reality, destabilizing societies at a scale and speed that dwarfs current disinformation challenges.'[12] Amid multiple competing narratives designed to spread confusion and cynicism, state secrecy becomes less paramount; non-acknowledgement is key.

The rise of open-source investigation conducted by amateur groups could add to the confusion and further muddy the landscape. Bellingcat, the most familiar of such collectives, has high standards and operates responsibly, but what happens when others catch up? As the American scholar Amy Zegart worries, 'a thin line separates the wisdom of crowds from the danger of mobs. The herd is often wrong – and when it is, the costs can be high.' She points to the aftermath of the Boston Marathon bombing in 2013 when amateur sleuths turned to the internet and social media to hunt the terrorists but caught the wrong men. 'The crowdsourced investigation quickly devolved into a digital witch-hunt.'[13] Open-source intelligence has a flip side in that it will not necessarily unearth truths and deter covert actions. Instead, competing amateurs could offer competing truths in a world in which covert action operates within a fog of confusion not secrecy.

The final trend shaping the future of covert action is one of privatization. States are increasingly outsourcing operations to private companies. As we have seen, groups like Wagner now play a role in secret wars. Why sponsor unreliable violent rebel groups when you can hire mercenaries? This will only increase. US intelligence forecasts that state interventions over the coming decades 'are likely to involve more armed proxies, private military companies, hackers, and terrorist organizations as governments seek to reduce risks and costs for conducting attacks'.[14] Although mercenaries have been around for millennia, with the French being particularly infamous in post-imperial Africa, many scholars agree that private military companies will be the proxy-war wagers of the future.[15]

We have also seen how the same is true of influence operations, as countries across the globe increasingly outsource disinformation to PR firms and others. The Internet Research Agency was a private company allegedly run by a Putin ally, allowing deniability and distance. It did, however, receive intense scrutiny after the 2016 US presidential election from American law enforcement and intelligence. In response, Russia outsourced disinformation work targeting the subsequent US election even further to – often unwitting – people working for short-lived companies in Ghana, Mexico and Nigeria.[16] Russia is not alone. In 2020, Facebook attributed a French propaganda operation targeting the Central African Republic to protagonists associated with the French military, rather than the French military itself.

The use of private companies will continue into the future. Importantly, outsourcing creates more confusion, again obfuscating attempts to expose and hold states to account. It comes at the price of loss of control. Outsourcing risks firms competing with each other for contracts and becoming more aggressive in their operations, or simply taking shortcuts, where they go for easy wins based on spurious metrics, and take the money and run. This will make operations messier still.

Covert action will continue. There will still be plenty of operations in which the hidden hand is genuinely untraceable, more sensed than seen, but there will also be plenty which are implausibly deniable. Covert action is an intangible, yet significant part of international politics. It is difficult to know, and not just because of the secrecy involved.

Covert action spans a whole range of subterranean activities, from propaganda campaigns to cyber sabotage, from disrupting a terrorist attack to training and arming rebels. Leaders turn towards it to influence events, communicate with select audiences, or simply to cause chaos. It can be secretive; it can be performative. At heart, though, the hidden hand disrupts, subverts and undermines the adversary. Covert action may be evasive, but it is not going away. For better or worse, secret state-craft is a part of life. We need to better understand it, wield it and defend against it.

This is not some game of spies played out in the shadows or the backstreets of Berlin. Assassination may only directly affect an unlucky few, but disinformation, subversion and disruption affect all of us. In December 2021, the chief of MI6 warned of Chinese attempts to exploit the open nature of our society to distort public debate and political decision-making. Democracy does not necessarily die in darkness; neither will it end in a flash and a bang. Rather than a coup or violent insurrection, it will be the steady drumbeat of subversion and disruption carried out in broad daylight that has the most corrosive effect. We are a sitting target so long as our polarized communities and toxic populism create divisions that adversaries can readily exploit. We must not let them.

ACKNOWLEDGEMENTS

This book morphed out of a module I teach at the University of Nottingham on covert action and unacknowledged intervention. First and foremost, I would therefore like to thank my wonderful students. They have not only been guinea pigs for many an anecdote, but their insightful questions, comments and criticisms have shaped the book's argument. This is a team effort. I'm also grateful to the School of Politics for allowing me to teach such a fun, research-led module.

I am very grateful to various experts who read chapters for me: Chun-yi Lee, Dov Levin, Natalie Martin, Andrew Mumford, Vladimir Rauta, Luca Trenta, Damien Van Puyvelde and J.D. Work. J.D. patiently talked me, a luddite historian, through cyber, gave helpful feedback on drafts, and didn't seem to mind me asking embarrassing questions. Hugo Drochon offered expert guidance as I went down various rabbit holes about the nature of truth. It's been a humbling experience; a reminder that the more you know about a subject the more you don't know. Covert action is becoming a rich field of academic study with so many outstanding scholars. I've drawn on a wide range of literature and hope that I've done justice to their arguments.

Thanks to my agent, Martin Redfern at Northbank Talent Management. Without his encouragement, I would not have started this project. Thanks also to James Nightingale and the team at Atlantic for believing in me and giving me licence to tell this story in a way that hopefully balances academic rigour with wider appeal. Tamsin Shelton, once again, has been a copy-editor extraordinaire, picking me up on the wild overuse of the word 'notorious'. I'm also grateful to my dad for checking over my French translations.

A few friends and colleagues deserve special thanks for providing particular support along the way. Richard Aldrich is a hero (he doesn't let me thank him in our co-authored books, so let me say it here: the man is a wonder and has done so much for a generation of young scholars from diverse backgrounds). Michael Goodman set me off down the covert action route over a decade ago. Loch Johnson and Mark Stout have encouraged from the US. David Gill, Caitlin Milazzo and Andrew Mumford have kept me going.

Most of all, I'm grateful to Joanne. This is the first book not dedicated to her, but I hope she doesn't take it personally.

Rory Cormac
Beeston, 2022

ENDNOTES

Abbreviations

FCO: Foreign and Commonwealth Office
IISS: International Institute for Strategic Studies
IRD: Information Research Department
ISC: Intelligence and Security Committee of Parliament
NSA: National Security Agency
ODNI: Office of the Director of National Intelligence
TNA: The National Archives

PROLOGUE

1. President Joseph Biden, 'Interim National Security Strategic Guidance', The White House, 2021: https://www.whitehouse.gov/wp-content/uploads/2021/03/NSC-1v2.pdf
2. President Joseph Biden, 'Remarks by President Biden on America's Place in the World', The White House, 4/2/21: https://www.whitehouse.gov/briefing-room/speeches-remarks/2021/02/04/remarks-by-president-biden-on-americas-place-in-the-world/
3. ODNI, 'Annual Threat Assessment of the US Intelligence Community' (2021): https://www.dni.gov/files/ODNI/documents/assessments/ATA-2021-Unclassified-Report.pdf
4. Prime Minister Boris Johnson, 'Foreword from the Prime Minister' in 'Global Britain in a Competitive Age: The Integrated Review of Security, Defence, Development and Foreign Policy' (Crown, 2021), p. 6.
5. Gordon Corera, 'Racism Fuelling Far-Right Threat in UK – MI5's Ken McCallum Warns', *BBC News*, 14/7/21.

6. Annabel Goldie, 'Britain's Real Life 007 have "Licence to Kill" Renewed after 60 Year Gap', *Mirror*, 15/8/20.

7. Rebecca Camber, 'Spy Chief Wants to Recruit More Women and Ethnic Minorities and Describes Plan as "Mission Critical" for the Secret Service', MailOnline, 11/5/21.

8. Aldrich and Moran, 'Delayed Disclosure', pp. 291–306.

INTRODUCTION

1. Porter, *The False Promise of the Liberal Order*.

2. Myers, *Watching the Door*, p. 136.

3. Knott, *Secret and Sanctioned*.

4. Haslam, *Near and Distant Neighbours*, pp. 278–9.

5. 'Ministry of State Security (Stasi), "Notes on Statements made by Comrade Colonel General Kryuchkov"', 3/10/83, History and Public Policy Program Digital Archive, BStU, MfS, Abt. X, Nr. 2020, S. 8–15. Translated by Bernd Schaefer. https://digitalarchive.wilsoncenter.org/document/119321

6. See Devine, *Spymaster's Prism*.

7. See Cormac, *Disrupt and Deny*, pp. 74, 109, ch. 9.

8. Marc Polymeropoulos, '"Defend Forward": What the CIA has done since 1947', *Washington Examiner*, 28/6/21.

9. Nick Bisley, 'The US–China Rivalry is not a new Cold War. It is Way More Complex and Could Last Longer', *The Conversation*, 26/8/20.

10. Monaghan, *Dealing with the Russians*, pp. 23–6.

11. Clack and Selisny, 'From Beijing Bloggers to Whitehall Writers: Observations on the "Invisible War"', p. 266.

12. See Bale, *The Darkest Side of Politics*, pp. 46–59.

13. Quoted in Jack Murphy and Zack Dorfman, '"Conspiracy is hard": Inside the Trump Administration's secret plan to kill Qassem Soleimani', *Yahoo News*, 8/5/21.

14. Waldman, *Vicarious Warfare*, p. 190.

15. See Daugherty, *Executive Secrets*, ch. 2.

16. Knott, *Secret and Sanctioned*, p. 20.

17. O'Rourke, *Covert Regime Change*, ch. 2.

18. Waldman, *Vicarious Warfare*, p. 86.

19. Giles, 'Russian Information Warfare', p. 150.

20. Brantly, 'A Brief History of Fake', p. 27.
21. Nehring, 'Active and Sharp Measures', p. 21.
22. Giles, 'Russian Information Warfare', p. 141; Galeotti, *Russian Political War*, p. 54. Schultz and Godson, *Dezinformatsia*, p. 193; Gioe, Goodman and Frey, 'Unforgiven', pp. 561–75.
23. Galeotti, *Russian Political War*, pp. 88–9.
24. Amy McKinnon, 'What's This Unit of Russian Spies that Keeps Getting Outed?', *Foreign Policy*, 1/7/20.
25. Richard Moore, speech at IISS, 30/11/21.
26. Rid, *Active Measures*, p. 7.
27. Giles, 'Russian Information Warfare', p. 140.
28. Galeotti, *Russian Political War*, p. 3.
29. Headquarters, Department of the US Army, 'Chinese Tactics', Army Techniques Publication, ATP7-100.3 (August 2021), p. 1–6.
30. Eftimiades, *Chinese Espionage*.
31. Hamilton and Ohlberg, *Hidden Hand*, p. 17.
32. Kania, 'The Ideological Battlefield', p. 42.
33. Hamilton and Ohlberg, *Hidden Hand*, pp. 142–3; Charon et Jeangène Vilmer, 'Les Opérations d'influence chinoises', ch. 3.
34. Eftimiades, *Chinese Espionage*, p. 2.
35. Kania, 'The Ideological Battlefield', p. 43.
36. Hamilton and Ohlberg, *Hidden Hand*, p. 1; see also Belo, 'Conflict in the absence of war', pp. 73–91.
37. Aldrich and Cormac, *The Secret Royals*, p. 17.
38. Mandeep Dhami, 'Behavioural Science Support for JTRIG's (Joint Threat Research and Intelligence Group's) Effects and Online HUMINT operations', DSTL, 10/3/11, available online via the National Security Archive.
39. Chopin and Oudet, *Renseignement et Sécurité*, pp. 138–63; de Marolles, 'La Tradition Française de l'Action Invisible', pp. 337–8.
40. Von Bülow, 'Myth or Reality?', pp. 787–820.
41. See Nouzille, *Les Tueurs de la République*; Powell, *France's Wars in Chad*.
42. Quoted in Nouzille, *Les Tueurs de la République*, p. 24.
43. Nathalie Guibert, 'La Guerre Sècrete de la France en Libye', *Le Monde*, 23/2/16.
44. Nouzille, *Les Tueurs de la République*, p. 7.
45. Bergman, *Rise and Kill First*.

46. Ibid., p. 61.
47. Raffi Berg, 'Red Sea Diving Resort: The Holiday Village Run by Spies', *BBC News*, 5/8/19.
48. Kahana, 'Covert Action', pp. 78–9.
49. Wege, 'Iranian intelligence organizations', pp. 287–98.
50. National Intelligence Council, 'Foreign Threats to the 2020 US Federal Elections' (2021): https://www.dni.gov/files/ODNI/documents/assessments/ICA-declass-16MAR21.pdf
51. Bezci, *Turkish Intelligence and the Cold War.*
52. Sirrs, *A History of the Egyptian Intelligence Service*, pp. 192–3, 67.
53. Winchell, 'Pakistan's ISI', pp. 374–88.
54. Shaffer, 'Unraveling India's Foreign Intelligence', p. 260.
55. Winchell, 'Pakistan's ISI', pp. 374–88.
56. See Sirrs, *Pakistan's Inter-Services Intelligence Directorate*, pp. 240–45.
57. Jayshree Bajoria, 'RAW: India's External Intelligence Agency', Council on Foreign Relations (2008); John Chalmers and Sanjeev Miglani, 'Indian Spy's Role Alleged in Sri Lankan President's Election Defeat', *Reuters*, 18/1/15.
58. IISS, 'Cyber Capabilities and National Power: A Net Assessment', *International Institute for Strategic Studies Research Papers* (2021), p. 139.
59. Inkster, 'War in an Age of Uncertainty', p. 284.
60. Cormac, Walton and Van Puyvelde, 'What Constitutes Successful Covert Action?', pp. 1–18.
61. Muldoon is apt to cite. Fond of linguistic covert operations, his poems are exercises in how actions create unintended consequences for which the agent is held responsible. Sounds familiar. See Robbins, 'Paul Muldoon's Covert Operations', pp. 266–99.
62. Melley, *The Covert Sphere*; see also Ehrhart, 'Postmodern warfare and the blurred boundaries between war and peace', pp. 263–75; Coker, 'Post-modern war', pp. 7–14.

CHAPTER 1

1. Bergman, *Rise and Kill First*, p. xxii.
2. Devine, *Spymaster's Prism*, pp. 43–4.

3. See also Luca Trenta, *The President's Kill List*.

4. Ivan Lledo-Ferrer and Damien van Puyvelde, 'Assassination: An Increasingly Uninhibited Instrument of Power', IRSEM (May 2020.

5. Thanks to Luca Trenta for pointing this out.

6. Trenta, 'Death by Reinterpretation'.

7. Hayes, *Queen of Spies*, pp. 178, 181.

8. Desmond de Silva, *The Report of the Patrick Finucane Review* (The Stationery Office, 2012); see also Punch, *State Violence*.

9. Beesley, *The Official History of Cabinet Secretaries*, p. 555.

10. Jerome Starkey, 'The Real 007s', *Sun*, 7/6/21.

11. Bergman, *Rise and Kill First*, p. xxiv.

12. O'Rourke, *Covert Regime Change*, pp. 74–5.

13. Peter Kornbluh (ed.), 'CIA Assassination Plot Targeted Cuba's Raul Castro', National Security Archives Briefing Book #757, 16/4/21.

14. William Harvey, 'Transcript of Hearing, Witness: Harvey, William, K.', 11/7/75: https://www.archives.gov/files/research/jfk/releases/157-10011-10053.pdf

15. See Bauer, *Hitlers zweiter Putsch*.

16. Thanks to Nick Sitter for alerting me to this example.

17. Sirrs, *Pakistan's Inter-Services Intelligence Directorate*, p. 135.

18. Sirrs, *A History of the Egyptian Intelligence Service*, p. 171.

19. Hussain Sharfi, 'Sudan and the assassination attempt on President Mubarak in June 1995', pp.454–72.

20. See Galeotti, *Storm-333*.

21. Kevin Klose, 'Soviet Union Denies Involvement in Coup in Afghanistan', *Washington Post*, 31/12/79. Thanks to Tom Waldman for sharing this.

22. Bergman, *Rise and Kill First*, p. 263; Anon., 'Trial in Killing of Gemayel Kin Leads to Syria', *Washington Post*, 8/2/84; see also David Kennedy and Leslie Brünetta, 'Lebanon and the US Intelligence Community: Case Study', p. 41. This article, a write-up of a wider case managed by the CIA's Center for the Study of Intelligence, states that the assassination was 'almost surely at Syrian direction'. Available at: https://www.cia.gov/static/44abb397fa8ce2ed6c911123185446d0/Lebanon-and-Intel-Community.pdf.

23. O'Brien, 'The Use of Assassination as a Tool of State Policy', pp. 107–42.

24. Michael Walzer, 'Difficult to Draw a Bead on Issue of Targeted Killing', *Los Angeles Times*, 8/9/03, p. A27.

25. Waldman, *Vicarious Warfare*, p. 204.

26. Cunliffe, 'Hard target espionage in the information era'; William M. Arkin, 'Inside the Military's Secret Undercover Army', *Newsweek*, 17/5/21; Jenna McClaughlin and Zach Dorfman, 'Shattered: Inside the Secret Battle to Save America's Undercover Spies in the Digital Age', *Yahoo News*, 30/12/19.

27. See Gioe, Goodman and Frey, 'Unforgiven', pp. 561–75.

28. Deborah Haynes, 'Living in the Grey Zone – MI5 and the Russia Threat', Into the Grey Zone podcast (2021).

29. Gioe, Goodman and Frey, 'Unforgiven', pp. 561–75.

30. Martin Banks, 'Jamal Khashoggi Killing was "Message" to Deter Saudi Regime Opposition', *Parliament Magazine*, 5/12/19.

31. Bergman, *Rise and Kill First*, p. xxiii.

32. Van Puyvelde, 'French paramilitary actions during the Algerian war of Independence'.

33. Robinson, 'The Future of Special Operations: Beyond Kill and Capture', pp. 110–12.

34. Data from the Bureau of Investigative Journalism's Drone Warfare database, available at: https://www.thebureauinvestigates.com/projects/drone-war

35. Carvin, 'The Trouble with Targeted Killing', pp. 529–55.

36. Wilner, 'Targeted Killings in Afghanistan', pp. 307–29.

37. Bergman, *Rise and Kill First*, p. xxiii.

38. Dear, 'Beheading the Hydra?', pp. 293–337; Abrahms and Mierau, 'Leadership Matters', pp. 830–51; Varriale Carson, 'Assessing the Effectiveness of High-Profile Targeted Killings in the "War on Terror"', pp. 191–220; Jordan, 'When Heads Roll', pp. 719–55.

39. O'Brien, 'The Use of Assassination as a Tool of State Policy', pp. 107–42.

CHAPTER 2

1. Obama, *A Promised Land*, p. 675.
2. Wirtz, 'The Abbottabad raid and the theory of special operations'; Obama, *A Promised Land*, p. 695.
3. David Robarge, 'Covert Action', *Lawfare* podcast, 17/3/21.
4. Anon., 'Israel Court Backs Targeted Kills', *BBC News*, 14/12/06; Scott Wilson, 'Israeli High Court Backs Military on its Policy of "Targeted Killings"', *Washington Post*, 14/12/06.
5. Trenta, 'The Obama administration's conceptual change', pp. 69–93.
6. Dexter Filkins, 'The Shadow Commander', *New Yorker*, 23/9/13.
7. Julian Borger, 'Woodward tells how Allies Tried to Rein in "Childish" Trump's Foreign Policy', *Guardian*, 11/9/20; Jack Murphy and Zack Dorfman, '"Conspiracy is hard": Inside the Trump Administration's secret plan to kill Qassem Soleimani', *Yahoo News*, 8/5/21.
8. Ibid.
9. Ibid.
10. Ibid.
11. Ruxandra Vlad's doctoral thesis offers an excellent overview of the shifting debate about imminence. See Vlad, 'Striking the Shadow Commander', pp. 150–80; Claudia Grisales and Jessica Taylor, 'Trump Says Killing of Iranian General Was Necessary to "Stop War" not "Start One"', *NPR*, 3/1/20; Shane Harris *et al.*, 'Trump Now Claims Four Embassies Were Under Threat from Iran, Raising Fresh Questions About Intelligence Reports', *Washington Post*, 10/1/20.
12. See press release for Senator Chris Van Hollen (D-MD), 'Van Hollen Joins Murphy, Democratic Senators in Requesting Classified Briefing on Evidence Underlying Imminent Attacks on US Embassies', 14/1/20.
13. Thanks to Luca Trenta for pointing this out.
14. Vlad, 'Striking the Shadow Commander', pp. 171–2.
15. See Elliot Setzer, 'U.N. Special Rapporteur Release Report on Drone Strikes and Soleimani Killing', *Lawfare*, 8/7/20.
16. Jack Murphy and Zack Dorfman, '"Conspiracy is hard": Inside

the Trump Administration's secret plan to kill Qassem Soleimani', *Yahoo News*, 8/5/21.

17. Vlad, 'Striking the Shadow Commander', pp. 175, 205; Zachary Cohen, 'Barr and Pompeo shift justification for Iran strike from "imminent" threat to deterrence', *CNN*, 14/1/20.

18. Banka and Quinn, 'Killing Norms Softly', pp. 665–703.

19. Ibid.; Pozen, 'The leaky Leviathan', p. 560; Perina, 'Black holes and open secrets', pp. 507–83.

20. Melley, *The Covert Sphere*, pp. 8–9. Emphasis in original.

21. Tolz, Hutchings, Chatterje-Doody and Crilley, 'Mediatization and journalistic agency'.

22. Manor, 'The Russians are Laughing!'; Joel Gunter and Olga Robinson, 'Sergei Skripal and the Russian disinformation game', *BBC News*, 9/9/18; Chernobrov, 'Strategic Humour'.

23. Duncan, *In the Thick of It*, p. 364.

24. ODNI, 'Assessing the Saudi Government's role in the killing of Jamal Khashoggi' (2021): https://www.dni.gov/files/ODNI/documents/assessments/Assessment-Saudi-Gov-Role-in-JK-Death-20210226.pdf

25. Abrahams and Leber, 'Comparative Approaches to Mis/Disinformation'.

26. Bergman, *Rise and Kill First*, p. xxii.

27. Dear, 'Beheading the Hydra?', p. 295.

28. Urban, *Task Force Black*; Cormac, *Disrupt and Deny*.

29. ISC, *UK Lethal Drone Strikes in Syria* (Crown, 2017).

30. Lara Marlowe, 'How France strove to eliminate terrorists on its "kill list"', *Irish Times*, 6/1/17.

31. Nouzille, *Les Tueurs de la République*, pp. 18–19, 407.

32. Bergen and Sims, 'America's Drone Wars Outside of Conventional Warzones', p. 471.

33. Trenta, 'Death by Reinterpretation'.

34. Ibid.

35. Ibid.

36. ISC, *Russia Report* (Crown, 2020).

37. Private information.

38. Duncan, *In the Thick of It*, p. 356.

CHAPTER 3

1. Reuters staff, 'Wuhan Lockdown "Unprecedented"', *Reuters*, 23/1/20.
2. Charon et Jeangène Vilmer, 'Les Opérations d'influence chinoises', p. 592.
3. See Miriam Matthews et al, 'Superspreaders of Malign and Subversive Information on COVID-19' (RAND, 2021); 'Behind China's Twitter Campaign, A Murky Support Chorus', *New York Times*, 9/6/20.
4. Charon et Jeangène Vilmer, 'Les Opérations d'influence chinoises', pp. 595–7.
5. Lijian Zhao, Twitter, 12/3/20.
6. Charon et Jeangène Vilmer, 'Les Opérations d'influence chinoises', ch. 6.
7. Carly Miller *et al.*, 'Sockpuppets Spin COVID Yarns: An Analysis of PRC-attributed June 2020 Twitter Takedown', Stanford Internet Observatory (2020).
8. Jennifer Rankin, 'EU says China behind huge wave of COVID-19 disinformation', *Guardian*, 10/6/20.
9. Joshua Kurlantzick, 'How China Ramped Up Disinformation Efforts During the Pandemic', Council on Foreign Relations (2020).
10. EU vs Disinfo, 'Short Assessment of Narratives and Disinformation Around the COVID-19 Pandemic' (2021): https://euvsdisinfo.eu/eeas-special-report-update-short-assessment-of-narratives-and-disinformation-around-the-covid-19-pandemic-update-december-2020-april-2021/
11. Mwende Maweu, '"Fake Elections"?' p. 63.
12. Samantha Bradshaw *et al.*, *Industrialized Disinformation: 2020 Global Inventory of Organized Social Media Manipulation* (Oxford Internet Institute, 2021).
13. Cohen *et al.*, *Combating Foreign Disinformation on Social Media*, p. 10.
14. Samantha Bradshaw *et al.*, *Industrialized Disinformation: 2020 Global Inventory of Organized Social Media Manipulation* (Oxford Internet Institute, 2021).
15. Owen Jones, 'Propaganda, Fake News and Fake Trends', pp. 1389–415.

16. For discussion see Baggini, *A Short History of Truth*, p.62.

17. Samantha Bradshaw *et al.*, *Industrialized Disinformation: 2020 Global Inventory of Organized Social Media Manipulation* (Oxford Internet Institute, 2021).

18. Ibid.

19. Owen Jones, 'Disinformation Superspreaders', pp. 431–7.

20. Samantha Bradshaw *et al.*, *Industrialized Disinformation: 2020 Global Inventory of Organized Social Media Manipulation* (Oxford Internet Institute, 2021).

21. Ibid.; Shelby Grossman and Khadeja Ramali, 'Outsourcing Disinformation', *Lawfare*, 13/12/20.

22. Jack Stubbs and C. Shawn Eib, 'Coordinated Inauthentic Bee-havior', Graphika (2021): https://graphika.com/reports/coordinated-inauthentic-bee-havior/

23. Shelby Grossman and Khadeja Ramali, 'Outsourcing Disinformation', *Lawfare*, 13/12/20; Josh Goldstein and Shelby Grossman, 'How Disinformation Evolved in 2020', Brookings Institute, 4/1/21; Max Fisher, 'Disinformation For Hire: A Shadowy Industry is Quietly Booming', *New York Times*, 25/7/21.

24. Quoted in Taylor, *Munitions of the Mind*, p. 1.

25. Aldrich and Cormac, *The Secret Royals*, p. 393.

26. See Wanless and Pamment, 'How Do You Define a Problem Like Influence?', pp. 1–14.

27. Turner, 'Covert Action', p. 112.

28. Brantly, 'A Brief History of Fake', pp. 27–8.

29. Ibid., p. 35.

30. Selvage, 'Operation "Denver"', p. 4; Douglas Selvage and Christopher Nehring, 'Operation Denver: KGB and Stasi Disinformation Regarding Aids', Wilson Center (2019).

31. For an overview see Blackburn, *Truth*.

32. Wanless and Pamment, 'How Do You Define a Problem Like Influence?', pp. 1–14.

33. See McIntyre, *Post-Truth*, p. 13.

34. Rid, *Active Measures*, pp. 426–7.

35. Giles, *Moscow Rules*, p. 110.

36. Wanless and Pamment, 'How Do You Define a Problem Like Influence?', pp. 1–14.

37. Taylor, *Munitions of the Mind*, p. 3.
38. See Carl Miller, *The Death of the Gods*, pp. 256–8.
39. Samantha Bradshaw *et al.*, *Industrialized Disinformation: 2020 Global Inventory of Organized Social Media Manipulation* (Oxford Internet Institute, 2021); Carl Miller, *Death of the Gods*, pp. 222–4.
40. Ian Cobain, '"This is Woke": The Media Outfit That's Actually a UK Counter-Terror Programme', *Middle East Eye*, 15/8/19.
41. Churchill College Archives: 'Herbert Harold Tucker, OBE, transcript of interview by J. Hutson, 19 April 1996, British Diplomatic Oral History Project 11'.
42. Cormac, 'The Information Research Department, Unattributable Propaganda, and Northern Ireland, 1971–1973', p. 1089.
43. McIntyre, *Post-Truth*, pp. 6–11.
44. IRD, 'Loyal African Brothers leaflet No. 657', September 1965, TNA, FCO 168/2386; IRD, 'Loyal African Brothers leaflet No. 661', January 1966, TNA, FCO 168/2387.
45. IRD, 'Exposure of Diallo Telli', October 1966, TNA, FCO 168/2920; IRD, Rayner to [redacted], 24 March 1969, TNA, FCO 168/3900.
46. IRD, 'World Muslim Brotherhood (No. 5) Poison gas', February 1967, TNA, FCO 168/2921.
47. Blackburn, *Truth*, p. xv.
48. For discussion of 'creative truths', see Baggini, *A Short History of Truth*, pp. 61–8.
49. Blackburn, *Truth*, pp. 19–22.
50. Ministry of Defence, *Allied Joint Doctrine for Psychological Operations*, Allied Joint Publication 3.10.1 (NATO Standardization Office, 2014), pp. 1–6.
51. See D'Ancona, *Post-Truth*.
52. Benkler, Faris and Roberts, *Network Propaganda*.
53. Crilley, 'International relations in the age of "post-truth" politics', pp. 417–25.
54. McIntyre, *Post-Truth*, pp. 5, 11.
55. For discussion see Baggini, *A Short History of Truth*, ch. 1.
56. Johnson, 'Reflections on the ethics and effectiveness of America's "third option"', pp. 669–85.
57. Rid, *Active Measures*, p. 426.

58. William Arkin, 'When Seeing and Hearing Isn't Believing', *Washington Post*, 1/2/99.

59. Rid, *Active Measures*, p. 426.

CHAPTER 4

1. Graphika and Stanford Internet Observatory, 'More-Troll Combat' (2020): https://public-assets.graphika.com/reports/graphika_stanford_report_more_troll_kombat.pdf

2. Mare, Mabweazara and Moyo, '"Fake News" and Cyber-Propaganda in Sub-Saharan Africa', pp. 1–12; Wahutu, 'Fake News and Journalistic "Rules of the Game"', p. 14.

3. Rid, *Active Measures*, p. 402.

4. Dawson and Innes, 'How Russia's Internet Research Agency Built Its Disinformation Campaign', pp. 245–56.

5. Ibid.

6. Robert Mueller, *Report on the Investigation into Russian Interference in the 2016 Presidential Election, Vol. 1* (2019).

7. Rid, *Active Measures*, pp. 406–7.

8. Pier, 'Commanding the Trend', pp. 100–01.

9. Lukito, 'Coordinating a Multi-Platform Disinformation Campaign', pp. 238–55.

10. See FCO 168/4596.

11. Kragh and Åsberg, 'Russia's strategy for influence through public diplomacy and active measures', pp. 773–816.

12. Alistair Coleman and Matilda Welin, 'Greenland Minister at Centre of Fake Letter Affair', *BBC Monitoring*, 13/11/19; Jacob Gronholt-Pedersen, 'Denmark Accuses Russia, China, Iran of Espionage Threat', *Reuters*, 13/1/22.

13. Bolsover and Howard, 'Computational Propaganda and Political Big Data'.

14. Hall Jamieson, *Cyberwar*, pp. 131–5.

15. Rid, *Active Measures*, p. 403.

16. Cohen *et al.*, *Combating Foreign Disinformation on Social Media*, p. 23.

17. Swanbeck, 'How to Understand Iranian Information Operations'.

18. For an exception see Briant, 'Lessons from the Cambridge

Analytica Crisis: Confronting Today's (Dis)information Challenges', pp. 125–7.

19. Tom Cheshire, 'Behind the Scenes at Donald Trump's UK Digital War Room', *Sky News*, 22/10/16.

20. BBC, 'Cambridge Analytica: The Data Firm's Global Influence', *BBC News*, 22/3/18.

21. Mwende Maweu, '"Fake Elections"?', pp. 62–76; see also Ekdale and Tully, 'African Elections as a Testing Ground', p. 33.

22. See discussion in Miskimmon *et al.*, *Strategic Narratives*, ch. 1.

23. Ibid., p. 2.

24. Fitzgerald and Brantly, 'Subverting Reality', pp. 215–40; Pomerantsev, *Nothing Is True and Everything Is Possible*.

25. Bjola and Papadakis, 'Digital Propaganda, Counterpublics, and the Disruption of the Public Sphere', p. 186.

26. Rid, *Active Measures*, p. 11.

27. Sonja Swanbeck, 'How to Understand Iranian Information Operations', *Lawfare*, 19/2/21.

28. Brian Bennett, 'Iran Steps Up Efforts to Sow Discord Inside the US', *Time*, 9/6/21.

29. Cohen *et al.*, *Combating Foreign Disinformation on Social Media*, p. 12.

30. Headquarters, Department of the US Army, 'Chinese Tactics', Army Techniques Publication, ATP7-100.3 (August 2021), pp. 1–14.

31. Cohen *et al.*, *Combating Foreign Disinformation on Social Media*, p. 19.

32. Kania, 'The Ideological Battlefield', p.48.

33. Jean-Baptiste Jeangène Vilmer and Paul Charon, 'Russia as a Hurricane; China as Climate Change: Different ways of Information Warfare', *War on the Rocks*, 21/1/20.

34. Ibid.

35. Emma Graham-Harrison, 'China's Communist Party Ran Campaign to Discredit BBC, Thinktank Finds', *Guardian*, 4/3/21.

36. Sarah Cook, 'Beijing is Getting Better at Disinformation on Global Social Media', *The Diplomat*, 30/3/21; Cardiff University Crime and Security Research Institute, 'China Linked Influence Operation on Twitter Detected Engaging with the US Presidential Election' (2021), pp. 14–15.

37. Cohen *et al.*, *Combating Foreign Disinformation on Social Media*, pp. 24, 26.
38. Romerstein, 'Disinformation as a KGB Weapon in the Cold War', pp. 54–67.
39. Freelon and Wells, 'Disinformation as Political Communication', pp. 145–56.
40. Plattner, 'Democracy Embattled', pp. 5–10; Pomerantsev, *This Is Not Propaganda*, p. 236; Bennett and Livingston, 'The Disinformation Order', pp. 122–39.
41. Rob Joyce cited in Jean-Baptiste Jeangène Vilmer and Paul Charon, 'Russia as a Hurricane; China as Climate Change: Different ways of Information Warfare', *War on the Rocks*, 21/1/20.
42. Ken McCallum, untitled first public speech (2020): https://www.mi5.gov.uk/news/director-general-ken-mccallum-makes-first-public-address
43. Quoted in Rory Cormac, 'George Kennedy Young: Banker, Writer, Soldier, Spy', Engelsberg Ideas, 14/12/20.
44. See Blackstock, *The Strategy of Subversion*, ch. 2
45. Romerstein, 'Soviet Agents of Influence', pp. 12, 23–4.
46. Rid, *Active Measures*, ch. 18.
47. Ibid., ch. 20.
48. Unknown [illegible], 'SPA in Ecuador', September 1962, FCO168/682.
49. McWilliam, 'SPA in Chile', 24/9/62, FCO168/674.
50. Anonymous, 'The Longer Telegram', *Atlantic* (2020).
51. James Kynge *et al.*, 'Inside China's Secret "Magic Weapon" for Worldwide Influence', *Financial Times*, 26/10/17.
52. Anne-Marie Brady, 'Magic Weapons: China's Political Influence Activities under Xi Jinping', Wilson Center (2017).
53. Charon et Jeangène Vilmer, 'Les Opérations d'influence chinoises', pp. 38–9.
54. Kynge *et al.*, 'Inside China's Secret "Magic Weapon"'.
55. Josh Rudolf and Thomas Morley, *Covert Foreign Money: Financial Loopholes Exploited by Authoritarians to Fund Political Interference in Democracies* (Alliance for Securing Democracies, 2020), p. 74.
56. James Kynge *et al.*, 'Inside China's Secret "Magic Weapon" for Worldwide Influence', *Financial Times*, 26/10/17.

57. Richard Moore, speech at IISS, 30/11/21.

58. Gordon Corera and Jennifer Scott, 'MI5 Warning of "Chinese Agent" in Parliament', *BBC News*, 13/1/22.

59. Robert Fife and Steven Chase, 'Canada's Spy Agency Warns MPs to Beware of Influence Operations from China', *Globe and Mail*, 11/1/22.

60. Stephen Mosher, 'Testimony Presented to the Sub-Committee on Oversight and Investigations, House Committee on Foreign Affairs' (2012); Anne-Marie Brady, 'Magic Weapons: China's Political Influence Activities under Xi Jingping', Wilson Center (2017).

61. Peter Hartcher, '"Insidious": Former ASIO Boss Warns on Chinese Influence in Australia', *Sydney Morning Herald*, 22/11/19.

62. Hugo Gye, 'Commons Foreign Affairs Chief Tom Tugendhat hit By Chinese "Psyops" Attack', *i News*, 9/4/21.

63. Deborah Haynes, 'Head of MI5 Ken McCallum Warns "Regular People" Being Targeted by Foreign Spies', *Sky News*, 14/7/21.

64. BBC, 'US Labels Confucius Institute a Chinese "Foreign Mission"', *BBC News*, 14/8/20.

65. Fulda and Missal, 'Mitigating threats to academic freedom in Germany', p. 7.

66. Ibid., p. 8.

67. Foreign Affairs Select Committee, 'A Cautious Embrace: Defending Democracy in an Age of Autocracies' (Crown, 2019).

68. Martin Thorley, 'Huawei, the CSSA and Beyond: Latent Networks and Party Influence within Chinese Institutions', *The Asia Dialogue*, 5/7/19.

69. Johnson, 'Spies and Scholars in the United States', pp. 1–21.

70. Kotek, *Students and the Cold War*, p. 103; Burkett, 'The National Union of Students and Transnational Solidarity, 1958-68', pp. 539–55.

71. IRD, 'WFDY letter and Declaration', May 1963, TNA, FO 1110/2363.

72. Cormac, 'The currency of covert action'.

73. David Robarge, 'Covert Action', *Lawfare* podcast, 17/3/21.

74. John Prados and Arturo Jiminez-Bacardi, 'The Overthrow of Cheddi Jagan in British Guiana', National Security Archive, 6/4/20.

75. ACSI to Army Chief of Staff, 'Ideas on How to Harm the Castro/Communist Regime', 21/1/63; https://www.archives.gov/files/research/jfk/releases/2018/docid-32423712.pdf

76. Griffin, 'French military policy in the Nigerian Civil War', 1967–1970, p. 120.

77. Kirshner, 'Currency and Coercion in the Twenty-first Century'.

78. Liss, 'Making Monetary Mischief', pp. 29–38.

79. Kirshner, 'Currency and Coercion in the Twenty-first Century', p. 6.

80. Kartikaya Sharma, 'Pakistan Officially Printing Fake Indian Currency Notes', *India Today*, 6/11/14; Vaishali Basu Sharma, 'Is the Spectre of Fake Indian Currency Coming in from Pakistan Back to Haunt Us?', *The Wire*, 25/10/19.

81. Tim Maurer *et al.*, 'Towards a Global Norm Against Manipulating the Integrity of Financial Data', *Cyber Policy Initiative Working Paper Series* (Carnegie Endowment for International Peace, 2016), pp. 24–5, 26; Rid, *Cyber War Will Not Take Place*, p. 6.

CHAPTER 5

1. Schmidt, *Foreign Intervention in Africa*, p. 184.

2. Levin, *Meddling in the Ballot Box*; Shimer, *Rigged*. In particular see Levin's dataset: 'Partisan Electoral Intervention by the Great Powers'.

3. Josh Rudolf and Thomas Morley, *Covert Foreign Money: Financial Loopholes Exploited by Authoritarians to Fund Political Interference in Democracies* (Alliance for Securing Democracies, 2020).

4. Quirk, 'Lawfare in the Disinformation Age', pp. 538–9.

5. Pratik Jakhar, 'Analysis: Fake News Fears Grip Taiwan Ahead of Local Poll', *BBC Monitoring*, 21/11/18.

6. ISC, *Russia Report* (Crown, 2020).

7. See for example, Barbara McQuade, 'Biden's Election Probe Focuses on Rudy Giuliani. But Not How You Think', *MSNBC*, 29/5/21; Dan Friedman and David Corn, 'The Crazy Last Days of Rudy Giuliani and Steve Bannon', *Motherjones*, 29/1/20.

8. Reuters, 'Rudy Giuliani Suffers Hair Malfunction as he Makes More Baseless Voter Fraud Allegations', *Guardian*, 19/11/20.

9. Emma-Jo Morris and Gabrielle Fonrouge, 'Smoking Gun Email Reveals How Hunter Biden Introduced Ukrainian Businessman to VP Dad', *New York Post*, 14/10/20.

10. Natasha Bertand, 'Hunter Biden Story is Russian Disinformation, Dozens of Former Intelligence Officials Say', Politico, 19/10/20.

11. The intelligence report did not name this documentary or channel but news outlets claimed the details aligned. E.g., see Ken Dilanian, 'Russia Tried to Help Trump in 2020, Iran Tried to Hurt Him and China Stayed Out of it says New Report', NBC News, 16/3/21.

12. National Intelligence Council, 'Foreign Threats to the 2020 US Federal Election' (2021): https://www.dni.gov/files/ODNI/documents/assessments/ICA-declass-16MAR21.pdf

13. Ibid.

14. Ibid.

15. O'Brien, 'The Quiet Option', p. 37.

16. Rudolf and Morley, *Covert Foreign Money*, p. 1.

17. Committee on Foreign Relations, US Senate, 'Putin's Asymmetric Assault on Democracy in Russia and Europe: Implications for US National Security' (2017).

18. Rudolf and Morley, *Covert Foreign Money*, p. 18.

19. UK Foreign Affairs Committee, 'Putin's Gold: Russian Corruption in the UK' (Crown, 2018).

20. Belton, *Putin's People*, pp. 399–400.

21. UK Foreign Affairs Committee, 'Putin's Gold: Russian Corruption in the UK' (2018), p. 6.

22. Joseph R. Biden Jr and Michael Carpenter, 'How to Stand Up to the Kremlin', *Foreign Affairs*, 5/12/17.

23. UK Foreign Affairs Committee, 'Putin's Gold: Russian Corruption in the UK' (2018), p. 7.

24. Rudolf and Morley, 'Covert Foreign Money', p. 58.

25. Cormac, *Disrupt and Deny*, pp. 41, 95.

26. Shimer, *Rigged*, ch.4; see also Kellerhoff and Von Kostka, *Capital of Spies*, p.121; Andrew and Gordievsky, *KGB*, p. 514.

27. Rid, *Active Measures*. Thanks also to Dov Levin for pointing this out.

28. Kim Zetter, 'How Close Did Russia Really Come to Hacking the 2016 Election?' *Politico*, 26/12/19.

29. See Shimer, *Rigged*, chs. 9–10.

30. ISC, *Russia Report* (Crown, 2020).

31. Levin, *Meddling in the Ballot Box*, pp. 28, 226.

32. Levin, 'When the Great Power Gets a Vote', pp. 189–202.

33. Greg Heffer, 'Cameron "Personally Requested Obama's Back of the Queue Warning"', *Sky News*, 2/7/18.

34. Levin, *Meddling in the Ballot Box*, pp. 40–41.

35. Ibid.

36. O'Rourke, *Covert Regime Change*; Poznansky, *In the Shadow of International Law*.

37. Levin, 'When the Great Power Gets a Vote', pp. 189–202.

38. Levin, *Meddling in the Ballot Box*, pp. 267–70; Shimer, *Rigged*, pp. 113–15.

39. Ibid.; ibid.

40. Levin, *Meddling in the Ballot Box*, pp. 267–70.

41. John Prados and Arturo Jiminez-Bacardi, 'The Overthrow of Cheddi Jagan in British Guiana', National Security Archive, 6/4/20.

42. Ibid.

43. Ibid.

44. O'Rourke, *Covert Regime Change*, pp. 83–9.

45. Ibid., pp. 85–94; Levin, 'A Vote for Freedom?', pp. 839–68.

46. Levin, 'Will you still love me tomorrow?'

CHAPTER 6

1. Her Majesty's Government, 'PM statement on the death of His Majesty Sultan Qaboos bin Said al Said, Sultan of Oman' (2021): https://www.gov.uk/government/news/pm-statement-on-the-death-of-his-majesty-sultan-qaboos-bin-said-al-said-sultan-of-oman

2. Duncan, *In the Thick of It*, p. 117.

3. Luttwak, *Coup d'État*, p. 12.

4. Ibid., p. 2.

5. Cormac, *Disrupt and Deny*, pp. 187–8.

6. Hebditch and Connor, *How to Stage a Military Coup*, pp. 24–30.

7. Poznansky, 'The Psychology of Overt and Covert Intervention', pp. 1, 6.

8. Luttwak, *Coup d'État*, pp. 2–3.
9. Ibid., pp. 6–17.
10. Ibid., ch. 2.
11. O'Rourke, *Covert Regime Change*, p. 65.
12. Kate Doyle and Peter Kornbluh (eds) 'CIA and Assassinations: The Guatemala documents', *National Security Archive Briefing Book No.4* [nd].
13. David, 'Soviet Involvement in Third World Coups', pp. 3–36.
14. Andrew and Mitrokhin, *The Mitrokhin Archive II*, p. 17.
15. Griffin, 'French military policy in the Nigerian Civil War, 1967–1970', p. 115; see also Bat, *Le Syndrome Foccart*.
16. R. W. Johnson, 'The President's Man', *London Review of Books*, 17/10/95.
17. Bat, 'Le secteur N (Afrique) et la fin de la Guerre froide', pp. 43–56; Bat, *Le Syndrome Foccart*, p.401; Nouzille, *Les Tueurs de la République*, p.106.
18. Bat, *Le Syndrome Foccart*, pp. 402–3; Nouzille, *Les Tueurs de la République*, pp. 106–8; Hebditch and Connor, *How to Stage a Military Coup*, p. 136.
19. Powell, *France's Wars in Chad*, pp. 240–41.
20. Simon, *O Brasil contra a democracia*; see also Peter Kornbluh and Savannah Bock (eds), 'Brazil Abetted Overthrow of Allende in Chile', *National Security Archive Briefing Books*, no. 753 (2021).
21. Ibid.
22. Anon., 'Australian Spies Aided and Abetted CIA in Chile', National Security Archive, 10/9/21.
23. O'Rourke, *Covert Regime Change*, pp. 77–9.
24. Luttwak, *Coup d'État*, p. 92.
25. For more practical tactical guides see Luttwak, *Coup d'État* and Hebditch and Connor, *How to Stage a Military Coup*.
26. Aldrich, 'Uganda, Southern Sudan and the Idi Amin Coup', pp. 1109–139.
27. Ibid.
28. ISC, *Russia Report* (Crown, 2020).
29. Richard Moore, speech at IISS, 30/11/21.
30. Martin Chulov and Michael Safi, 'Phone Intercepts Shine More Light on Jordanian Prince's Alleged Coup Attempt', *Guardian*, 30/5/21.

31. Mehul Srivastava and Andrew England, 'Inside Jordan's Royal Crisis: Why the Prince Turned to Tribal Leaders for Support', *Financial Times*, 18/4/21.

32. Anon., 'Report: Saudi crown prince backed Israel plan to overthrow Jordan king', *Middle East Monitor*, 20/4/21; Martin Chulov and Michael Safi, 'Did Jordan's Closest Allies Plot to Unseat its King?', *Guardian*, 26/5/21; David Ignatius, 'Opinion: Inside the Palace Intrigue in Jordan and a Thwarted "Deal of the Century"', *Washington Post*, 11/6/21.

33. Simon Tisdall, 'Russia May Regret Kyrgyzstan Coup', *Guardian*, 21/4/10.

34. Vasabjit Banerjee and Timothy Rich, 'Diamonds and the Crocodile: China's role in the Zimbabwe Coup', *The Diplomat*, 22/11/17.

CHAPTER 7

1. D'Ancona, *In It Together*, p. 172

2. Nouzille, *Les Tueurs de le République*, pp. 364–5.

3. Martin Chulov, 'Gaddafi's Last Moments: "I Saw the Hand Holding the Gun and I Saw it Fire"', *Guardian*, 20/10/12.

4. Rauta, '"Proxy War"', pp. 1–24.

5. Grauer and Tierney, 'The Arsenal of Insurrection', p. 268.

6. Hughes, 'Syria and the Perils of Proxy Warfare', p. 523.

7. Mumford, 'Proxy Warfare and the Future of Conflict', pp. 40–46.

8. Ben Rhodes, 'Inside the White House During the Syrian "Red Line" Crisis', *The Atlantic*, 3/6/18.

9. Poznansky, 'Feigning Compliance', pp. 72–84.

10. Rauta, 'Proxy Warfare and the Future of Conflict', pp. 1–10.

11. See Krieg, 'Externalizing the burden of war', pp. 97–113; Lee, *Crippling Leviathan*.

12. Griffin, 'French military policy in the Nigerian Civil War,' pp. 114–35; see also R. W. Johnson, 'The President's Man', *London Review of Books*, 17/10/95.

13. Berkowitz, 'Delegating Terror', pp. 709–48.

14. Although, clearly, democracies can be coercive when pursuing ambitious objectives too.

15. Rauta, 'Proxy Warfare and the Future of Conflict'.

16. Tabatabai, 'Other side of the Iranian coin: Iran's counterterrorism apparatus', pp. 181–207.
17. Rauta, 'Proxy Warfare and the Future of Conflict'; Gleis and Berti, *Hezbollah and Hamas*.
18. Inna Rudolf, 'The Sunnis of Iraq's "Shia" Paramilitary Powerhouse', The Century Foundation (2020): https://tcf.org/content/report/sunnis-iraqs-shia-paramilitary-powerhouse/?agreed=1
19. Rauta, 'Proxy Warfare and the Future of Conflict'; Mumford, *Proxy Warfare*, pp. 51–3.
20. Jack Watling, *Iran's Objectives and Capabilities: Deterrence and Subversion*, RUSI Occasional Paper, 2019.
21. Declan Walsh *et al.*, 'In a Dangerous Game of Cat and Mouse, Iran Eyes New Targets in Africa', *New York Times*, 15/2/21.
22. Byman and Kreps, 'Agents of Destruction'; Berkowitz, 'Delegating Terror'.
23. Marshall, *Prisoners of Geography*, pp. 141–4.
24. Ibid.
25. Akbarzadeh, Gourlay and Ehteshami, 'Iranian proxies in the Syrian conflict: Tehran's "forward-defence" in action', pp. 2, 21.
26. Mumford, *Proxy Warfare*, pp. 41–4.
27. David Robarge, 'Covert Action', *Lawfare* podcast, 17/3/21.
28. O'Rourke, *Covert Regime Change*, p. 26. Other successful operations, such as in Guatemala, also included promoting coups and influencing elections.
29. Tobin, 'The Myth of the "Afghan Trap"', p. 248.
30. Weiner, *Legacy of Ashes*, p. 444.
31. See Woodward, *Veil*, pp.96, 157; Anon., 'Enabling a Dictator', Human Rights Watch (2016).
32. Schmidt, *Foreign Intervention in Africa*, pp. 186–7; Powell, *France's Wars in Chad*, pp. 279–80. For a detailed account see Mireval, *Tchad*.
33. Woodward, *Veil*, pp. 96–7.
34. See Sirrs, *Pakistan's Inter-Services Intelligence Directorate*, p.43; Raman, *The Kaoboys of R&AW*; Samant, *Operation X*; Shaffer, 'Indian spies inside Pakistan', pp.727–42; Shaffer, 'Unraveling India's Foreign Intelligence', pp. 252–89.
35. Long, 'CIA–MI6 psychological warfare and the subversion of communist Albania in the early Cold War', pp. 787–807.

36. Michael Kofman *et al.*, 'Lessons from Russia's Operations in Crimea and Eastern Ukraine' (RAND Corporation, 2017).

37. International Crisis Group, 'Rebels Without a Cause: Russia's Proxies in Eastern Ukraine', International Crisis Group Report no.254 (2019).

38. Lee, *Crippling Leviathan*, pp. 9–10.

39. See Marshall, *Prisoners of Geography*, ch. 7.

40. Sirrs, *Pakistan's Inter-Services Directorate*, p. 43.

41. Lee, *Crpipling Leviathan*, p. 49; Swami, 'Failed Threats and Flawed Fences'.

42. Berkowitz, 'Delegating Terror'; Wolf, 'Pakistan and State-Sponsored Terrorism in South Asia'; Ahsan Butt, 'What the Kulbhushan Jadhav Saga Reveals About India and Pakistan's Balochistan Problem', *The Diplomat*, 11/1/18.

43. Constantino, 'The India–Pakistan Rivalry in Afghanistan', pp. 9–10.

44. William Hague, Hansard, 7/3/11, cm643.

45. See Holland, 'Operation PBHistory', pp. 300–32.

46. Aldrich, 'American Journalism and the Landscape of Secrecy', pp. 189–209.

47. Kurlantzick, *A Great Place to Have a War.*

48. Denécém, 'France', p. 144.

49. Devine, *Spymaster's Prism*, p. 181.

50. Fiona Hamilton, 'Defence chief warns attacks online could lead to real war', *The Times*, 11/1/20; Deborah Haynes, 'The Gathering Storm', Into the Grey Zone podcast (2021).

51. Moore, 'Selling to Both Sides', pp. 325–47.

52. Schultz, 'The Enforcement Problem in Coercive Bargaining', pp. 281–312; Gleditsch *et al.*, 'Fighting at Home, Fighting Abroad', pp. 479–506.

53. Reeder, 'Civil War and the Severity of Militarized Interstate Disputes', pp. 1–8.

54. Thanks to Vladimir Rauta for pointing this out.

55. Carson, *Secret Wars.*

56. Gould and Stel, 'Strategic Ignorance and the Legitimation of Remote Warfare'.

57. Austin Carson, 'Russia and the US just defused a potential crisis in Syria – and showed us how to back away from a war', Monkey Cage, 20/02/18.

58. Ibid.
59. Carson and Yarhi-Milo, 'Covert Communication', pp. 124–56.
60. Quoted in ibid., p. 152.
61. Al Saud, *The Afghanistan File*, p.40; Carson and Yarhi-Milo, 'Covert Communication', p. 153.
62. Rauta, 'Proxy Warfare and the Future of Conflict: Take Two'.
63. Byman and Kreps, 'Agents of Destruction'; Akbarzadeh and Ibrahimi, 'The Taliban', pp. 764–82.
64. Al Saud, *The Afghanistan File*, pp. 40, 87.
65. Waldman, *Vicarious Warfare*, p. 110.
66. Rauta, 'Proxy agents, auxiliary forces, and sovereign defection', pp. 91–111.
67. Monaghan, 'The "War" in Russia's Hybrid Warfare', p. 65.
68. Cormac and Aldrich, 'Grey Is the New Black', pp. 477–94.
69. Renz, 'Russia and "hybrid warfare"', pp. 283–300.

CHAPTER 8

1. Reyntjens, *The Great African War*, pp. 48–58.
2. Byman *et al.*, *Trends in Outside Support for Insurgent Movements*, p. 18. Thanks to Vladimir Rauta for alerting me to this example.
3. Devine and Mattingly, 'The Iran–Contra Affair and the Afghan Task Force', p. 220.
4. Lee, *Crippling Leviathan*, p. 55.
5. Boutton and Dolan, 'Enemies in the Shadows', pp. 146–59.
6. Thanks to Vladimir Rauta for pointing this out.
7. LeoGrande, *Our Own Backyard*, p. 413.
8. Byman, 'Understanding, and Misunderstanding, State Sponsorship of Terrorism'.
9. Duncan, *In the Thick of It*, p. 287.
10. Alan Duncan, 'Oral Evidence: Libya: Examination of Intervention and Collapse and the UK's Future Policy Options', 19/1/16, answer to Q392.
11. Alastair Burt MP, 'Libya: Armed Conflict, Question for Foreign and Commonwealth Office' (2018): https://questions-statements.parliament.uk/written-questions/detail/2018-03-22/133856
12. Lord Richards, 'Oral evidence: Libya: Examination of intervention and collapse and the UK's future policy options', HC 520 (2016).

13. Anon., 'Army Announces Special Ops Army Ranger Regiment', Ministry of Defence press release, 23/3/21.

14. Krishnan, 'Controlling partners and proxies in pro-insurgency paramilitary operations', pp. 544–60.

15. Pattison, 'The Ethics of Arming Rebels', pp. 455–71.

16. Smith, 'Secret but constrained', pp. 685–707.

17. See Johnson, *National Security Intelligence*.

18. Pattison, 'The Ethics of Arming Rebels', pp. 455–71.

19. Raman, *The Kaoboys of R&AW*, p. 26.

20. Patrick Wintour *et al.*, 'Johnson Says Saudi Arabia is a "Puppeteer" in Middle East Proxy Wars', *Guardian*, 7/12/16.

21. Rauta, 'A Structural Relational Analysis of Party Dynamics in Proxy Wars', pp. 449–67; Krishnan, 'Controlling Partners and Proxies'.

22. Sirrs, *A History of the Egyptian Intelligence Service*, pp. 140–41.

23. Hughes, *My Enemy's Enemy*, pp. 117–121.

24. Yadav, *RAW*, p. 107.

25. Hughes, *My Enemy's Enemy*, p. 49; Krishnan, *Why Paramilitary Operations Fail*, p. 145.

26. Krishnan, *Why Paramilitary Operations Fail*, p. 145.

27. Krieg, 'Externalizing the burden of war', pp. 109–10.

28. Krishnan, *Why Paramilitary Operations Fail*, p. 147.

29. Quoted in Johnson, 'National Security Intelligence in the United States', p. 613.

30. Krishnan, *Why Paramilitary Operations Fail*, p. 149.

31. Lee, *Crippling Leviathan*, ch. 5.

32. Bapat, 'Understanding State Sponsorship of Militant Groups,' pp. 1–29.

33. Mumford, *Proxy Warfare*, p. 57.

34. See Moghadam and Wyss, 'The Political Power of Proxies', pp. 119–57; Ashley Lane, 'Iran's Islamist Proxies in the Middle East, Wilson Center, 20/5/21.

35. Krieg, 'Externalizing the burden of war', p. 100.

36. Voß, 'Plausibly deniable', pp. 37–60.

37. Michael Weiss *et al.*, 'The Fallen Mercenaries in Russia's Dark Army', *New Lines Magazine*, 19/12/21.

38. Marten, 'Russia's use of semi-state security forces', pp. 181–204.

39. Nader Ibrahim and Ilya Barabanov, 'The Lost Tablet and the Secret Documents', *BBC News*, 11/8/21.

40. Amy McKinnon, 'Russia's Wagner Group Doesn't Actually Exist', *Foreign Policy*, 6/7/21.
41. National Intelligence Council, 'Global Trends 2040: A More Contested World', NIC 2021-02339 (2021), p. 105.
42. Mumford, *Proxy Warfare*, p. 82.
43. Voß, 'Plausibly deniable', pp. 37–60.
44. Ibid.
45. Marten, 'Russia's use of semi-state security forces', pp. 198–9.

CHAPTER 9

1. As pointed out by Damien Van Puyvelde.
2. Rob Evans and Paul Brown, 'France Blamed MI6 for Rainbow Warrior', *Guardian*, 28/11/05.
3. Domínguez, 'The @#$%& Missile Crisis', p. 311.
4. Andrew and Mitrokhin, *The Mitrokhin Archive II*, p. 464.
5. The first example of a cyberattack causing physical damage was a test, known as the Aurora Generator test, conducted in a lab. Thanks to Damien Van Puyvelde for pointing this out.
6. Lucy Fisher and Chris Smyth, 'GCHQ in cyberwar on anti-vaccine propaganda,' *The Times*, 9/11/20; see also Deborah Haynes, 'Cyber Power Part II', Into the Grey Zone podcast (2021).
7. See IISS, 'Cyber Capabilities and National Power: A Net Assessment', International Institute for Strategic Studies Research Papers (2021).
8. Kim Zetter and Huib Modderkolk, 'How a Secret Dutch Mole Aided the US-Israeli Stuxnet Cyber Attack on Iran', *Yahoo News*, 2/9/19.
9. Jake Wallis Simons, 'Mossad Recruited Top Iranian Scientists to Blow Up Key Nuclear Facility', *Jewish Chronicle,* 2/12/21.
10. Jon Gambrell, 'Ex-Mossad Chief Signals Israel Attacked Iran Nuclear Assets', *AP News*, 12/6/21.
11. Jake Wallis Simons, 'Mossad Recruited Top Iranian Scientists to Blow Up Key Nuclear Facility', *Jewish Chronicle*, 2/12/21.
12. Farnaz Fassihi, 'Burning Ships in Iran Add to String of Dozens of Explosions and Fires', *New York Times*, 15/7/20.
13. Michelle Weise Bockmann, 'Tanker "Sabotage" of UAE Puts Shipping on Alert', *Lloyds List*, 13/5/19.

14. H. I. Sutton, 'Spate of Attacks on Ships in Middle East Points to Iran-Backed Group', *US Naval Institute News*, 6/1/21.

15. Mark Landler *et al.*, 'US Puts Iran on Notice and Weighs Response to Attack on Oil Tankers', *New York Times*, 14/6/19.

16. Patrick Kingsley *et al.*, 'Israel's Shadow War with Iran Moves Out to Sea', *New York Times*, 26/3/21.

17. Martin Chulov and Dan Sabbagh, 'British Tanker Among Two Crew Killed in Attack on Israeli-Linked Oil Tanker off Oman', *Guardian*, 30/7/21.

18. J. D. Work and Richard Harknett, 'Troubled Vision: Understanding Recent Israeli-Iranian Offensive Cyber Exchanges', *Atlantic Council*, 22/7/20.

19. Collins and Frantz, *Fallout*.

20. 'US Reviews Secret Program to Sabotage Iranian Missiles and Rockets', *New York Times*, 13/2/19.

21. Reed, *At the Abyss*.

22. Gus Weiss, 'Disrupting the Soviets: The Farewell Dossier', CIA (1996): https://www.cia.gov/static/887689795bd91ed08ca926a2f6 278ee4/The-Farewell-Dossier.pdf

23. Paterson, 'Fixation with Cuba', pp. 137–8.

24. Anon., 'Cyberwar and Sabotage', *Newsweek*, 30/5/99.

25. Ibid.

26. Dana Priest, 'US Role at a Crossroads in Mexico's Intelligence War on the Cartels', *Washington Post*, 27/4/13.

27. Patrick Sanders, speaking at Chatham House event entitled 'Digital Competition: The UK's Cyber-Response to Online Real World Threats', 14/12/20.

28. Her Majesty's Government, 'Global Britain in a Competitive Age: The Integrated Review of Security, Defence, Development and Foreign Policy' (Crown, 2021).

29. Heng, 'The "Transformation of War" Debate', pp. 69–91; Coker, *War in an Age of Risk*, pp. 99–100.

30. Aldrich, 'Beyond the Vigilant State', pp. 889–902.

31. IISS, 'Cyber Capabilities and National Power: A Net Assessment', International Institute for Strategic Studies Research Papers (2021), p. 63.

32. For discussion see Jowett and O'Donnell, *Propaganda and Persuasion*, pp. 207–8.

33. Cogan, 'Hunters Not Gatherers', pp. 304–21.
34. Bergman, *Rise and Kill First*, pp. 234–6.
35. Damien Van Puyvelde, 'French Paramilitary Actions and the Algerian War of Independence', Wilson Center: Sources and Methods (2021): https://www.wilsoncenter.org/blog-post/french-paramilitary-actions-and-algerian-war-independence
36. Von Bülow, 'Myth or Reality?', pp. 787–820.
37. Ibid.
38. Ibid.
39. Bellingcat Investigations Team, 'Senior GRU Leader Directly Involved with Czech Arms Depot Explosion', *Bellingcat*, 20/4/21.
40. Gordon Corera, 'Salisbury Poisoning Suspects "Linked to Czech Blast"', *BBC News*, 18/4/21.
41. This is more recently debated in Leahy, *Intelligence War Against the IRA*, which claims the effect has been exaggerated, and Edwards, *Agents of Influence*, which points to covert operations as an important factor underpinning the peace deal.
42. Kiras, *Special Operations and Strategy*, pp. 75–81.
43. Al Saud, *The Afghanistan File*, pp. 55–7, 85.
44. Jonsson and Seely, 'Russian Full-Spectrum Conflict', pp. 1–22.
45. Anon., 'Ukraine Detains Man Accused of Leading Sabotage Group for Russia-Backed Separatists', *Radio Free Europe*, 16/2/21.
46. Finlan, 'A dangerous pathway?', pp. 255–75.
47. Kiras, *Special Operations and Strategy*, pp. 75–81.

CHAPTER 10

1. Lindsay, 'Stuxnet and the Limits of Cyber Warfare', pp. 365–404.
2. Kim Zetter, 'An Unprecedented Look at Stuxnet, the World's First Digital Weapon', *Wired*, 3/1/14.
3. Kim Zetter, 'Inside the Cunning, Unprecedented Hack of Ukraine's Power Grid', *Wired*, 3/3/16.
4. Anon., 'Iran Cyberattack Could Have Sickened Hundreds', *Times of Israel*, 1/6/20.
5. Ken McCallum, untitled speech, 14/10/20.
6. Ciaran Martin, 'GCHQ chief: The threat of a rogue cyber-attack keeps me awake at night', *The Times*, 30/8/20.

7. Robert Chesney, 'The CIA, Covert Action and Operations in Cyberspace', *Lawfare*, 15/7/20.

8. See Gartzke, 'The Myth of Cyberwar', pp. 41–73.

9. Gartzke and Lindsay, 'Weaving Tangled Webs', pp. 343–5.

10. Kreps and Schneider, 'Escalation firebreaks in the cyber, conventional, and nuclear domains', pp. 1–11.

11. Van Puyvelde and Brantly, *Cybersecurity*, p. 73.

12. Joshua Rovner, 'Why Restraint in the Real World Encourages Digital Espionage', *War on the Rocks*, 8/12/21.

13. Kaminska, 'Restraint under conditions of uncertainty', pp. 1–15; Kello, 'Cyber legalism', pp. 1, 4.

14. Akoto, 'Accountability and cyber conflict', pp. 1–22.

15. Maschmeyer, 'The Subversive Trilemma', p. 55.

16. Joshua Rovner, 'Cyberwar as an Intelligence Context', War on the Rocks, 16/9/19.

17. Whyte, 'Developed States' Vulnerability to Economic Disruption Online', pp. 417–32.

18. Brown and Fazal, '#SorryNotSorry', pp. 401–17.

19. Gartzke and Lindsay, 'Weaving Tangled Webs: Offense, Defense, and Deception in Cyberspace', pp. 316–48.

20. Rid and Buchanan, 'Attributing Cyber Attacks', p. 25.

21. David Sanger, 'Obama Order Sped Up Wave of Cyberattacks Against Iran', *New York Times*, 1/6/12; Sanger, *Confront and Conceal*.

22. IISS, 'Cyber Capabilities and National Power: A Net Assessment', International Institute for Strategic Studies Research Papers (2021), p. 97.

23. Buchanan, *The Cyber Security Dilemma*.

24. Jordan Williams, 'Durbin says alleged Russian hack "virtually a declaration of war"', *The Hill*, 16/12/20; Joel Gehrke, 'Romney likens hack to "Russian bombers flying undetected" over US mainland', *Washington Examiner*, 17/12/20.

25. Willett, 'Lessons of the SolarWinds Hack', p. 10.

26. Shimer, *Rigged*.

27. Thanks to J. D. Work for pointing this out.

28. Yevgeny Vindman, 'Is the SolarWinds Cyberattack an Act of War? It is if the United States Says It Is', *Lawfare*, 26/1/21.

29. Willett, 'Lessons of the SolarWinds Hack', p. 13.

30. Weiss, 'The Lavon Affair', pp. 58–68.
31. Mainwaring, 'Division D', pp. 623–40.
32. Thanks to J. D. Work for pointing this out.
33. Thanks to Richard Aldrich for pointing this out.
34. GCHQ press release, 'National Cyber Force Transforms Country's Cyber Capabilities to Protect the UK', 19/11/20.
35. Fischerkeller and Harknett, 'Deterrence is Not a Credible Strategy for Cyberspace', pp. 381–93.
36. See US Department of Defense, 'Summary of US Department of Defence Cyber Strategy' (2018): https://media.defense.gov/2018/Sep/18/2002041658/1/1/1/CYBER_STRATEGY_SUMMARY_FINAL.PDF
37. IISS, 'Cyber Capabilities and National Power: A Net Assessment', International Institute for Strategic Studies Research Papers (2021), p. 172.
38. Healey, 'The implications of persistent (and permanent) engagement in cyberspace', pp. 1–15.
39. Valeriano *et al.*, *Cyber Strategy*, pp. 2–3, 80.
40. Ibid.
41. Ibid., pp. 185, 187.
42. Maschmeyer, 'The Subversive Trilemma', p. 71.
43. Ibid., pp. 72–7.
44. Thanks to J. D. Work for pointing this out.
45. The above examples, China, North Korea and Iran, come from the dataset in Valeriano *et al.*, *Cyber Strategy*.
46. IISS, 'Cyber Capabilities and National Power: A Net Assessment', International Institute for Strategic Studies Research Papers (2021), p. 120.
47. Maher, 'The covert campaign against Iran's nuclear program'; Mahsa Rouhi, 'Explosion at Natanz: Why Sabotaging Iran's Nuclear Program Could Backfire', *Bulletin of Atomic Scientists*, 15/7/20.
48. See discussion in Maher, 'The covert campaign against Iran's nuclear program'.
49. Maher, 'The covert campaign against Iran's nuclear program'.
50. John Glaser, 'Cyberwar on Iran Won't Work: Here's Why', CATO Institute (2017).
51. Christopher Hope, 'MI6 Chief Sir John Sawers: We Foiled Iranian Nuclear Weapons Bid', *Telegraph*, 12/7/12.

52. Thanks to Damien Van Puyvelde for pointing this out.
53. John Glaser, 'Cyberwar on Iran Won't Work: Here's Why', CATO Institute (2017).
54. Valeriano *et al.*, *Cyber Strategy*, p. 197.
55. Maschmeyer, 'The Subversive Trilemma', pp. 62–5.
56. See Buchanan, *The Hacker and the State*.
57. Sanger, *Confront and Conceal*.
58. Joe Devanny *et al.*, 'The National Cyber Force that Britain Needs?', Cyber Security Research Group, King's College London (2021).

CHAPTER 11

1. Anon., *How to be a Spy: The World War Two SOE Training Manual* (Dundurn, 2004).
2. David Robarge, 'Covert Action', *Lawfare* podcast, 17/3/21.
3. Treverton, *Covert Action*, p. 193.
4. Ibid., pp. 189, 201.
5. Waldman, *Vicarious Warfare*, pp. 109, 192.
6. Sirrs, *A History of the Egyptian Intelligence Service*, pp. 192–3.
7. Treverton, *Covert Action*, p. 201.
8. Zach Dorfman *et al.*, 'Exclusive: Secret Trump Order Gives CIA More Powers to Launch Cyberattacks', *Yahoo News*, 15/7/20.
9. Waldman, *Vicarious Warfare*, p. 191.
10. David Robarge, 'Covert Action', *Lawfare* podcast, 17/3/21.
11. Richelson, *Sword and Shield*, pp. 137, 146.
12. Sergei Naryshkin interview with BBC, *BBC News*, 18/5/21.
13. 'Russians Detained in Chad Desert Say They Are Tourists', *Reuters*, 23/6/21.
14. Cormac, *Disrupt and Deny*, pp. 170–71.
15. See O'Rourke, *Covert Regime Change*; Levin, *Meddling in the Ballot Box*.
16. TNA: 'WPC Circular – Solzhenitsyn and European Security', April 1974, FCO 95/2176.
17. Devine, *Spymaster's Prism*, p. 15.
18. Joe Devanny *et al.*, 'The National Cyber Force that Britain Needs?', Cyber Security Research Group, King's College London (2021); see also Gordon Corera, 'UK's National Cyber Force Comes out of the Shadows', *BBC News*, 20/11/20.

19. Michael Poznansky, 'Confronting Cyber Threats: Challenges and Opportunities', Modern War Institute, 26/7/21.

20. Nouzille, *Les Tueurs de la République*, p. 29.

21. Devine and Mattingly, 'The Iran–Contra Affair and the Afghan Task Force', p. 219.

22. Smith, 'Secret but Constrained', pp. 685–707.

23. Johnson, 'Hybrid War and Its Countermeasures', pp. 41–163.

24. ISS, 'Cyber Capabilities and National Power: A Net Assessment', International Institute for Strategic Studies Research Papers (2021), p. 110.

25. Quoted in Galeotti, *Russian Political War*, pp. 88–9.

26. Ehrhart, 'Postmodern warfare and the blurred boundaries between war and peace', pp. 263–75.

27. Maher, 'The covert campaign against Iran's nuclear program'.

28. For a recent discussion of intelligence generally as a system of transnational knowledge circulation see Hoffmann, 'Circulation, not Cooperation'.

29. Crile, *Charlie Wilson's War*, pp. 200–2.

30. Kim Zetter and Huib Modderkolk, 'Revealed: How a secret Dutch mole aided the US–Israeli Stuxnet cyberattack on Iran', *Yahoo News*, 2/9/19.

31. Hoffmann, 'Circulation, not Cooperation'.

32. Sirrs, 'The perils of multinational intelligence coalitions', pp. 36–47.

33. Private information.

34. Abramovici, 'The World Anti-Communist League', p. 125.

35. Van Dongen *et al.*, 'Introduction', p.12.

36. Hänni, 'A Global Crusade against Communism', pp. 161–74.

37. Devine, *Spymaster's Prism*, pp. 164–5.

38. Wilson, 'Four Types of Russian Propaganda', pp. 77–81.

39. Kragh and Åsberg, 'Russia's strategy for influence through public diplomacy and active measures', pp. 773–816.

40. Poznansky, 'Revisiting Plausible Deniability'.

41. For discussion see Johnson, *The Third Option*, pp. 233–4.

42. Rogin, '"Make My Day!"', p. 101.

43. Nouzille, *Les Tueurs de la République*, p. 219.

44. Barry, 'Covert action can be just', pp. 375–90.

45. Poznansky, 'Stasis or Decay?', pp. 815–26.

46. Fabre, 'The Case for Foreign Electoral Subversion', pp. 283–92.
47. IISS, 'Cyber Capabilities and National Power: A Net Assessment', International Institute for Strategic Studies Research Papers (2021), p. 36.
48. Fisher and Smyth, 'GCHQ in cyberwar on anti-vaccine propaganda'.
49. GCHQ, 'National Cyber Force Transforms Country's Cyber Capabilities to Protect the UK', press release, 19/11/21.
50. Landon-Murray, Mujkic and Nussbaum, 'Disinformation in Contemporary U.S. Foreign Policy', pp. 512–22.

CONCLUSION

1. Gordon Corera, 'Washington Seeks to Expose Russian Intelligence Activity', *BBC News*, 15/4/21.
2. Arthur P. B. Laudrain, 'France's New Offensive Cyber Doctrine', *Lawfare*, 26/2/19.
3. Robert Chesney, 'Sanctioning Russia for SolarWinds: What Normative Line did Russia Cross?', *Lawfare*, 15/4/21; White House, 'Fact Sheet: Imposing Costs for Harmful Foreign Activities by the Russian Government', 15/4/21.
5. Ibid.
6. Rogin, '"Make My Day!"', p. 102.
7. Eason, Daddow and Cormac, 'From secrecy to accountability', pp. 542–60.
8. Babiracki, 'Putin's postmodern war with the west'.
9. Bay-Cheng, 'Pixelated Memories', p. 327; Jones, 'Sarin Gas Heartbreak', p. 64.
10. Jones, 'Sarin Gas Heartbreak', pp. 61–4.
11. Egloff and Smeets, 'Publicly attributing cyber attacks'.
12. Betsy Woodruff Swan and Bryan Bender, 'Spy chiefs look to declassify intel after rare plea from 4-star commanders', Politico, 26/4/21.
13. Paul R. Pillar, 'Intelligence Agencies Should Not Be Propaganda Organs', *National Interest*, 9/5/21.
14. Egloff and Smeets, 'Publicly attributing cyber attacks'.
15. Otto and Spaniel, 'Doubling Down', pp. 500–11.
16. Ibid.

17. Gabriel Band, 'A Government Practitioner's Guide to Countering Online Foreign Covert Influence', *Lawfare*, 22/7/21.

18. Ibid.

19. Egloff and Smeets, 'Publicly attributing cyber attacks'.

20. NSA, 'NSA, Partners Release Cybersecurity Advisory on Brute Force Global Cyber Campaign' (2021): https://www.nsa.gov/news-features/press-room/Article/2677750/nsa-partners-release-cybersecurity-advisory-on-brute-force-global-cyber-campaign/

21. Roula Khalaf, 'Alex Younger: The Russians Did Not Create the Things that Divide Us, We Did That', *Financial Times*, 30/9/20; Ken McCallum, untitled first public address, Security Service (2020): https://www.mi5.gov.uk/news/director-general-ken-mccallum-makes-first-public-address

22. Brantly, 'A Brief History of Fake', p. 38.

23. Lockhart, 'How Effective Are Covert Operations?' p. 45.

24. See Chernobrov and Briant, 'Competing Propagandas', p. 1.

25. Cormac, Walton and Van Puyvelde, 'What Constitutes Successful Covert Action?'.

26. Shimer, *Rigged*, pp. 39–40.

27. Mistry, 'Approaches to Understanding the Inaugural CIA Covert Operation in Italy', pp. 249–50.

28. Ramazani, 'Who Lost America?', pp. 5–21.

29. Cullather, *Secret History*, p. 97.

30. Echevarria, *Reconsidering the American Way of War*, p. 136.

31. O'Rourke, *Covert Regime Change*, p. 120.

32. Anon., 'Threat Report: The State of Influence Operations, 2017–2020', Facebook (2021): https://about.fb.com/wp-content/uploads/2021/05/IO-Threat-Report-May-20-2021.pdf

33. Gabriel Band, 'A Government Practitioner's Guide to Countering Online Foreign Covert Influence', *Lawfare*, 22/7/21.

34. Anon., 'Threat Report: The State of Influence Operations, 2017–2020', Facebook (2021).

35. @ReutersFacts, Twitter, 18/8/21.

36. Cohen *et al.*, *Combating Foreign Disinformation on Social Media*, pp. 74–6.

37. Ibid., pp. 87, 91.

38. Jankowicz, *How to Lose the Information War*, p. 194.

39. Ciaran Martin, 'Cyber "Deterrence": A Brexit Analogy', *Lawfare*, 15/1/21.

40. James Cleverly, Hansard, 20/1/21, cm880.

41. Harry Cole and Jerome Starkey, 'Tanker Warfare: Angry Boris Johnson Warns Iran of Consequences for Killing Brit at Sea in Drone Strike', *Sun*, 2/8/21.

42. Kaminska, 'Restraint under conditions of uncertainty'.

43. Jack Goldsmith, 'Empty Threats and Warnings on Cyber', *Lawfare*, 12/7/21.

44. Perri Adams *et al.*, 'Responsible Cyber Offense', *Lawfare*, 2/8/21.

45. Kello, 'Cyber legalism', pp. 1, 4.

46. Wilson, 'Four Types of Russian Propaganda', pp. 77–81.

47. Kahne and Bowyer, 'Educating for Democracy in a Partisan Age', pp. 3–34; De Paor and Heravi, 'Information literacy and fake news', pp. 1–8; McDougall, 'Media Literacy vs Fake News', pp. 29–45.

48. Wright, 'Post-Truth, Postmodernism and Alternative Facts', pp. 17–29.

49. Crilley and Chatterje-Doody, 'Security studies in the age of "post-truth" politics', pp. 166–70.

50. See Braw, *The Defender's Dilemma*.

51. Elisabeth Braw, 'Building a Wall of Denial Against Gray-Zone Aggression', American Enterprise Institute (2021); Ciaran Martin, 'Cyber "Deterrence": A Brexit Analogy', *Lawfare*, 15/1/21.

52. Canadian Security Intelligence Service, 'Foreign Intelligence: Threats to Canada's Democratic Process' (July 2021): https://www.canada.ca/en/security-intelligence-service/corporate/publications/foreign-interference-threat-to-canadas-democratic-process.html#toc18

53. Cohen *et al.*, *Combating Foreign Disinformation on Social Media*, pp. 43, 47.

54. See Jankowicz, *How to Lose the Information War*, p. 200.

55. See Jankowicz, *How to Lose the Information War*.

56. Colley, Granelli and Altuis, 'Disinformation's Societal Impact', pp. 89–140.

57. McIntyre, *Post-Truth*, p.158.

58. Bjola and Papadakis, 'Digital Propaganda, Counterpublics, and the Disruption of the Public Sphere', pp. 204–7.

59. Mare, Mabweazara and Moyo, '"Fake News" and Cyber-Propaganda in Sub-Saharan Africa', pp. 1–12.
60. Braw, *The Defender's Dilemma*.

EPILOGUE

1. Jenna McClaughlin and Zach Dorfman, 'Shattered: Inside the Secret Battle to Save America's Undercover Spies in the Digital Age', *Yahoo News*, 30/12/19.
2. Prince, *Civilian Warriors*, pp. 342–3.
3. Duncan, *In the Thick of It*, p. 247.
4. Cormac and Aldrich, 'Grey Is the New Black', pp. 477–94.
5. Florini, 'The End of Secrecy', pp. 50–63.
6. Jenna McClaughlin and Zach Dorfman, 'Shattered: Inside the Secret Battle to Save America's Undercover Spies in the Digital Age', *Yahoo News*, 30/12/19.
7. Ibid.; Cunliffe, 'Hard target espionage in the information era'; William M. Arkin, 'Inside the Military's Secret Undercover Army', *Newsweek*, 17/5/21.
8. Reisman and Baker, *Regulating Covert Action*, p. 14.
9. Waldman, *Vicarious Warfare*, p. 209.
10. Andrew Roth, 'European MPs Targeted by Deepfake Video Calls Imitating Russian Opposition', *Guardian*, 22/4/21.
11. National Intelligence Council, 'Global Trends 2040: A More Contested World', NIC 2021-02339 (2021), p. 65.
12. Ibid., p. 63.
13. Amy Zegart, 'Spies Like Us: The Promise and Peril of Crowdsourced Intelligence', *Foreign Affairs* (July/August 2021).
14. National Intelligence Council, 'Global Trends 2040: A More Contested World', NIC 2021-02339 (2021), p. 104.
15. Mumford, *Proxy Warfare*, p. 80.
16. National Intelligence Council, 'Foreign Threats to the 2020 US Federal Elections' (2021): https://www.dni.gov/files/ODNI/documents/assessments/ICA-declass-16MAR21.pdf, p.4.

BIBLIOGRAPHY

Abrahams, Alexei, and Leber, Andrew, 'Comparative Approaches to Mis/Disinformation. Electronic Armies or Cyber Knights? The Sources of Pro-Authoritarian Discourse on Middle East Twitter', *International Journal of Communication*, 15 (2021): 1173–1199

Abrahms, Max, and Mierau, Jochen, 'Leadership Matters: The Effects of Targeted Killings on Militant Group Tactics,' *Terrorism and Political Violence*, 29/5 (2017): 830–51

Abramovici, Pierre, 'The World Anti-Communist League: Origins, Structures and Activities', in Luc Van Dongen *et al.* (eds), *Transnational Anti-Communism and the Cold War* (Palgrave Macmillan, 2014): 113–29

Akbarzadeh, Shahram, Gourlay, William, and Ehteshami, Anoushiravan, 'Iranian proxies in the Syrian conflict: Tehran's "forward-defence" in action', *Journal of Strategic Studies* (iFirst, 2022): 1–24

Akbarzadeh, Shahram, and Ibrahimi, Niamatullah, 'The Taliban: a new proxy for Iran in Afghanistan?', *Third World Quarterly*, 41/5 (2020): 764–82

Akoto, William, 'Accountability and cyber conflict: examining institutional constraints on the use of cyber proxies', *Conflict Management and Peace Science* (iFirst, 2021): 1–22

Al Saud, Prince Turki Alfaisal, *The Afghanistan File* (Arabian Publishing, 2021)

Aldrich, Harriet, 'Uganda, Southern Sudan and the Idi Amin Coup', *The Journal of Imperial and Commonwealth History*, 48/6 (2020): 1109–39

Aldrich, Richard J., 'American Journalism and the Landscape of

Secrecy: Tad Szulc, the CIA and Cuba', *History*, 100/340 (2015): 189–209

Aldrich, Richard J., 'Beyond the Vigilant State: Globalisation and Intelligence', *Review of International Studies*, 35/4 (2009): 889–902

Aldrich, Richard J., and Cormac, Rory, *The Secret Royals: Spying and the Crown from Victoria to Diana* (Atlantic, 2021)

Aldrich, Richard J., and Cormac, Rory, *The Black Door: Spies: Secret Intelligence and British Prime Ministers* (William Collins, 2016)

Aldrich, Richard J., and Moran, Christopher R., '"Delayed Disclosure": National Security, Whistle-Blowers and the Nature of Secrecy', *Political Studies*, 67/2 (2019): 291–306

Andrew, Christopher, and Mitrokhin, Vasili, *The Mitrokhin Archive II: The KGB and the World* (Allen Lane, 2005)

Andrew, Christopher, and Gordievsky, Oleg, *KGB: The Inside Story* (HarperCollins, 1990)

Arendt, Hannah, *The Origins of Totalitarianism* (Meridian Books, 1958)

Babiracki, Patryk, 'Putin's postmodern war with the west', *The Wilson Quarterly* (Winter 2018)

Baggini, Julian, *A Short History of Truth: Consolations for a Post Truth World* (Quercus, 2017)

Bale, Jeffrey M., *The Darkest Side of Politics, I: Postwar Fascism, Covert Operations and Terrorism* (Routledge, 2018)

Banka, Andris, and Quinn, Adam, 'Killing Norms Softly: US Targeted Killing, Quasi-secrecy and the Assassination Ban', *Security Studies*, 27/4 (2018): 665–703

Bapat, Navin A., 'Understanding State Sponsorship of Militant Groups,' *British Journal of Political Science*, 42/1 (2012): 1–29

Barry, James A., 'Covert action can be just', *Orbis*, 37/3 (1993): 375–90

Bat, Jean-Pierre, 'Le secteur N (Afrique) et la fin de la Guerre froide', *Relations Internationales*, 165/1 (2016): 43–56

Bat, Jean-Pierre, *Le Syndrome Foccart: Politique Francaise En Afrique, 1959 a Nos Jours* (Gallimard, 2012)

Bauer, Kurt, *Hitlers zweiter Putsch: Dollfuß, die Nazis und der 25. Juli 1934* (Residenz Verlag, 2014)

Bay-Cheng, Sarah, 'Pixelated Memories: Performance, Media, and Digital Technology', *Contemporary Theatre Review*, 27/3 (2017): 324–39

Beesley, Ian, *The Official History of Cabinet Secretaries* (Routledge, 2016)

Belo, Dani, 'Conflict in the absence of war: a comparative analysis of China and Russia engagement in gray zone conflicts', *Canadian Foreign Policy Journal*, 26/1 (2020): 73–91

Belton, Catherine, *Putin's People: How the KGB Took Back Russia and Then Took on the West* (William Collins, 2021)

Benkler, Yochai, Faris, Robert, and Roberts, Hal, *Network Propaganda: Manipulation, Disinformation, and Radicalization in American Politics* (Oxford University Press, 2018)

Bennett, W. Lance, and Livingston, Steven, 'The Disinformation Order: Disruptive communication and the decline of democratic institutions', *European Journal of Communication*, 33/2 (2018): 122–39

Bergen, Peter, and Sims, A.G., 'America's Drone Wars Outside of Conventional Warzones', in Michael A. Sheehan *et al.* (eds), *Routledge Handbook of US Counterterrorism and Irregular Warfare Operations* (Routledge, 2021): 460–76

Bergman, Ronan, *Rise and Kill First: The Secret History of Israel's Targeted Assassinations* (Random House, 2018)

Berkowitz, Jeremy M., 'Delegating Terror: Principal–Agent Based Decision Making in State Sponsorship of Terrorism,' *International Interactions*, 44:4 (2018): 709–48

Bezci, Egemen, *Turkish Intelligence and the Cold War: The Turkish Secret Service, the US and the UK* (IB Tauris, 2020)

Bjola, Corneliu and Papadakis, Kryssianna, 'Digital Propaganda, Counterpublics, and the Disruption of the Public Sphere', in Timothy Clack and Robert Johnson (eds), *The World Information War: Western Resilience, Campaigning and Cognitive Effects* (Routledge, 2021)

Blackburn, Simon, *Truth: A Guide for the Perplexed* (Penguin, 2005)

Blackstock, Paul, *The Strategy of Subversion: Manipulating the Politics of Other Nations* (Quadrangle, 1954)

Bolsover, Gillian, and Howard, Philip, 'Computational Propaganda and Political Big Data: Moving Towards a More Critical Research Agenda', *Big Data*, 5/4 (2017): 273–6

Boutton, Andrew, and Dolan, Thomas M., 'Enemies in the Shadows: On the Origins and Survival of Clandestine Clients', *International Studies Quarterly*, 65/1 (2021): 146–59

Brantly, Aaron F., 'A Brief History of Fake: Surveying Russian Disinformation from the Russian Empire through the Cold War and to the Present', in Christopher Whyte *et al.* (eds), *Information Warfare in the Age of Cyber Conflict* (Routledge, 2021)

Braw, Elisabeth, *The Defender's Dilemma: Identifying and Deterring Gray-Zone Aggression* (AEI Press, 2022)

Briant, Emma L., 'Lessons from the Cambridge Analytica Crisis: Confronting Today's (Dis)information Challenges', *The Journal of Intelligence, Conflict, and Warfare*, 3/3 (2021): 125–7

Brown, Joseph M., and Fazal, Tanisha M., '#SorryNotSorry: Why states neither confirm nor deny responsibility for cyber operations', *European Journal of International Security*, 6/4 (2021): 401–17

Buchanan, Ben, *The Hacker and the State: Cyber Attacks and the New Normal of Geopolitics* (Harvard University Press, 2020)

Buchanan, Ben, *The Cyber Security Dilemma* (Oxford University Press, 2017)

Burkett, Jodi, 'The National Union of Students and Transnational Solidarity, 1958–68', *European Review of History*, 21/4 (2014): 539–55

Byman, Daniel, 'Understanding, and Misunderstanding, State Sponsorship of Terrorism', *Studies in Conflict & Terrorism* (iFirst, 2020)

Byman, Daniel, *et al.*, *Trends in Outside Support for Insurgent Movements* (RAND, 2005)

Byman, Daniel, and Kreps, Sarah E., 'Agents of Destruction? Applying Principal-Agent Analysis to State-Sponsored Terrorism', *International Studies Perspectives*, 11/1 (2010): 1–18

Carson, Austin, *Secret Wars: Covert Conflict in International Politics* (Princeton University Press, 2018)

Carson, Austin, and Yarhi-Milo, Keren, 'Covert Communication: The Intelligibility and Credibility of Signaling in Secret', *Security Studies*, 26/1 (2017): 124–56

Carvin, Stephanie, 'The Trouble with Targeted Killing', *Security Studies*, 21/3 (2012): 529–55

Charon, Paul, et Jeangène Vilmer, Jean-Baptiste, 'Les Opérations d'influence chinoises. Un moment machiavélien, rapport de l'Institut de recherche stratégique de l'École militaire (IRSEM)', Paris, Ministère des Armées, 2e édition, 2021

Chernobrov, Dimitry, 'Strategic Humour: Public Diplomacy and Comic Framing of Foreign Policy Issues', *The British Journal of Politics and International Relations* (iFirst, 2021)

Chernobrov, Dimitry, and Briant, Emma L., 'Competing Propagandas: How the United States and Russia represent mutual propaganda activities', *Politics* (iFirst, 2020): 1–17

Chopin, Olivier, and Oudet, Benjamin, *Renseignement et Sécurité* (Armand Colin, 2019)

Clack, Timothy, and Selisny, Louise, 'From Beijing Bloggers to Whitehall Writers: Observations on the "Invisible War"', in Timothy Clack and Robert Johnson (eds), *The World Information War: Western Resilience, Campaigning and Cognitive Effects* (Routledge, 2021): 259–280

Clarke, Richard A., and Knake, Robert, *Cyber War: The Next Threat to National Security and What to Do About It* (HarperCollins, 2010)

Cogan, Charles, 'Hunters Not Gatherers: Intelligence in the Twenty-first Century', *Intelligence and National Security*, 29/2 (2004): 304–21

Cohen, Raphael S., *et al.*, *Combating Foreign Disinformation on Social Media: Study Overview and Recommendations* (RAND, 2021)

Coker, Christopher, *War in an Age of Risk* (Polity, 2009)

Coker, Christopher, 'Post-modern war', *The RUSI Journal*, 143/3 (1998): 7–14

Colley, Thomas, Granelli, Francesca, and Altuis, Jente, 'Disinformation's Societal Impact: Britain, Covid and Beyond', *Defence Strategic Communications*, 8 (2020): 89–140

Collins, Catherine, and Frantz, Douglas, *Fallout: The True Story of the CIA's Secret War on Nuclear Trafficking* (Free Press, 2011)

Constantino, Zachary, 'The India–Pakistan Rivalry in Afghanistan', USIP Special Report, no. 462 (US Institute of Peace, 2020)

Cormac, Rory, 'The currency of covert action: British special political action in Latin America, 1961–64', *Journal of Strategic Studies* (iFirst, 2020)

Cormac, Rory, *Disrupt and Deny: Spies, Special Forces and the Secret Pursuit of British Foreign Policy* (Oxford University Press, 2018)

Cormac, Rory, and Aldrich, Richard J., 'Grey Is the New Black: Covert Action and Implausible Deniability', *International Affairs*, 94/3 (2018): 477–94

Cormac, Rory, 'The Information Research Department, Unattributable Propaganda, and Northern Ireland, 1971–1973: Promising Salvation but Ending in Failure?', *English Historical Review*, 131/552 (2016): 1074–104

Cormac, Rory, Walton, Calder, and Van Puyvelde, Damien, 'What Constitutes Successful Covert Action? Evaluating Unacknowledged Interventionism in Foreign Affairs', *Review of International Studies* (iFirst, 2021): 1–18

Crile, George, *Charlie Wilson's War* (Atlantic Books, 2002)

Crilley, Rhys, 'International relations in the age of "post-truth" politics', *International Affairs*, 94/2 (2018): 417–25

Crilley, Rhys, and Chatterje-Doody, Precious, 'Security studies in the age of "post-truth" politics: in defence of poststructuralism', *Critical Studies on Security*, 7/2 (2019): 166–70

Cullather, Nick, *Secret History: The CIA's Classified Account of its Operations in Guatemala, 1952–54* (Stanford University Press, 1999)

Cunliffe, Kyle S., 'Hard target espionage in the information era: new challenges for the second oldest profession', *Intelligence and National Security* (iFirst, 2021)

D'Ancona, Matthew, *Post-truth: The New War on Truth and How to Fight Back* (Ebury Press, 2017)

D'Ancona, Matthew, *In It Together: The Inside Story of the Coalition Government* (Penguin, 2004)

Daugherty, William, *Executive Secrets: Covert Action and the Presidency* (University Press of Kentucky, 2004)

David, Steven, 'Soviet Involvement in Third World Coups', *International Security*, 11/6 (1986): 3–36

Davies, Robert, 'The SADF's Covert War Against Mozambique', in Jacklyn Cook (ed.), *War and Society: The Militarisation of South Africa* (David Philip, 1989): 103–15

Dawson, Andrew, and Innes, Martin, 'How Russia's Internet Research Agency Built its Disinformation Campaign', *Political Quarterly*, 90/2 (2019): 245–56

de Marolles, Alain, 'La Tradition Française de l'Action Invisible', in Pierre Lacoste (ed.), *Le Renseignement à la Française* (Economica, 1999)

De Paor, Saoirse, and Heravi, Bahareh, 'Information literacy and fake news: How the field of librarianship can help combat the epidemic of fake news', *The Journal of Academic Librarianship*, 46/5 (2020): 1–8

de Wijze, Stephen, 'Targeted killing: a "dirty hands" analysis', *Contemporary Politics*, 15/3 (2009): 305–20

Dear, Keith, 'Artificial Intelligence, Security and Society', in Timothy Clack and Robert Johnson (eds), *The World Information War: Western Resilience, Campaigning and Cognitive Effects* (Routledge, 2021): 231–256

Dear, Keith, 'Beheading the Hydra? Does Killing Terrorist or Insurgent Leaders Work?', *Defence Studies*, 13/3 (2013): 293–337

Denécém, Eric, 'France: The Intelligence Services' Historical and Cultural Context', in Bob de Graaff *et al.* (eds), *Handbook of European Intelligence Cultures* (Rowman and Littlefield, 2016): 135–46

Devine, Jack, *Spymaster's Prism: The Fight Against Russian Aggression* (Potomac Books, 2021)

Devine, Jack, and Mattingly, Amanda, 'The Iran–Contra Affair and the Afghan Task Force: Lessons in Covert Action', in Michael A. Sheehan *et al.* (eds), *Routledge Handbook of US Counterterrorism and Irregular Warfare Operations* (Routledge, 2021): 212–22

Domínguez, Jorge I., 'The @#$%& Missile Crisis: (Or, What Was "Cuban" about U.S. Decisions during the Cuban Missile Crisis?)', *Diplomatic History*, 24/2 (2000): 305–15

Downes, Alexander B., *Catastrophic Success: Why Foreign Imposed Regime Change Goes Wrong* (Cornell University Press, 2021)

Duncan, Alan, *In The Thick of It: The Private Diaries of a Minister* (William Collins, 2021)

Eason, Thomas, Daddow, Oliver, and Cormac, Rory, 'From secrecy to accountability: The politics of exposure in the Belgrano affair', *The British Journal of Politics and International Relations*, 22/3 (2020): 542–60

Echevarria II, Antulio, *Reconsidering the American Way of War: US Military Practice from the Revolution to Afghanistan* (Georgetown University Press, 2014)

Edwards, Aaron, *Agents of Influence: Britain's Secret Intelligence War Against the IRA* (Merrion Press, 2021)

Eftimiades, Nicholas, *Chinese Espionage: Operations and Tactics* (Vitruvian Press, 2020)

Egloff, Florian J., and Smeets, Max, 'Publicly attributing cyber attacks: a framework', *Journal of Strategic Studies* (iFirst, 2021)

Ehrhart, Hans-Georg, 'Postmodern warfare and the blurred boundaries between war and peace', *Defense & Security Analysis*, 33/3 (2017): 263–75

Ekdale, Brian, and Tully, Melissa, 'African Elections as a Testing Ground: Comparing Coverage of Cambridge Analytica in Nigerian and Kenyan Newspapers', *African Journalism Studies*, 40/4 (2019): 27–43

Fabre, Cécile, 'The Case for Foreign Electoral Subversion', *Ethics & International Affairs*, 32/3 (2018): 283–92

Finlan, Alastair, 'A dangerous pathway? Toward a theory of special forces', *Comparative Strategy*, 38/4 (2019): 255–75

Fischerkeller, Michael P., and Harknett, Richard J., 'Deterrence is Not a Credible Strategy for Cyberspace,' *Orbis*, 61/3 (2017): 381–93

Fitzgerald, Chad W., and Brantly, Aaron F., 'Subverting Reality: The Role of Propaganda in 21st Century Intelligence', *International Journal of Intelligence and CounterIntelligence*, 30/2 (2017): 215–40

Florini, Ann, 'The End of Secrecy', *Foreign Policy*, 111 (1998): 50–63

Foot, M. R. D., *SOE in France* (Her Majesty's Stationery Office, 1969)

Freelon, Deen, and Wells, Chris, 'Disinformation as Political Communication', *Political Communication*, 37/2 (2020): 145–56

Fulda, Andreas, and Missal, David, 'Mitigating threats to academic freedom in Germany: the role of the state, universities, learned societies and China', *The International Journal of Human Rights* (iFirst, 2021)

Galeotti, Mark, *STORM-333: KGB and Spetsnaz Seize Kabul, Soviet-Afghan War 1979* (Osprey, 2021)

Galeotti, Mark, *Russian Political War: Moving Beyond the Hybrid* (Routledge, 2019)

Galeotti, Mark, 'Hybrid, ambiguous, and non-linear? How new is Russia's "new way of war"?', *Small Wars & Insurgencies*, 27/2 (2016): 282–301

Gartzke, Erik, 'The Myth of Cyberwar: Bringing War in Cyberspace Back Down to Earth', *International Security*, 38/2 (2013): 41–73

Gartzke, Eric, and Lindsay, Jon R., 'Weaving Tangled Webs: Offense, Defense, and Deception in Cyberspace', *Security Studies*, 24/2 (2015): 316–48

Giles, Keir, 'Russian Information Warfare', in Timothy Clack and Robert Johnson (eds.) *The World Information War: Western Resilience, Campaigning and Cognitive Effects* (Routledge, 2021)

Giles, Keir, 'Russian Information Warfare: Construct and Purpose', in Christopher Whyte *et al*, (eds), *Information Warfare in the Age of Cyber Conflict* (Routledge, 2021)

Giles, Keir, *Moscow Rules: What Drives Russia to Confront the West* (Brookings Institution Press, 2018)

Gioe, David, Goodman, Michael S., and Frey, David S., 'Unforgiven: Russian intelligence vengeance as political theatre and strategic messaging', *Intelligence and National Security*, 34/4 (2019): 561–75

Gleditsch, Kristian, *et al.*, 'Fighting at Home, Fighting Abroad: How Civil Wars Lead to International Disputes', *The Journal of Conflict Resolution*, 52/4 (2008): 479–506

Gleis, Joshua L., and Berti, Benedetta, *Hezbollah and Hamas: A Comparative Study* (Johns Hopkins University Press, 2012)

Gould, Lauren, and Stel, Nora, 'Strategic Ignorance and the Legitimation of Remote Warfare: The Hawija Bombardments', *Security Dialogue* (iFirst, 2021)

Grauer, Ryan, and Tierney, Dominic, 'The Arsenal of Insurrection: Explaining Rising Support for Rebels', *Security Studies*, 27/2 (2018): 263–95

Griffin, Christopher, 'French military policy in the Nigerian Civil War, 1967–1970', *Small Wars & Insurgencies*, 26/1 (2015): 114–35

Hamilton, Clive, and Ohlberg, Mareike, *Hidden Hand: Exposing How the Chinese Communist Party is Reshaping the World* (Oneworld, 2020)

Hänni, Adrian, 'A Global Crusade against Communism: The Cercle in the "Second World War"', in Luc Van Dongen *et al.* (eds), *Transnational Anti-Communism and the Cold War* (Palgrave Macmillan, 2014): 161–74

Haslam, Jonathan, *Near and Distant Neighbours: A New History of Soviet Intelligence* (Oxford University Press, 2015)

Hayes, Paddy, *Queen of Spies: Daphne Park, Britain's Cold War Spymaster* (Duckworth Overlook, 2015)

Healey, Jason, 'The implications of persistent (and permanent) engagement in cyberspace', *Journal of Cybersecurity*, 5/ 1 (2019): 1–15

Hebditch, David, and Connor, Ken, *How to Stage a Military Coup: From Planning to Execution* (Skyhorse Publishing Inc, 2017)

Heng, Yee-Kuang, 'The "Transformation of War" Debate', *International Relations,* 20/1, (2006): 69–91

Hoffmann, Sophia, 'Circulation, not Cooperation: Towards a new understanding of intelligence agencies as transnationally constituted knowledge providers', *Intelligence and National Security* (iFirst, 2021)

Holland, Max, 'Operation PBHistory: The Aftermath of SUCCESS', *International Journal of Intelligence and Counterintelligence,* 17/2 (2004): 300–32

Hughes, Geraint, 'Syria and the Perils of Proxy Warfare', *Small Wars and Insurgencies,* 25/3 (2014): 522–38

Hughes, Geraint, *My Enemy's Enemy: Proxy Warfare in International Relations* (Sussex Academic Press, 2012)

Hussain Sharfi, Mohammed, 'Sudan and the assassination attempt on President Mubarak in June 1995: a cornerstone in ideological reverse', *Journal of Eastern African Studies,* 12/3 (2018): 454–72

Inkster, Nigel, 'War in an Age of Uncertainty', in Timothy Clack and Robert Johnson (eds), *The World Information War: Western Resilience, Campaigning and Cognitive Effects* (Routledge, 2021): 281–286

Jamieson, Kathleen Hall, *Cyberwar: How Russian Hackers and Trolls Helped Elect a President* (Oxford University Press, 2018)

Jankowicz, Nina, *How to Lose the Information War: Russia, Fake News and the Future of Conflict* (Bloomsbury, 2020)

Johnson, Loch K., *The Third Option: Covert Action and American Foreign Policy* (Oxford University Press, 2022)

Johnson, Loch K., 'Reflections on the ethics and effectiveness of America's "third option": covert action and U.S. foreign policy', *Intelligence and National Security,* 35/5 (2020): 669–85

Johnson, Loch K., 'Spies and Scholars in the United States: Winds of Ambivalence in the Groves of Academia', *Intelligence and National Security,* 34/1 (2019): 1–21

Johnson, Loch K., *National Security Intelligence* (Polity, 2017)

Johnson, Loch K., 'National Security Intelligence in the United States: A Performance Checklist', *Intelligence and National Security,* 26/5 (2011): 607–15

Johnson, Robert, 'Hybrid War and Its Countermeasures: A Critique of the Literature', *Small Wars & Insurgencies,* 29/1 (2018): 141–63

Jones, Matt, 'Sarin Gas Heartbreak: Theatre and Post-Truth Warfare in Syria', *Theatre Journal*, 72/1 (2020): 61–79

Jonsson, Oscar, and Seely, Robert, 'Russian Full-Spectrum Conflict: An Appraisal After Ukraine', *The Journal of Slavic Military Studies*, 28/1 (2015): 1–22

Jordan, Jenna, 'When Heads Roll: Assessing the Effectiveness of Leadership Decapitation', *Security Studies*, 18/4 (2009): 719–55

Joseph, Michael F., and Poznansky, Michael, 'Media technology, covert action, and the politics of exposure', *Journal of Peace Research*, 55/3 (2018): 320–35

Jowett, Garth, and O'Donnell, Victoria, *Propaganda and Persuasion* (Sage, 2015)

Kahana, Ephraim, 'Covert Action: The Israeli Experience', in Loch K. Johnson (ed.), *Strategic Intelligence Vol. 3: Covert Action – Behind the Veils of Secret Foreign Policy* (Praeger Security International, 2007): 61–82

Kahne, Joseph, and Bowyer, Benjamin, 'Educating for Democracy in a Partisan Age: Confronting the Challenges of Motivated Reasoning and Misinformation', *American Educational Research Journal*, 54/1 (2017): 3–34

Kaminska, Monica, 'Restraint under conditions of uncertainty: Why the United States tolerates cyberattacks', *Journal of Cybersecurity*, 7/1 (2021): 1–15

Kania, Elsa B., 'The Ideological Battlefield: China's Approach to Political Warfare in an Age of Cyber Conflict', in Christopher Whyte *et al.* (eds), *Information Warfare in the Age of Cyber Conflict* (Routledge, 2021): 42–53

Keller, Franziska B., Schoch, David, Stier, Sebastian, and Yang, JungHwan, 'Political Astroturfing on Twitter: How to Coordinate a Disinformation Campaign', *Political Communication*, 37/2 (2020): 256–80

Kellerhoff, Sven Felix, and Von Kostka, Bernd, *Capital of Spies: Intelligence Agencies in Berlin during the Cold War* (Casemate, 2021)

Kello, Lucas, 'Cyber legalism: why it fails and what to do about it', *Journal of Cybersecurity*, 7/1 (2021): 1–15

Kiras, James D., *Special Operations and Strategy: From World War II to the War on Terrorism* (Routledge, 2007)

Kirshner, Jonathan, 'Currency and Coercion in the Twenty-first Century', *European University Institute Working Papers*, 2005/13 (2013)

Knott, Stephen, *Secret and Sanctioned: Covert Action and the American Presidency* (Oxford University Press, 1996)

Kotek, Joel, *Students and the Cold War* (Palgrave Macmillan, 1996)

Kragh, Martin, and Åsberg, Sebastian, 'Russia's strategy for influence through public diplomacy and active measures: the Swedish case', *Journal of Strategic Studies*, 40/6 (2017): 773–816

Kreps, Sarah, and Schneider, Jacquelyn, 'Escalation firebreaks in the cyber, conventional, and nuclear domains: moving beyond effects-based logics', *Journal of Cybersecurity*, 5/1 (2019): 1–11

Krishnan, Armin, 'Controlling partners and proxies in pro-insurgency paramilitary operations: the case of Syria', *Intelligence and National Security*, 34/4 (2019): 544–60

Krishnan, Armin, *Why Paramilitary Operations Fail* (Palgrave, 2018)

Kurlantzick, Joshua, *A Great Place to Have a War: America in Laos and the Birth of a Military CIA* (Simon & Schuster, 2017)

Landon-Murray, Michael, Mujkic, Edin, and Nussbaum, Brian, 'Disinformation in Contemporary U.S. Foreign Policy: Impacts and Ethics in an Era of Fake News, Social Media, and Artificial Intelligence', *Public Integrity*, 21/5 (2019): 512–22

Leahy, Thomas, *Intelligence War Against the IRA* (Cambridge University Press, 2020)

Lee, Melissa M., *Crippling Leviathan: How Foreign Subversion Weakens the State* (Cornell University Press, 2020)

LeoGrande, William M., *Our Own Backyard: The United States in Central America, 1977–1992* (University of North Carolina Press, 1998)

Levin, Dov, 'Will you still love me tomorrow? Partisan electoral interventions, foreign policy compliance, and voting in the UN', *International Interactions* (iFirst, 2021)

Levin, Dov, *Meddling in the Ballot Box: The Causes and Effects of Partisan Electoral Interventions* (Oxford University Press, 2020)

Levin, Dov, 'A Vote for Freedom? The Effects of Partisan Electoral Interventions on Regime Type', *Journal of Conflict Resolution*, 63/4 (2018): 839–68

Levin, Dov, 'When the Great Power Gets a Vote: The Effects of Great Power Electoral Interventions on Election Results', *International Studies Quarterly*, 60/2 (2016): 189–202

Libicki, Martin, 'The Convergence of Information Warfare', in Christopher Whyte *et al.* (eds), *Information Warfare in the Age of Cyber Conflict* (Routledge, 2021): 15–26

Lindsay, John, 'Stuxnet and the Limits of Cyber Warfare', *Security Studies*, 22/3 (2013): 365–404

Liss, Jodi, 'Making Monetary Mischief: Using Currency as a Weapon', *World Policy Journal*, 24/4 (2007/8): 29–38

Lockhart, James, 'How Effective Are Covert Operations? The CIA's Intervention in Chile, 1964–73', *Marine Corps University Journal*, 10/1 (2019): 21–49

Long, Stephen, 'CIA–MI6 psychological warfare and the subversion of communist Albania in the early Cold War', *Intelligence and National Security*, 35/6 (2020): 787–807

Lukito, Josephine, 'Coordinating a Multi-Platform Disinformation Campaign: Internet Research Agency Activity on Three U.S. Social Media Platforms, 2015 to 2017', *Political Communication*, 37/2 (2020): 238–55

Luttwak, Edward N., *Coup d'État: A Practical Handbook*, revised edn (Harvard University Press, 2016)

Mager Stellman, Jeanne, *et al.*, 'The extent and patterns of usage of Agent Orange and other herbicides in Vietnam', *Nature*, 422 (2003): 681–87

Maher, Richard, 'The covert campaign against Iran's nuclear program: Implications for the theory and practice of counterproliferation', *Journal of Strategic Studies* (iFirst, 2019)

Mainwaring, Sarah, 'Division D: Operation Rubicon and the CIA's Secret SIGINT Empire', *Intelligence and National Security*, 35/5 (2020): 623–40

Manor, Ilan, 'The Russians are Laughing! The Russians are Laughing! How Russian Diplomats Employ Humour in Online Public Diplomacy', *Global Society* (iFirst, 2020)

Mare, Admire, Mawindi Mabweazara, Hayes, and Moyo, Dumisani, '"Fake News" and Cyber-Propaganda in Sub-Saharan Africa: Recentering the Research Agenda', *African Journalism Studies*, 40/4 (2019): 1–12

Marshall, Tim, *Prisoners of Geography: Ten Maps that Tell You Everything You Need to Know about Global Politics* (Elliott and Thompson, 2016)

Marten, Kimberly, 'Russia's use of semi-state security forces: the case of the Wagner Group', *Post-Soviet Affairs*, 35/3 (2019): 181–204

Maschmeyer, Lennart, 'The Subversive Trilemma: Why Cyber Operations Fall Short of Expectations', *International Security*, 46/2 (2021): 51–90

McDougall, Julian, 'Media Literacy vs Fake News: Critical Thinking, Resilience and Civic Engagement', *Media Studies*, 10/19 (2019): 29–45

McIntyre, Lee, *Post-Truth* (MIT Press, 2018)

Melley, Timothy, *The Covert Sphere: Secrecy, Fiction and the National Security State* (Cornell University Press, 2012)

Mireval, Damien, *Tchad, les guerres secrètes de la France: Les arcanes du renseignement français (1969–1990)* (VA Press, 2021)

Miskimmon, Alister, *et al.*, *Strategic Narratives: Communication Power and the New World Order* (Routledge, 2013)

Mistry, Kaeten, 'Approaches to Understanding the Inaugural CIA Covert Operation in Italy: Exploding Useful Myths', *Intelligence and National Security*, 26/2–3 (2011): 246–68

Moghadam, Assaf, and Wyss, Michel, 'The Political Power of Proxies: Why Nonstate Actors Use Local Surrogates', *International Security*, 44(/4 (2020): 119–57

Monaghan, Andrew, *Dealing with the Russians* (Polity, 2019)

Monaghan, Andrew, 'The "War" in Russia's Hybrid Warfare', *Parameters*, 45/4 (2015)

Moore, Matthew, 'Selling to Both Sides: The Effects of Major Conventional Weapons Transfers on Civil War Severity and Duration', *International Interactions*, 38/3 (2012): 325–47

Msindo, Enocent, 'Winning hearts and minds': Crisis and Propaganda in Colonial Zimbabwe, 1962–1970', *Journal of Southern African Studies*, 35/3 (2009): 663–81

Mumford, Andrew, *Proxy Warfare* (Polity, 2013)

Mumford, Andrew, 'Proxy Warfare and the Future of Conflict', *The RUSI Journal*, 158/2 (2013): 40–46

Mwende Maweu, Jacinta, '"Fake Elections"? Cyber Propaganda, Disinformation and the 2017 General Elections in Kenya', *African Journalism Studies*, 40/4 (2019): 62–76

Myers, Kevin, *Watching the Door: A Memoir, 1971–1978* (Lilliput, 2006)

Nehring, Christopher, 'Active and Sharp Measures: Cooperation between the Soviet KGB and Bulgarian State Security', *Journal of Cold War Studies*, 23/4 (2021): 3–33

Ncube, Lyton, 'Digital Media, Fake News and Pro-Movement for Democratic Change (MDC) Alliance Cyber-Propaganda during the 2018 Zimbabwe Election', *African Journalism Studies*, 40/4 (2019): 44–61

Nouzille, Vincent, *Les Tueurs de la République: Assassinats et Opérations Spéciales des Services Secrets* (Fayard, 2016)

O'Brien, Kevin, 'The Use of Assassination as a Tool of State Policy: South Africa's Counter-Revolutionary Strategy 1979–92 (Part II)', *Terrorism and Political Violence*, 13/2 (2001): 107–42

O'Rourke, Lindsey, *Covert Regime Change: America's Secret Cold War* (Cornell University Press, 2018)

Obama, Barack, *A Promised Land* (Viking, 2020)

Otto, Jacob, and Spaniel, William, 'Doubling Down: The Danger of Disclosing Secret Action', *International Studies Quarterly*, 65/2 (2021): 500–511

Owen Jones, Marc, 'Disinformation Superspreaders: The Weaponization of COVID-19 Fake News in the Persian Gulf and Beyond', *Global Discourse*, 10/4 (2020): 431–7

Owen Jones, Marc, 'Propaganda, Fake News and Fake Trends: The Weaponization of Twitter Bots in the Gulf Crisis', *International Journal of Communication*, Vol. 3 (2019): 1389–415

Pantucci, Rafaello, and Lain, Sarah, *China's Eurasian Pivot* (Routledge, 2017)

Parker, Celia G., 'The UK National Security Council and misuse of intelligence by policy makers: reducing the risk?', *Intelligence and National Security*, 35:7 (2020): 990–1006

Paterson, Thomas G., 'Fixation with Cuba: The Bay of Pigs, Missile Crisis, and Covert War Against Cuba', in Thomas G. Paterson (ed.), *Kennedy's Quest for Victory: American Foreign Policy, 1961–63* (Oxford University Press, 1989)

Pattison, James, 'The Ethics of Arming Rebels', *Ethics and International Affairs*, 29/4 (2015): 455–71

Perina, Alexandra, 'Black holes and open secrets: the impact of covert action on international law', *Columbia Journal of Transnational Law*, 53/3 (2015): 507–83

Pier, Jarred, 'Commanding the Trend: Social Media as Information Warfare', in Christopher Whyte *et al.* (eds), *Information Warfare in the Age of Cyber Conflict* (Routledge, 2021): 88–113

Plattner, Marc F., 'Democracy Embattled', *Journal of Democracy*, 31/1 (2020): 5–10

Pomerantsev, Peter, *This Is Not Propaganda: Adventures in the War Against Reality* (Public Affairs, 2019)

Pomerantsev, Peter, *Nothing Is True and Everything Is Possible* (Faber and Faber, 2015)

Porter, Patrick, *The False Promise of the Liberal Order: Nostalgia, Delusion and the Rise of Trump* (Polity, 2020)

Pouget, Émile, *Le Sabotage* (Charles H. Kerr and Co., 1912)

Powell, Nathaniel K., *France's Wars in Chad: Military Intervention and Decolonisation in Africa* (Cambridge University Press, 2020)

Powell, Nathaniel K., 'The "Cuba of the West"? France's Cold War in Zaïre, 1977–1978', *Journal of Cold War Studies*, 18/2 (2016): 64–96

Pozen, David, 'The leaky Leviathan: why the government condemns and condones unlawful disclosures of information', *Harvard Law Review*, 127/512 (2013): 512–635

Poznansky, Michael, 'The Psychology of Overt and Covert Intervention,' *Security Studies* (iFirst, 2021)

Poznansky, Michael, *In the Shadow of International Law: Secrecy and Regime Change in the Postwar World* (Oxford University Press, 2020)

Poznansky, Michael, 'Revisiting Plausible Deniability', *Journal of Strategic Studies* (iFirst, 2020)

Poznansky, Michael, 'Feigning Compliance: Covert Action and International Law', *International Studies Quarterly*, 63/1 (2019): 72–84

Poznansky, Michael, 'Stasis or Decay? Reconciling Covert War and the Democratic Peace', *International Studies Quarterly*, 59/4 (2015): 815–26

Prince, Erik, *Civilian Warriors: The Inside Story of Blackwater* (Penguin, 2013)

Punch, Maurice, *State Violence, Collusion and the Troubles: Counterinsurgency, Government Deviance and Northern Ireland* (Pluto, 2012)

Quirk, Sean P., 'Lawfare in the Disinformation Age: Chinese Interference in Taiwan's 2020 Elections', *Harvard International Law Journal*, 62/2 (2021): 525–67

Raman, B., *The Kaoboys of R&AW: Down Memory Lane* (Lancer Publishers, 2007)

Ramazani, R. K., 'Who Lost America? The Case of Iran', *The Middle Eastern Journal*, 36:1 (1982): 5–21

Rauta, Vladimir, '"Proxy War" – A Reconceptualisation', *Civil Wars*, 23/1 (2021): 1–24

Rauta, Vladimir, 'Proxy Warfare and the Future of Conflict: Take Two', *The RUSI Journal*, 165/2 (2020): 1–10

Rauta, Vladimir, 'A Structural Relational Analysis of Party Dynamics in Proxy Wars', *International Relations*, 32/4 (2018): 449–67

Rauta, Vladimir, 'Proxy agents, auxiliary forces, and sovereign defection: assessing the outcomes of using non-state actors in civil conflicts', *Southeast European and Black Sea Studies*, 16/1 (2016): 91–111

Reed, Thomas, *At the Abyss: An Insider's History of the Cold War* (Presidio, 2005)

Reeder, Bryce W., 'Civil War and the Severity of Militarized Interstate Disputes', *Research and Politics* (2014): 1–8

Reisman, Michael, and Baker, James, *Regulating Covert Action* (Yale University Press, 2011)

Renz, Bettina, 'Russia and "hybrid warfare"', *Contemporary Politics*, 22/3 (2016): 283–300

Reyntjens, Filip, *The Great African War: Congo and Regional Geopolitics, 1996–2006* (Cambridge University Press, 2009)

Richelson, Jeffrey, *Sword and Shield: Soviet Intelligence and Security Apparatus* (Ballinger, 1986)

Rid, Thomas, *Active Measures: The Secret History of Disinformation and Political Warfare* (Macmillan USA, 2020)

Rid, Thomas, *Cyber War Will Not Take Place* (Hurst, 2013)

Rid, Thomas, and Buchanan, Ben, 'Attributing Cyber Attacks', *Journal of Strategic Studies*, 38:1–2 (2015): 4–37

Robbins, Michael, 'Paul Muldoon's Covert Operations', *Modern Philology*, 109/2 (2011): 266–99

Robinson, Linda, 'The Future of Special Operations: Beyond Kill and Capture', *Foreign Affairs*, 91 (2012): 110–12

Rogers, Paul, *et al.*, 'Biological Warfare against Crops', *Scientific American*, 280/6 (1999): 70–75

Rogin, Michael, '"Make My Day!": Spectacle as Amnesia in Imperial Politics', *Representations*, 29 (1990): 99–123

Romerstein, Herbert, 'Disinformation as a KGB Weapon in the Cold War', *Journal of Intelligence History*, 1/1 (2001): 54–67

Romerstein, Herbert, *Soviet Agents of Influence* (Center for Intelligence Studies, 1991)

Samant, M. N. R., *Operation X: The Untold Story of India's Naval War in East Pakistan* (HarperCollins, 2019)

Sanger, David, *Confront and Conceal: Obama's Secret Wars and Surprising Use of American Power* (Crown Publishers, 2012)

Schmidt, Elizabeth, *Foreign Intervention in Africa: From the Cold War to the War on Terror* (Cambridge University Press, 2013)

Schultz, Kenneth A., 'The Enforcement Problem in Coercive Bargaining: Interstate Conflict Over Rebel Support in Civil Wars', *International Organization*, 64/02 (2010): 281–312

Schultz, Richard, and Godson, Roy, *Dezinformatsia: Active Measures in Soviet Strategy* (Pergamon-Brassey's, 1984)

Selvage, Douglas, 'Operation "Denver": The East German Ministry for State Security and the KGB's AIDS Disinformation Campaign, 1986–1989 (Part 2)', *Journal of Cold War Studies*, 23/3 (2021): 4–80

Shaffer, Ryan, 'Indian spies inside Pakistan: South Asian human intelligence across borders', *Intelligence and National Security*, 34/5 (2019): 727–42

Shaffer, Ryan, 'Unraveling India's Foreign Intelligence: The Origins and Evolution of the Research and Analysis Wing', *International Journal of Intelligence and CounterIntelligence*, 28/2 (2015): 252–89

Shimer, David, *Rigged: America, Russia and One Hundred Years of Covert Electoral Interference* (William Collins, 2020)

Simon, Roberto, *O Brasil contra a democracia: A ditadura, o golpe no Chile e a Guerra Fria na América do Sul* (Companhia das Letras, 2021)

Sirrs, Owen L., 'The perils of multinational intelligence coalitions: Britain, America and the origins of Pakistan's ISI', *Intelligence and National Security*, 33/1 (2018): 36–47

Sirrs, Owen L., *Pakistan's Inter-Services Intelligence Directorate: Covert Action and Internal Operations* (Routledge, 2017)

Sirrs, Owen L., *A History of the Egyptian Intelligence Service: A History of the Mukhabarat, 1910–2009* (Routledge, 2010)

Smith, Gregory, 'Secret but constrained: The impact of elite opposition on covert operations', *International Organization*, 73:3 (2019): 685–707

Stampnitzky, Lisa, 'Truth and consequences? Reconceptualizing the politics of exposure', *Security Dialogue*, 51/6 (2021): 597–613

Stempel, John, 'Covert Action and Diplomacy' in Loch K. Johnson (ed.), *Strategic Intelligence Vol. 3: Covert Action – Behind the Veils of Secret Foreign Policy* (Praeger Security International, 2007): 145–56

Swami, Praveen, 'Failed Threats and Flawed Fences: India's Military Responses to Pakistan's Proxy War', *India Review*, 3/2 (2004): 147–70

Tabatabai, Ariane M., 'Other side of the Iranian coin: Iran's counterterrorism apparatus', *Journal of Strategic Studies*, 41/1–2 (2018): 181–207

Taylor, Philip M., *Munitions of the Mind: A History of Propaganda from the Ancient World to the Present Day*, 3rd edn (Manchester University Press, 2003)

Tolz, Vera, Hutchings, Stephen, Chatterje-Doody, Precious, and Crilley, Rhys, 'Mediatization and journalistic agency: Russian television coverage of the Skripal poisonings', *Journalism* (iFirst, 2020)

Trenta, Luca, *The President's Kill List: Assassination and US Foreign Policy Since the Cold War* (Edinburgh University Press, 2022)

Trenta, Luca, 'Death by Reinterpretation: Dynamics of Norm Contestation and the US Ban on Assassination in the Reagan Years', *Journal of Global Security Studies* (iFirst, 2021)

Trenta, Luca, 'The Obama administration's conceptual change: Imminence and the legitimation of targeted killings', *European Journal of International Security*, 3/1 (2018): 69–93

Treverton, Gregory, *Covert Action: The Limits of Intervention in the Postwar World* (Basic Books, 1987)

Turner, Michael A., 'Covert Action: An Appraisal of the Effects of Secret Propaganda', in Loch K. Johnson (ed.), *Strategic Intelligence Vol. 3: Covert Action – Behind the Veils of Secret Foreign Policy* (Praeger Security International, 2007): 107–18

Urban, Mark, *Task Force Black: The Explosive True Story of the SAS and the Secret War in Iraq* (Abacus, 2017)

Valeriano, Brandon, *et al.*, *Cyber Strategy: The Evolving Character of Power and Coercion* (Oxford University Press, 2018)

Van Dongen, Luc, *et al.*, 'Introduction', in Luc Van Dongen *et al.* (eds), *Transnational Anti-Communism and the Cold War* (Palgrave Macmillan, 2014)

Van Puyvelde, Damien, 'French paramilitary actions during the Algerian War of Independence, 1956–1958', *Intelligence and National Security* (iFirst, 2021)

Van Puyvelde, Damien, and Brantly, Aaron F., *Cybersecurity: Politics, Governance and Conflict in Cyberspace* (Polity, 2019)

Varriale Carson, Jennifer, 'Assessing the Effectiveness of High-Profile Targeted Killings in the "War on Terror": A Quasi Experiment', *Criminology and Public Policy*, 16/1 (2017): 191–220

Vlad, Ruxandra, 'Striking the Shadow Commander' (University of Warwick PhD thesis, 2021)

Von Bülow, Mathilde, 'Myth or Reality? The Red Hand and French Covert Action in Federal Germany during the Algerian War, 1956–61', *Intelligence and National Security*, 22/6 (2007): 787–820

Voß, Klaas, 'Plausibly deniable: mercenaries in US covert interventions during the Cold War, 1964–1987', *Cold War History*, 16/1 (2016): 37–60

Wahutu, J. Siguru, 'Fake News and Journalistic "Rules of the Game"', *African Journalism Studies*, 40/4 (2019): 13–26

Waldman, Thomas, *Vicarious Warfare: American Strategy and the Illusion of War on the Cheap* (Bristol University Press, 2021)

Wanless, Alicia, and Pamment, James, 'How Do You Define a Problem Like Influence?', *Journal of Information Warfare*, 18/3 (2009): 1–14

Wege, Carl Anthony, 'Iranian intelligence organizations', *International Journal of Intelligence and Counter Intelligence*, 10/3 (1997): 287–98

Tim Weiner, *Legacy of Ashes: The History of the CIA* (Anchor, 2008)

Weiss, Leonard, 'The Lavon Affair: How a False Flag Operation Led to War and the Israeli Bomb', *Bulletin of the Atomic Scientists*, 69/3 (2013): 58–68

Welch, David, 'A Brief History of Propaganda: "A Much Maligned and Misunderstood Word"', in Timothy Clack and Robert Johnson (eds), *The World Information War: Western Resilience, Campaigning and Cognitive Effects* (Routledge, 2021)

Whyte, Christopher, 'Developed States' Vulnerability to Economic Disruption Online', *Orbis*, 60/3 (2016): 417–32

Willett, Marcus, 'Lessons of the SolarWinds Hack', *Survival*, 63/2 (2021): 7–26

Williamson, David, *The Polish Underground, 1939–1947* (Pen and Sword Military, 2012)

Wilner, Alex, 'Targeted Killings in Afghanistan: Measuring Coercion and Deterrence in Counterterrorism and Counterinsurgency', *Studies in Conflict & Terrorism*, 33/4 (2012): 307–29

Wilson, Andrew, 'Four Types of Russian Propaganda', *Aspen Review*, No. 4 (2015): 77–81

Winchell, Sean P., 'Pakistan's ISI: The Invisible Government', *International Journal of Intelligence and Counterintelligence*, 16/3 (2003): 374–88

Wirtz, James J., 'The Abbottabad raid and the theory of special operations', *Journal of Strategic Studies* (iFirst, 2021)

Wolf, Siegfried O., 'Pakistan and State-Sponsored Terrorism in South Asia', in P. Casaca and S. Wolf (eds), *Terrorism Revisited: Islamism, Political Violence and State Sponsorship* (Springer, 2017)

Woodward, Bob, *Veil: The Secret Wars of the CIA, 1981–1987* (Simon & Schuster, 2007)

Wright, Colin, 'Post-Truth, Postmodernism and Alternative Facts', *New Perspectives*, 26/3 (2018): 17–29

Yadav, Yatish, *RAW: A History of India's Covert Operations* (Westland, 2020)

INDEX

374   **HOW TO STAGE A COUP**